I Can Make You Hate

CHARLIE BROOKER

I Can Make You Hate

faber and faber

guardianbooks

First published in 2012
by Faber and Faber Limited
Bloomsbury House
74–77 Great Russell Street
London WC1B 3DA

Published with Guardian Books
Guardian Books is an imprint of Guardian Newspapers Ltd

Typeset by Donald Sommerville
Printed in England by CPI Group (UK) Ltd, Croydon, CR0 4YY

A CIP record for this book
is available from the British Library

ISBN 978–0–571–29502–9

2 4 6 8 10 9 7 5 3 1

CONTENTS

For Covey

INTRODUCTION

This book contains a lot of words, each of which had to be typed by hand. Consider that next time you're complaining about writing not being a proper job.

All the words in this book were individually typed, letter-by-letter – see what I mean about the truly gargantuan level of effort involved? – between August 2009 and July 2012.

And as you will soon discover, some of them weren't merely typed, but were then fed into an autocue and read aloud on television. That's an unnecessarily opaque way of saying 'I've included bits of scripts from some TV shows I was on.'

My previous collections of scribble have alternated chapters full of TV review columns with other, more general writings. But since I quit writing the *Screen Burn* column roughly halfway through this book, this time around everything's presented in chronological order, unfurling like a long, inky turd.

Not that you have to sit down and read it all in sequence. I recommend dipping in at random. Easy if you're reading this on paper: not so simple if you've chosen the snazzy and futuristic 'ebook' edition. Unless I'm mistaken, ebooks don't yet offer you the option to read books in 'shuffle' mode, on the basis that the result would be meaningless chaos, unless you're reading *The Way I See It* by Sir Alan Sugar, in which case it's a stunning improvement.

Anyway, I hope you enjoy the book. Don't take anything in it too seriously, and don't glue it to the end of a Kalashnikov and carry out an atrocity. Apart from that, do what you want with it. It's yours now.

Charlie Brooker,
London, 2012

PART ONE

In which the author has an out-of-body experience, is shaken to discover that the Chancellor of the Exchequer is slightly younger than he is, and decides there is too much 'stuff' in the world.

Screened for your pleasure
23/08/2009

Try not to bellow with fear and/or excitement, but video screens are coming to magazines. Next month, thousands of copies of vapid US showbiz journal *Entertainment Weekly* will contain a slimline electronic display capable of showing forty minutes of video, activated when you open the magazine. As an added bonus, if you dip it in the bath while reading it, you'll instantly win a free forty-minute full-body electroconvulsive therapy session (although sadly, for legal reasons, I have to point out that isn't true).

This tragic news is no surprise. Screens have us surrounded.

Last week I stood on a tube platform watching a Persil commercial being digitally projected in HD on to the opposite wall, to give me something to stare at while waiting for my delayed train. It showed gurgling kiddywinks in polar-white clothes gambolling in a field at the height of summer, tumbling and rolling and skipping and laughing, as if the sheer supernatural luminance of their outfits had somehow short-circuited their minds.

The contrast between the faces in the advert and the faces on the platform couldn't have been more marked. In the advert, all smiles. On the platform, morose expressions laminated by a thin sheen of grime and sweat; hangdog mugs smeared with London.

There's no air-con on the underground, so on a hot day people quickly resemble clothed piglets trapped in a can waiting for the air to run out. In these circumstances, the Persil ad was downright sarcastic; not a harmless video, but a magic window showing what life could be, if only you weren't stuck in a stinking, clammy pipe, jostling for space with fellow victims.

The underground also has video adverts lining the escalators. Where once stood rows of little posters with the occasional blob of dried chewing gum stuck to the nose of a beaming model, now stand rows of plasma screens displaying animated versions of movie posters and slogans for chain stores, and no one knows where to stick their gum any more because the pictures slide around.

It's impossible not to be slightly impressed, not to think, 'Ooh, I'm in *Minority Report*,' even as you glide by for the 10,000th time. The screens seem to belong there more than the real people trundling past them. Ad-world looks so vivid and clean, we humans are grotty streaks in a toilet pan by comparison.

They should ban us flesh-scum from using the escalators, and lovingly place glossy examples of technology on there instead: MacBooks, iPods, shiny white smoothie makers, Xbox 360s and so on; one brilliant white machine quietly perched atop each step, screens advertising *Ice Age 3D* mirrored in their gleaming minimalist surfaces as they scroll steadily upwards, ascending into the light. Hey, it's their destiny. We can use the stairs.

At London's Westfield shopping centre – picture the Duty Free section of a twenty-second-century spaceport – a series of 'information centres' vaguely resembling giant iPhones stand dotted around the echoing floorspace.

If you want to know where to buy some jeans, simply tap the interactive touchscreen and it instantly returns 500 different store names with step-by-step directions on how to find them.

And if you want to know where to buy a radio or some comics or maybe just something with a bit of character to it, simply tap it again and it'll sit there ignoring you; judging you somehow, like a mutely brooding obelisk – until you can't bear the chill any longer and run screaming from the complex, passing across 2,000 CCTV screens as you go.

If a Victorian gentleman arrived in present-day London, he'd think we'd been invaded by glowing rectangles. The average single

Londoner's day runs as follows: you wake up and watch a screen until it tells you it's time to leave the house, at which point you step outside (appearing on a CCTV screen the moment you do so), catch a bus (with an LED screen on the outside and an LCD screen on the inside) to the tube station (giant screens outside; screens down the escalator; projected screens on the platform), to sit on a train and fiddle with your iPod (via the screen), arrive at the office (to stare at a screen all day), then head home to split your attention between the internet (the screen on your lap) and the TV (the screen in the corner) and your mobile (a handheld screen you hold conversations with).

All we city dwellers need is a screen to have sex with and the circle is complete. Panasonic is doubtless perfecting some hideous LCD orifice technology as we speak. Probably one that makes 3D adverts appear in your head at the point of orgasm. Coco Pops are so chocolatey they even turn the milk brown. Now pass me a tissue.

The absolute omnipresence of screens is still a recent occurrence – they've only become totally unavoidable in the last four years or so – but already I'm utterly acclimatised. When I venture into the moist green countryside, the lack of screens is stunning. I stare at wooden pub signs with dumb incomprehension.

The King's Head? Is that a film? Why isn't he moving? Is it a film about a king who can't move?

When a cow saunters by without so much as a single plasma display embedded in its hide, I instinctively film it on my phone, so I can see it on a screen where it won't freak me out. Then I email a recording to the folks back home, so they can look it up online and tell me what it is. Ooh: apparently it's a type of animal. I get it now, now it's on my screen.

Yes. Screens. If you want a picture of the future, imagine a screen pissing illuminated phosphor into a human face – forever.

A Thousand Mooing Wankers
28/08/2009

Animals, all of us: dying, desperate animals, alone in our skulls, in our souls, quietly tortured by our foreknowledge of death, wandering a mindless rock, baying with pain or killing each other.

That's the working week. Come Saturday we crave relief. Slumped, defeated in the corner, our flagellated cadavers scarcely held together by the gentle cocooning pressure of our armchairs, wearily we pivot our milky, despairing eyes in the direction of our television sets, seeking consolation or distraction or maybe just a little inconsequential merriment: a dab of balm to spread on these anguished bones, this empty heart.

And this is what you give us, universe? You give us *The X Factor*?

It doesn't even work right now. *The X Factor* is broken. They've changed the audition process. Bye bye claustrophobic rehearsal room, hello cavernous stadium. The wannabe singers used to perform *a cappella* in front of four poker-faced judges; now they have to perform karaoke in front of a thousand mooing wankers. The programme may have been a cruel machine before, but at least it worked. This latest build is a mess.

For starters, they've deleted the show's one joke: that the bad singers don't realise they're bad until the judges break the news. Now an ocean of cackling dimwits almost drowns them out the second they open their mouths. Consequently, the panel's comments come as no surprise. The mob's already beaten the contestants to the ground before Cowell can deliver his death blow.

What's more, the crowd's very presence amplifies the cruelty of the format to such a degree, even the smallest of guilty home chuckles is strangled at birth. In the first week, an overweight girl explained she'd been living in her car for six weeks because her family had been evicted from their house thanks to her dreadful singing. The audience tittered throughout. Even Cowell looked embarrassed as he eventually dismissed her from the stage after a few half-hearted insults.

Speaking of leaving the stage, the biggest absurdity of all is that the traditional moments of 'candid' note-comparing chit-chat between the judges, usually conducted as soon as an especially bad or good contestant vacates the room, now have to be performed panto-style, with raised voices, so they can be heard over the general audience hubbub.

'Y'know, I really liked him. That kid's got potential.'

'WHAT'S THAT LOUIS?'

'I said he's got potential.'

'HE'S FOCKING MENTAL?'

'No, POTENTIAL. And he's pitch-perfect.'

'DANNII'S A BITCH TO WORK WITH?'

'No, no – stop crying Dannii, what I said was . . . oh FORGET IT.' [*Exits Riverdancing*]

Aside from shattering the relatively intimate dynamic betwixt act and judge, holding each audition in a massive live venue has the added anti-bonus of making each conversation less enjoyable even simply from a technical perspective. Editing it must be a nightmare, what with crowd noise leaking over every comment.

Another thing: it pre-emptively wrecks the live shows. How can the viewer possibly salivate at the prospect of watching a successful auditionee cope in front of a live studio audience when they've already seen them slay an entire stadium in week one? Where's the jeopardy going to come from? Unless ITV suddenly reveal they'll be singing live in a Thunderdome, dodging cudgel blows as they belt out the best of Elton John, there'll be little or no sense of peril at all.

Even watching the 'good' performers is worse than ever. In *X Factor* world, you're only considered 'good' if you ostentatiously bend every note like Mariah Carey folding a theremin in half. Now each vocal boast is met with an instant standing ovation from the horde of oinking dumbos cramming every aisle. To tune in is to witness a shocking mass rally devoted to the slaughter of basic melody that sets music back fifty years.

The X Factor not only fails to provide consolation for the futile horrors of human existence – it's not even as good as it used to be.

The Omen
04/09/2009

At last weekend's Edinburgh TV festival, the annual MacTaggart Lecture was delivered by Niles Crane from *Frasier*, played with eerie precision by James Murdoch. His speech attacked the BBC, moaned about Ofcom and likened the British television industry to *The Addams Family*. It went down like a turd in a casserole.

Still, the *Addams Family* reference will have been well-considered because James knows a thing or two about horror households: he's the son of Rupert Murdoch, which makes him the closest thing the media has to Damien from *The Omen*.

That's a fatuous comparison, obviously. Damien Thorn, off-spring of Satan, was educated at Yale before inheriting a global business conglomerate at a shockingly young age and using it to hypnotise millions in a demonic bid to hasten Armageddon. James Murdoch's story is quite different. He went to Harvard.

Above all, Murdoch's speech was a call for the BBC's online news service to be curbed, scaled back, deleted, depleted, dragged to the wastebasket, and so on, because according to him, the dispersal of such free 'state-sponsored' news on the internet threatens the future of other journalistic outlets. Particularly those provided by News International, which wants to start charging for the online versions of its papers.

Yes Thorn – I mean, Murdoch – refers to the BBC as 'state-sponsored media', because that makes it sound bad (although not quite as bad as 'Satan-sponsored media', admittedly). He evoked the government's control of the media in Orwell's *1984*, and claimed that only commercial news organisations were truly capable of producing 'independent news coverage that challenges the consensus'.

I guess that's what the *News of the World* does when it challenges the consensus view that personal voicemails should remain personal, or that concealing a video camera in a woman's private home bathroom is sick and creepy (it magically becomes acceptable when she's Kerry Katona).

Another great example of independent consensus-challenging news coverage is America's Fox News network, home of bellicose human snail Bill O'Reilly and blubbering blubberball Glenn Beck. Beck – who has the sort of rubbery, chucklesome face that should ideally be either a) cast as the goonish sidekick in a bad frat-house sex comedy, or b) painted on a toilet bowl so you could shit directly on to it – has become famous for crying live on air, indulging in paranoid conspiracy theorising, and labelling Obama a 'racist' with 'a deep-seated hatred for white people or white culture'.

As a news source, Fox is about as plausible and useful as an episode of *Thundercats*. Still, at least by hiring Beck, they've genuinely challenged the stuffy consensus notion that people should only really be given their own show on a major news channel if they're sane.

The trouble is, once you've gasped or chuckled over the YouTube clips of his most demented excesses, he's actually incredibly boring: a fat clown with one protracted trick. His show consists of an hour of screechy, hectoring bullshit: a pudgy middle-aged right-winger sobbing into his shirt about how powerless he feels. It's an incredible performance, but it belongs in some kind of zoo, not on a news channel. But that's the Murdoch way.

Now there's a lengthy, valid, and boring debate to be had about the scope and suitability of some of the BBC's ambitions but, quite frankly, if their news website (a thing of beauty and a national treasure) helps us stave off the arrival of the likes of Beck – even tangentially, even only for another few years until the Tories take over and begin stealthily dismantling the Beeb while a self-interested press loudly eggs them on – then it deserves to be cherished and applauded.

To finish his speech, Murdoch claimed, 'The only reliable, durable, and perpetual guarantor of independence is profit.' Or to put it another way: greed is good.

Then he clopped off stage on his cloven hooves, guffing out a hot cloud of sulphur as he left.

NB: years after this article appeared, I co-wrote a comedy for Sky, although by then James Murdoch had stepped down from BSkyB. Incidentally, if you 'followed the money' up the chain of previous TV shows I've been involved with, you could arrive at Silvio Berlusconi, a man I once described on TV as 'an ejaculating penis with a Prime Minister attached to it'. And this book is published by Faber and Faber, a company owned and operated by the serial killer Dennis Nilsen.

Into the eighth dimension
06/09/2009

The sheer breadth of human knowledge is a wonderful thing. But sometimes it's scary. This morning I was aimlessly clicking my way around the BBC news site – which has become one of my favourite things in the world since I discovered just how much its very existence annoys James Murdoch – reading about the burial of Michael Jackson and the like, when my eye was drawn to an alarming headline.

'Galaxy's "cannibalism" revealed,' it read. This led to a story in the science section that calmly explained how a group of astronomers has decided that the Andromeda galaxy is expanding by 'eating' stars from neighbouring galaxies. Having studied Andromeda's outskirts in great detail, they discovered the fringes contained 'remnants of dwarf galaxies'.

It took me a couple of reads to establish that Andromeda wasn't literally chewing its way through the universe like an intergalactic Pac-Man, and that the 'remnants of dwarf galaxies' were living stars, not the immense galactic stools I'd envisaged. That was what had really frightened me: the notion that our entire solar system might be nothing more than a chunk of undigested sweetcorn in some turgid celestial bowel movement; that maybe black holes are actually almighty cosmological sphincters, squeezing solid waste into our dimension. What if the entire universe as we know it is essentially one big festival toilet?

That'd be a pretty good social leveller, come to think of it. So there, James Murdoch. You might well walk around thinking, 'Ooh, hooray for me, I'm the chairman and CEO of News Corporation Europe and Asia, not to mention chairman of SKY Italia and STAR TV, the non-executive chairman of British Sky Broadcasting, and a non-executive director of GlaxoSmithKline,' but at the end of the day you're just one of 900 trillion insignificant molecules in an all-encompassing turdiverse. And your glasses are rubbish.

Anyway, the astronomers who made the discovery about Andromeda deserve our awe and respect, because their everyday job consists of dealing with concepts so intense and overwhelming that it's a wonder their skulls don't implode through sheer vertigo. Generally speaking, it's best not to contemplate the full scope of the universe on a day-to-day basis because it makes a mockery of basic chores. It's Tuesday night and the rubbish van comes first thing Wednesday morning, so you really ought to put the bin bags out, but hey – if our sun were the size of a grain of sand, the stars in our galaxy would fill an Olympic-sized swimming pool, and if our entire galaxy were a grain of sand, the galaxies in our universe would fill several Olympic-sized swimming pools. So fuck the bin bags.

The human brain isn't equipped to house thoughts of this humbling enormity. Whenever I read a science article that nonchalantly describes the Big Bang, or some similarly dizzying reference to the staggering size and age and unknowable magnitude of everything, I feel like a sprite in an outdated platform game desperately straining to comprehend the machine code that put me there, even though that isn't my job: my job is to jump between two moving clouds and land feet-first on a mushroom without ever questioning why.

Perhaps astrophysics stories should come with a little warning. Just as graphically violent news reports tend to be preceded by a quick disclaimer advising squeamish viewers that the following footage contains shots of protesters hurling their own severed kneecaps at riot police – or whatever – maybe brain-mangling science reports likely to leave you nursing an unpleasant existential bruise for several hours should be flagged as equally hazardous. How can I flip channels and enjoy *Midsomer Murders* once I've been reminded of the crushing futility of everything? I can't get worked up about the murders in that kind of mood. Yeah, kill him. And her. And them. Fuck it. It's all just atoms in a vortex.

Not that the few scientists I know seem to suffer. In fact, they're unrelentingly calm and upbeat, like they've stumbled across a cosmic secret but aren't telling. One of my friends is married to a quantum physicist who, sickeningly, manages to combine an immense brain with a relaxed, down-to-earth, amused attitude to everything. He once tried to explain the characteristics of different theoretical dimensions to me.

Dimensions one to four I could just about cope with. The fifth made vague sense at a push. But the rest collapsed into terrifying babble. There was no foothold.

I swear, at one point he casually claimed the seventh dimension measured about half a metre in diameter and was shaped like a doughnut. That can't be right: either I've misremembered it because my brain deleted the explanation as it was going in, chewing it up and spitting it out before it could do damage, or – and this is just a wild theory – I'm too stupid to understand much in the realm of science beyond the difference between up and down, and the seventh dimension is beyond me. It might've been part of string theory (I like string theory, because I can at least hazily picture the strings). But this seventh dimension stuff was just gibberish.

God knows what the eighth dimension consists of. Probably two chalk moths and a puddle. Whatever it is, and wherever it lives, don't tell me. The binman's due and I don't want to know.

Live from St. Elsewhere
20/09/2009

Apologies if I sound a tad woozy, but yesterday I left planet Earth for some time and apparently enjoyed exploring some other reality while medical professionals did something fancy with my neck. It was a minor procedure. Minor by modern standards, that is.

The doctors casually performed the sort of everyday miracle that would've seen them worshipped as gods or drowned in the village pond if they'd done it in medieval times. But then, medieval peasants would run screaming from anything more complex than a turnip. Show them, say, a Nintendo Wii, and their minds would pop inside their skulls. Pop, pop, pop and down they fall, stupid green smocks and all.

Anyway, the fact I'm sitting here typing this proves nothing went wrong. Nothing was going to go wrong anyway, but that didn't stop me worrying. All I knew was this: they were going to stick a needle into my neck, right into the spine. Not too scary by surgical standards: it would only require a local anaesthetic. But it was precisely that fact which started my brain whirring.

I figured it was essential to remain still during this kind of procedure if I didn't want to wind up quadriplegic, which I didn't. What if, just at the crucial moment they stuck the needle in, I was seized by some awful Tourettes-like urge to suddenly jerk around on the slab, cackling like a madman in a rainstorm, deliberately severing my spinal cord against the cold, hard spike?

I'd have to be crazy to do that, obviously. But once the thought was in there, I couldn't rub it out. Even if I didn't actually snap and start twitching and flapping around, surely I'd be lying there fighting the urge, or at the very least fighting to suppress the urge from showing up in the first place? The more I thought about it, the more I became convinced I was going to do something appalling. It was like a mind virus.

Then I had another, even more terrible thought: what if I was lying there, desperately battling this loopy self-destructive brainstorm, when something altogether simpler yet equally destructive happened? Specifically: what if I sneezed? What if I sneezed just as the needle pierced my spine, and the doctors screamed and the nurses wept and I spent the rest of my life paralysed in bed, like the guy in *The Diving Bell and the Butterfly*, minus the consolation of having two pretty French women squabbling for my affections?

I'd have to spend years staring at the ceiling. I don't mind ceilings, but I've never glanced up at one and thought, 'Oooh, I could stare at you for the rest of my life.' Surely in this day and age, they could at least project films on the ceiling for me to watch? But that might be torture: what if they showed me nothing but Adam Sandler movies, and I couldn't fast-forward or hit stop, just sit there, blinking angrily, only the nurse hasn't noticed; no, she's busy looking up and laughing, laughing at the bit where Adam Sandler trips over the bench, or Adam Sandler gets hit on the nose with the basketball, she's laughing and I'm blinking and she hasn't noticed, and the blinks grow wetter and I realise I'm weeping, and Adam Sandler tumbles face-first into some dogshit and she laughs again, and I grit my mind and stare past the ceiling, stare past the sky, into deep space, and I focus a mental tractor beam composed of pure magnetic rage on a chunk of rock silently gliding through the blackness, and I stop it in its tracks and draw it towards the Earth, a 100-mile-wide asteroid swooping down to meet us, dragged down by me, until it collides with London, obliterating everything, an extinction-level event, billions of lives worldwide wiped out in the blink of an eye: my eye. My wrathful blinking eye. But don't blame me. Blame Sandler.

Anyway, in the event, I didn't have to worry about sneezing, or quadriplegia, or my *Medusa Touch* doomsday scenario, because the injection itself turned out to be fun. Yes, fun. Not because I'm into needles, but because they sedated me – and whatever drug they used was brilliant. So brilliant I don't want to know what it was, because I'd gladly kick a hospital to death for half a teaspoon of it. In an instant, I understood in my bones why people become heroin addicts.

I went light-headed, then more light-headed, and then I can't remember what happened. I was dimly aware of being moved back down a corridor. Before I knew it I was back in a cubicle, wondering whether they'd even been near my neck at all. The doctor came in to check on me, and I asked him if I'd been unconscious.

'No, no,' he said cheerfully, 'you were talking a fair bit.'

Talking? I was talking?

'Yes; we held a conversation with you throughout. You get a bit of amnesia, but that's it. It's good stuff.'

I've never had a blackout; never been knocked unconscious; never drunk so much I can't remember the night before. This wholesale deletion of recent memories is entirely new to me. And it's kind of creepy. During the blank phase, was I still me? If not, who was doing the talking on my behalf? Roger De Courcey? And where was I while this was happening? Delivering milk on the moon? Window-shopping in the afterlife? Hovering over Plymouth? Was I dead? Dead-ish? Or merely very obedient? Did they make me do terrible things with vegetables and film it and put it on the internet? Time will tell.

Whatever happened, whoever took over thankfully hadn't felt the need to flail like a salmon when the spike went in. Clearly they're more responsible and less neurotic than I am: they can have the job permanently if they like.

That evening, as I left the hospital, I realised I'd caught a cold. I spent the night sneezing and staring at the ceiling, keeping myself entertained by working out how to swear by blinking alone.

This is the news
25/09/2009

Finally, vegetables have a TV show of their very own. Not human vegetables. Don't be daft. This is way beneath them. I'm talking about actual vegetables: carrots, potatoes, turnips, cauliflowers ... such is the target audience for *Live From Studio Five*.

Clearly too stupid for human consumption, it is instead aimed squarely at cold, unfeeling lumps of organic matter with no discernible minds of their own. And it succeeds brilliantly at keeping them entertained. I watched last Monday's episode in the company of a clump of broccoli, and it was held in a rapt silence throughout. Well, most of the time. To be honest, I think it drifted off a bit during a Backstreet Boys report. And I had to slap it awake at the start of each ad break. Apart from that, it was spellbound.

Yes, here is a TV show that makes any and all previous accusations of 'dumbing down' seem like misplaced phoney-war hysteria. A show providing less mental nourishment than a baby's rattle. A show with a running order *Heat* magazine would consider frighteningly lightweight. A show that boasts Melinda Messenger as its intellectual touchstone. A show dumber than a blank screen and a low hum. Anyone who willingly tunes in to watch this really ought to be forced to work in the middle of a field for the rest of their life, well away from any technological devices (such as motor vehicles or microwave ovens) with which they might inadvertently cause harm to others.

In short: this is quite a stupid programme. It's hosted by Messenger, Ian Wright and Kate 'The Apprentice' Walsh. Inoffensive in isolation, once combined they demonstrate the sort of chemistry that could close a public swimming pool for twenty-five years. For one thing, they all stare and smile down the lens throughout, as though they've been asked to imagine the viewer is a backward child at a birthday party. Kate in particular grins like a woman being paid per square metre of dentistry.

According to the official website the show is 'a mix of celebrity interviews, gossip and banter wrapped around a popular news agenda that everyone's talking about'. In other words, it's a torrent of flavourless showbiz porridge interspersed with occasional VTs about Ronnie Biggs or twelve-year-old sex change patients or whatever else the tabloids are moaning about.

Last week they managed to wring twelve punishing minutes out of the 'Alesha Dixon on *Strictly*' debate, a story of interest only to people too dim to wipe themselves after a bowel movement without referring to an illustrated step-by-step instruction sheet at least six times during the process. First we were treated to a report summing up what the tabloids thought, including some vox pops in which random imbeciles shared their views. Then it cut back to the studio, where the hosts summarised what we'd just seen (for the benefit of the more forgetful carrots in the audience), before reading out emails in which some different random imbeciles shared their views. This was followed by a commercial break that included an advert desperately encouraging people to read books.

When the hosts aren't smiling or introducing VTs, they're sharing their opinions. For instance, last week Ian Wright read out a story about David Hasselhoff's alleged drink problem, and summed it up by saying, 'Wossee playing at? I mean, sort it out!' Then he did a sort of open-palmed 'It's-common-sense-innit' shrugging manoeuvre. Thus the issue was settled in time for the Bananarama interview.

Still, knocking the hosts is pointless. They're hardly trying to present *Newsnight*. But the VTs – astoundingly – are, in fact, created by actual news journalists. *Live From Studio Five* is a product of Sky News. Which makes it part of Five's news quota.

This – in case I haven't yet repeated the word 'news' often enough to hammer it home – is a news programme.

THIS IS THE NEWS. Melinda Messenger, Ian Wright and Kate Walsh are PRESENTING THE NEWS. In other words: welcome to the end of the world.

Like the faint smell of piss in a subway
27/09/2009

I admit it: I'm a bigot. A hopeless bigot at that: I know my particular prejudice is absurd, but I just can't control it. It's Apple. I don't like Apple products. And the better-designed and more ubiquitous they become, the more I dislike them. I blame the customers. Awful people. Awful. Stop showing me your iPhone. Stop stroking your MacBook. Stop telling me to get one.

Seriously, stop it. I don't care if Mac stuff is better. I don't care if Mac stuff is cool. I don't care if every Mac product comes equipped with a magic button on the side that causes it to piddle gold coins and resurrect the dead and make holographic unicorns dance inside your head. I'm not buying one, so shut up and go home. Go back to your house. I know, you've got an iHouse. The walls are brushed aluminium. There's a glowing Apple logo on the roof. And you love it there. You absolute MONSTER.

Of course, it's safe to assume Mac products are indeed as brilliant as their owners make out. Why else would they spend so much time trying to convert non-believers? They're not getting paid. They simply want to spread their happiness, like religious crusaders.

Consequently, nothing pleases them more than watching a PC owner struggle with a slab of non-Mac machinery. It validates their spiritual choice. Recently I sat in a room trying to write something on a Sony Vaio PC laptop which seemed to be running a special slow-motion edition of Windows Vista specifically designed to infuriate human beings as much as possible. Trying to get it to do anything was like issuing instructions to a depressed employee over a sluggish satellite feed. When I clicked on an application it spent a small eternity contemplating the philosophical implications of opening it, begrudgingly complying with my request several months later. It drove me up the wall. I called it a bastard and worse. At one point I punched a table.

This drew the attention of two nearby Mac owners. They hovered over and stood beside me, like placid monks.

'Ah: the delights of Vista,' said one.

'It really is time you got a Mac,' said the other.

'They're just better,' sang monk number one.

'You won't regret it,' whispered the second.

I scowled and returned to my infernal machine, like a dishevelled park-bench boozer shrugging away two pious AA recruiters by pulling a grubby, dented hip flask from his pocket and pointedly taking an extra deep swig. Leave me alone, I thought. I don't care if you're right. I just want you to die.

I know Windows is awful. Everyone knows Windows is awful. Windows is like the faint smell of piss in a subway: it's there, and there's nothing you can do about it. OK, OK: I know other operating systems are available. But their advocates seem even creepier, snootier and more insistent than Mac owners. The harder they try to convince me, the more I'm repelled. To them, I'm a sheep. And they're right. I'm a helpless, stupid, lazy sheep.

I'm also a masochist. And that's why I continue to use Windows – horrible Windows – even though I hate every second of it. It's grim, it's slow, everything's badly designed and nothing really works properly: using Windows is like living in a communist bloc nation circa 1981. And I wouldn't change it for the world, because I'm an abject fucking idiot and I hate myself, and this is what I deserve: to be sentenced to Windows for life.

That's why Windows works for me. But I'd never recommend it to anybody else, ever. This puts me in line with roughly everybody else in the world. No one has ever earnestly turned to a fellow human being and said, 'Hey, have you considered Windows?' Not in the real world at any rate.

Until now. Microsoft, hellbent on tackling the conspicuous lack of word-of-mouth recommendation, is encouraging people – real people – to host 'Windows 7 launch parties' to celebrate the 22 October release of, er, Windows 7. The idea is that you invite a group of friends – your real friends – to your home – your real home – and entertain them with a series of Windows 7 tutorials. So you show them how to burn a CD, how to make a little video, how to change the wallpaper, and how to, oh no, hang on it's not supposed to do that, oh, I think it's frozen, um, er, let me just, um, no that's not it, um, er, um, er, so how's it going with you and Kathy anyway, um, er, OK we'll see you around I guess.

To assist the party-hosting massive, they've also uploaded a series of spectacularly cringeworthy videos to YouTube, in which the four most desperate actors in the world stand around in a kitchen sharing tips on how best to indoctrinate guests in the wonder of Windows. If they were staring straight down the lens reading hints off a card it might be acceptable; instead they have been instructed to pretend to be friends. The result is the most nauseating display of artificial camaraderie since the horrific Doritos 'Friendchips' TV campaign (which caused 50,000 people to kill themselves in 2003, or should have done).

It's so terrible, it induces an entirely new emotion: a blend of vertigo, disgust, anger and embarrassment that I like to call 'shitasmia'. It not only creates this emotion: it defines it. It's the most shitasmic cultural artefact in history.

Still, bad though it is, I vaguely prefer the clumping, clueless, uncool, crappiness of Microsoft's bland Stepford gang to the creepy assurance of the average Mac evangelist. At least the grinning dildos in the Windows video are fictional, whereas eerie replicant Mac monks really are everywhere, standing over your shoulder in their charcoal pullovers, smirking with amusement at your hopelessly inferior OS, knowing they're better than you because they use Mac OS X v10.6 Snow Leopard.

Snow Leopard. SNOW LEOPARD.

I don't care if you're right. I just want you to die.

The Hookening
02/10/2009

When we look back at the 'noughties' – pausing briefly to gently vomit in protest at the hideous made-up word 'noughties' – we'll realise this was a golden age for absolute bollocks. Fun bollocks, maybe... but bollocks all the same.

Every new US show these days is fun bollocks. We've had the one where it's in real time (*24*), the one where they're stranded on a weird island (*Lost*), the one where they break out of prison (*Prison Break*), the one where the killer kills killers (*Dexter*) and the one where unfettered capitalism creates and destroys an entire underclass (*The Wire*).

Everything needs a hook, the hookier the better. Before long, we'll end up with the hookiest show possible: *The Hookening* – where everyone in the world suddenly passes out and wakes up 137 seconds later with a hook for a hand. Irritating for most of us; devastating for the jar industry.

We're not there yet, but who knows what could happen in six months' time? For now, we'll have to be content with *FlashForward*. It stars Joseph Fiennes as Mr Nice Cop with a Drink Problem, and it's a show in which everyone in the world passes out for 137 seconds and has a vision of the future six months from now. Weirder still, it's not strictly a vision: their consciousness has somehow raced forward in time, so they've experienced precisely what they'll be doing for around two minutes on 29 April 2010. Some are performing mundane actions, like reading the paper on the bog; others are doing exciting things, like being shot at. It's the world's biggest spoiler.

Having wandered off into futureworld for roughly half the length of an ad break, they're sucked back into the present, where naturally everyone's now a bit confused. And in some cases, dead. Because absolutely everyone blacked out simultaneously, there were countless car crashes, air disasters, chip-pan fires and so on, vividly depicted in scenes in which Joseph Fiennes wanders around a semi-destroyed LA gawping at various bits of CGI devastation. Helicopter crashes account for some of the worst damage, although several buildings appear to have burst into flames out of sheer confusion during the blackout. In one scene we get a glimpse of London; Big Ben is on fire. Presumably the bells overheated during the timequake.

(Incidentally I call it a 'timequake' because it seems vaguely similar to Kurt Vonnegut's novel *Timequake*, although apparently it's based on a different book, called, unsurprisingly, *FlashForward*.)

The rest of the story revolves around solving what caused the Great Leap Forward in the first instance. That's Fiennes's job. He saw himself in a big room full of clues, halfway towards solving the mystery, evading some bad guys. Oh, and drinking from a hip flask, so he knows he's going to fall off the wagon. Or does he? Yes! No! It rather depends on whether man truly has free will or not. Philosophers have wrestled with that one for centuries; this show promises to clear it up once and for all, and find room for a romantic subplot. Perhaps it was originally pitched with the working title *Adventures in Compatibilism: A Determinist Thought Experiment*.

Anyway, it's not bad: enjoyable bunkum in the manner of early *Lost*, although the paradox-heavy storyline easily overshadows the characters, who thus far could all be replaced by cardboard boxes with Character #1, Character #2 and so on scrawled on the front.

The fun comes in spotting flaws in the narrative. Such as: if everyone experienced the same bit of 'future', how come their future selves didn't seem aware the flash forward was going to happen? They were sitting in meetings, or running around, or watching TV. Nobody saw themselves saying 'Ooooh, this is the bit I saw six months ago.'

It's not a show, it's a puzzle. There are 10 billion other paradoxes in the storyline. How many can you find? (Answers on page 894, six months from now).

FlashForward *flopped, having painted itself into a billion logistical corners.*

Bewildered by the stuff-a-lanche
04/10/2009

I'm fairly certain I recently passed a rather pathetic tipping point, and now own more unread books and unwatched DVDs than my remaining lifespan will be able to sustain. I can't possibly read all these pages or watch all these movies before the grim reaper comes knocking. The bastard things are going to outlive me. It's not fair. They can't even breathe.

The other day I bought a DVD box set of Carl Sagan's astronomy epic *Cosmos*: by all accounts, one of the best documentary series ever made. On my way home, I made the mistake of carefully reading the back of the box, where I discovered it has a running time of 780 minutes. Thirteen hours. It's against my religion to only watch part of it – it's all or nothing. But thirteen hours? That's almost a marriage. The sheer weight of commitment is daunting. So it sits on the shelf, beside similarly unwrapped and unwatched obelisks. I'm not buying these things for myself any more. I'm preserving them for future generations.

DVD and book purchases fall into two main categories: the ones you buy because you really want to watch them, and the ones you buy because you vaguely think you should. Two years ago I bought Dostoevsky's *Crime and Punishment*, partly because I'd heard it was a good book and an easy read, but mainly because I figured reading it would make me cleverer – or at the very least, make me seem a bit cleverer to anyone sitting opposite me on the tube. I never read it. A few months ago, having forgotten I already owned a copy, I bought it again. This means I haven't read it twice.

And I haven't read it (twice) because it's got too much competition from all the other books I've bought but never read. Popular science books. Biographies. Classic works of fiction. Cult sci-fi and horror stories. Reference works. How-to guides. Graphic novels. I can't buy one book at a time: I have to buy at least four. Which makes it exponentially trickier to single out one to actually read. When I buy books, all I'm really doing is buying wall insulation, like a blackbird gathering twigs to make a nest.

Ditto DVDs. *Scenes From a Marriage* and *The Seventh Seal* – two well-regarded Ingmar Bergman films I bought during a short-lived fit of self-improvement. I should have thrown them in a bin on my way home from the shop. It's hard enough to choose between the two: am I in the mood for a lyrical ninety-two-minute meditation on death, or an unflinching three-hour portrayal of a dysfunctional relationship? Neither, as it turns out. They'd only be interrupted by emails and texts anyway.

Perhaps something more lightweight? They're sitting on the shelf in-between *JCVD* (a post-modern Jean-Claude Van Damme film) and season two of *Entourage*. I've never seen those either – partly because I feel guilty about not having watched the Bergman films first. Somehow I've purchased my way into a no-win situation.

Clearly, some sort of cull is in order. It's me or them. I pick them. My options need limiting. Last week I watched the first part of *Electric Dreams*, the 1900s house-style TV show where a family lives with old technology for several weeks. For episode one, they were stranded in the 1970s, with no internet, no DVDs or videos, and only three channels on the TV. It's fair to say the kids weren't massively impressed. It was all a bit Guantanamo for their liking. But to me the limited options looked blissful.

You couldn't lose yourself online, so if you didn't want to watch *Summertime Special* or *World in Action*, you had to read a book, go for a walk, or in extreme circumstances, strike up a conversation with a fellow human being.

But it wasn't just the limitations of the media themselves that appealed. This was thirty years ago. Fewer things had been created for them. Every day we humans gleefully churn out yet more books and films and TV shows and videogames and websites and magazine articles and blog posts and emails and text messages, all of it hanging around, competing for attention. Without leaving my seat I can access virtually any piece of music ever recorded, download any film ever made, order any book ever written. And the end result is that I hardly experience any of it.

It's too much. I've had it with choice. It makes my head spin.

Here's what I want: I want to be told what to read, watch and listen to. I want my hands tied. I want a cultural diet. I want a government employee to turn up on my doorstep once a month, carrying a single book for me to read. I want all my TV channels removed and replaced by a single electro-pipe delivering one pro-gramme or movie a day. If I don't watch it, it gets replaced by the following day's selection. I want all my MP3s deleted and replaced with one unskippable radio station playing one song after the other.

And every time I think about complaining, I want a minotaur to punch me in the kidneys and remind me how it was before.

In short: I've tried more. It's awful. I want less, and I want it now.

I eventually watched Scenes From a Marriage. *It was good. Still haven't got round to* The Seventh Seal *though.*

The Great Inescapable Time Disaster
11/10/2009

George Osborne's Tory conference speech last week left me in a state of shredded despair. Not because of anything he said, but because I'd just discovered he's younger than me. Only by two months, but still: younger.

In a correctly functioning universe, my advanced age would make me his superior. If I deliberately knocked a glass of milk on to the floor, he'd have to clean it up. He'd be on all fours, scrubbing desperately at the floorboards while I reclined in my chair, resting my feet on his back, reading the *Financial Times*, occasionally glancing over the top to harrumph at his efforts, grinding my heel into his spine to underline each criticism. You missed a bit, boy. For pity's sake, show some gumption. Tongue, Osborne! Use your bloody tongue!

Wild fantasy, of course: there's no way Osborne would prostrate himself before me, lapping up my mess like a prison cell Betty. He's of grander stock than I. He's worth ten thousand hundred billion pounds, wipes his arse on back issues of *Tatler*, attended a public school so swish that even its coat of arms looks down its nose at you, and spends his weekends running around his estate, dressed like the Planters 'Mr Peanut' mascot, wildly thrashing at the backs of chimney sweeps' legs with a cane. I went to a comprehensive and have the social standing of a plughole.

But I'm resigned to the class difference. It's the age difference that rankles. In my head, senior politicians are supposed to be older than I am – forever. No matter how much I age, part of their job is to be older and drier than me. At 38, Osborne feels too young for the world of politics. At 38, I feel too old for the world in general.

Age has been a lingering obsession of mine since I left my teens. However old I've been is too old.

At 26, I felt totally washed up.

At 32, I regretted wasting time worrying about my age as a 26-year-old, because now I was convinced I really was totally washed up.

At 38, I look back at my 32-year-old self and regret that he wasted time with those regrets about wasted time. Then I regret wasting my current time regretting regrets about regrets. This is pretty sophisticated regretting I'm doing. That's the sole advantage of ageing: I can now effortlessly consolidate my regrets into one manageable block of misery. Otherwise, by the age of 44, I'd need complex database software just to keep track of precisely how many things I'm regretting at once.

Age is an odd thing. As well as fretting about it, at every point in my life I've regarded those both above and below me on the age ladder with unwarranted contempt. Anyone younger was a barking idiot; anyone older, an outmoded embarrassment.

But rather than mellowing into acceptance as I ascend the ladder, my distaste for both groups sharpens into bitter focus. The young ones are even more idiotic because they don't appreciate how short-lived their youth will be, dammit – while the old ones are now a horrifying vision of a steadily approaching future. I'm not talking about OAPs, incidentally, but people just a few years older than I am now. To my eyes, they're walking victims of the Great Inescapable Time Disaster.

On a rational level, I know there's nothing wrong with ageing. If anything, it should be taken as a sign of continued success. Congratulations! You haven't dropped dead yet. But that doesn't stop me seeing each individual grey hair as a tiny shoot of failure. Like millions of us, I've been indoctrinated into believing the ageing process somehow reeks of indignity. I've been conditioned to view everything from the POV of a conceited twenty-something. My brain's lodged near the bottom of the ladder while my body clambers creakingly towards the top. Look at those silver flecks; that foul, rotting carcass: you stink of shame, you disgusting loser.

When you're young, anyone a decade older or more can seem like a gauche joke, tragically unaware of their own crashing irrelevance. They're either hopelessly out-of-touch (LOL! He's never heard of Lady Gaga!), embarrassingly immature (Ugh! He listens to Lady Gaga!) or hovering awkwardly in-between (Pff! He uses Lady Gaga as a catch-all reference for youth!). At the same time, you somehow believe that when – if – you ever grow to be so impossibly ancient yourself, you'll be wiser and less embarrassing. How could you not be? These people are just pathetic.

The good news is that when you get there, you *are* wiser – albeit only slightly. Chances are you're still flailing around, just as clueless about What Happens Next. Slightly more terrified at what the world might have in store, but slightly more confident in your ability to pilot a way through.

And the only real wisdom you've gained is a fresh understanding of just how ignorant and arrogant you were in the past: a realisation that the joke was ultimately on you. Pointing and laughing at your own destiny is futile. The harder you sneer at the old, the more uncomfortable you feel when you age.

And unless you die, you will age. Age and age and age, to a previously unimaginable degree, to the farthest reaches of 'age space' and beyond. To the point where, one day, the Shadow Chancellor is younger than you. At which point you experience a subtle, cathartic little death – and thus liberated, finally start to grow up and get on with it.

Pure blockheaded spite
16/10/2009

The funeral of Stephen Gately has not yet taken place. The man hasn't been buried yet. Nevertheless, Jan Moir of the *Daily Mail* has already managed to dance on his grave. For money.

It has been twenty minutes since I've read her now-notorious column, and I'm still struggling to absorb the sheer scope of its hateful idiocy. It's like gazing through a horrid little window into an awesome universe of pure blockheaded spite. Spiralling galaxies of ignorance roll majestically against a backdrop of what looks like dark prejudice, dotted hither and thither with winking stars of snide innuendo.

On the *Mail* website, it was headlined: 'Why there was nothing "natural" about Stephen Gately's death'. Since the official postmortem clearly ascribed the singer's death to natural causes, that headline contains a fairly bold claim.

Still, who am I to judge? I'm no expert when it comes to interpreting autopsy findings, unlike Moir. Presumably she's a leading expert in forensic science, paid huge sums of money to fly around the world lecturing coroners on her latest findings. Or maybe she just wants to gay-bash a dead man? Tragically, the only way to find out is to read the rest of her article.

She begins by jabbering a bit about untimely celebrity deaths, especially those whose lives are 'shadowed by dark appetites or fractured by private vice'. Not just Heath Ledger and Michael Jackson. No: she's eagerly looking forward to other premature snuffings.

'Robbie, Amy, Kate, Whitney, Britney; we all know who they are. And we are not being ghoulish to anticipate, or to be mentally braced for, their bad end: a long night, a mysterious stranger, an odd set of circumstances that herald a sudden death.'

Fair enough. I'm sure we all agree there's nothing 'ghoulish' whatsoever about eagerly imagining the hypothetical death of someone you've marked out as a potential cadaver on account of your ill-informed presumptions about their lifestyle. All she's doing is running a detailed celebrity-death sweepstake in her head. That's not ghoulish, that's fun. For my part, I've just put a tenner on Moir choking to death on her own bile by the year 2012. See? Fun!

Having casually prophesied the death of Robbie Williams and Co., Moir moves on to her main point: that Gately's death strikes her as a bit fishy ... 'All the official reports point to a natural death, with no suspicious circumstances ... But, hang on a minute. Something is terribly wrong with the way this incident has been shaped and spun into nothing more than an unfortunate mishap on a holiday weekend, like a broken teacup in the rented cottage.'

That's odd. I don't recall anyone equating the death with 'an unfortunate mishap on a holiday weekend'. I was only aware of shocked expressions of grief from those who knew or admired him, people who'd probably be moved to tears by Moir likening the tragedy to 'a broken teacup in the rented cottage'. But never mind that – 'shaped and spun' by whom, precisely? The coroner?

Incredibly, yes. Moir genuinely believes the coroner got it wrong: 'Healthy and fit 33-year-old men do not just climb into their pyjamas and go to sleep on the sofa, never to wake up again. Whatever the cause of death is, it is not, by any yardstick, a natural one.'

At this point, I dare to challenge the renowned international forensic pathologist Jan Moir, because I personally know of two other men (one in his twenties, one in his early thirties), who died in precisely this way. According to the charity Cardiac Risk in the Young (c-r-y.org.uk), 'Twelve apparently fit and healthy young people die in the UK from undiagnosed heart conditions' every single week. That's a lot of broken teacups, eh Jan?

Still, if his death wasn't natural 'by any yardstick', what did kill him? Moir knows: it was his lifestyle. Because Gately was, y'know ... homosexual. Having lanced this boil, Moir lets the pus drip out all over her fingers as she continues to type: 'The circumstances surrounding his death are more than a little sleazy,' she declares. 'Cowles and Gately took a young Bulgarian man back to their apartment. It is not disrespectful to assume that a game of canasta ... was not what was on the cards ... What happened afterwards is anyone's guess.'

Don't hold back, Jan. Have a guess. Draw us a picture. You specialise in celebrity death fantasies, after all.

'His mother is still insisting that her son died from a previously undetected heart condition that has plagued the family.' Yes. That poor, blinkered woman, 'insisting' in the face of official medical evidence that absolutely agrees with her.

Anyway, having cast aspersions over a tragic death, doubted a coroner and insulted a grieving mother, Moir's piece builds to its climax: 'Another real sadness about Gately's death is that it strikes another blow to the happy-ever-after myth of civil partnerships ... Gay activists are always calling for tolerance and understanding about same-sex relationships, arguing that they are just the same as heterosexual marriages ... in many cases this may be true. Yet the recent death of Kevin McGee, the former husband of *Little Britain* star Matt Lucas, and now the dubious events of Gately's last night raise troubling questions about what happened.'

Way to spread the pain around, Jan. Way to link two unrelated tragedies, Jan. Way to gay-bash, Jan.

Jan's paper, the *Daily Mail*, absolutely adores it when people flock to Ofcom to complain about something offensive, especially when it's something they've only learned about second-hand via an inflammatory article in a newspaper. So it would undoubtedly be delighted if, having read this, you paid a visit to the Press Complaints Commission website to lodge a complaint about Moir's article on the basis that it breaches sections 1, 5 and 12 of its code of practice.

After this article was written, over 25,000 people did indeed complain to the PCC about Jan Moir's article, although how many of them did so after reading this is anyone's guess. The PCC eventually found in favour of the Daily Mail, *saying that, although it was 'uncomfortable with the tenor of the columnist's remarks', censuring the paper would represent 'a slide towards censorship'.*

Which is fair enough, really. I think columnists should have the right to air offensive views, so I don't really know why I encouraged readers to lobby the doomed, meaningless PCC; I think I just wanted to use one of the Mail's own tactics against it – the paper often urges readers to complain to official bodies about things it deems offensive. But that's not really got anything to do with poor Stephen Gately. By implying Jan Moir had no right to spout her unpleasant bibble, I somehow ended up, to my mind, on the wrong side of a tricky freedom-of-speech debate.

Still, no matter what mistakes I may have made in the above column, and no matter where you stand on the freedom of speech, it's essential that we all try to learn from everything that happened – as a people, as a society. And ultimately the moral of the story and the single most important thing to remember is this: Jan Moir is a twat.

PART TWO

In which Jedward are born, Dubai is revealed to be a figment of the world's imagination, and snow falls from the sky to the amazement of Britain's rolling news networks.

Jedward: the Jenesis
16/10/2009

A bit of background, because let's face it no one remembers this stuff: at the time this article originally appeared, celebrity dance prick Anton Du Beke was in trouble for using the word 'Paki' during some ill-advised backstage tomfoolery, Dannii Minogue had upset X Factor *viewers with a mild gag about a contestant's sexuality, and following a blackmail attempt, US talk show giant David Letterman had made an on-air apology for having sex with members of his staff. Also, human beings had recently learned to walk on two legs.*

The times, they are a-jumpy. Really, when we're upset by something as simple as a man shouting a racially abusive term across a room full of people, or a woman teasing an aspiring pop star about his sexuality in front of 13 million viewers, isn't it time to wonder whether political correctness and basic human decency have gone too far? Apologies flutter through the airwaves like startled doves. 'Forgive me,' plead the transgressors, 'for I knowed not what I done. It was a joke! Geddit? Upsetting Pakis or poofs was the last thing on my mind. Really! And I'm sorry!'

From Anton Du Beke on *Strictly* to Dannii Minogue on *The X Factor*; at this rate, every show on TV will soon need to incorporate an on-air apology into its opening sequence. Unless, like Letterman, they make directly apologising down the lens a regular 'format point' in the programme itself. Christmas is traditionally the time when *Strictly* and *The X Factor* fight to see who can pull off the biggest climax, kicking ratings into the sky with displays of consummate showmanship. Instead, this year they'll be fighting to see which of their respective foot-in-mouth stars can issue the most spectacularly wretched request for forgiveness.

'Next on BBC1, Anton Du Beke prostrates himself before the cameras, sobbing with remorse while an entire Asian youth orchestra tramples up and down on his back.'

'Great Yuletide fun on ITV now: hilarious reparations as Dannii Minogue performs a selection of the biblical world's most hideous acts of penance in front of a panel of witheringly critical bisexual judges.'

Crikey. Unless I'm mistaken, both those shows would actually provide record-breaking Christmas Day viewing figures.

Now, on to business: *The X Factor*. The new format for the early audition shows (berks yelping in front of a massive screaming audience) left me wondering how the production team could possibly differentiate those instalments from the established format of the live episodes (berks yelping in front of a massive screaming audience). Saturday brought the answer: extra lighting.

Loads of lighting. They've dismantled the entire Las Vegas Strip and glued it round the walls of the studio. Everywhere you look, an impossibly bright neon tube; pulsing, blinking, flashing, strobing, scraping your retina off with its thumbnail ... *The X Factor*'s carbon footprint surely now dwarfs China's. To beat this next year, they'll have to scoop out the contestants' eyeballs and replace them with megawatt LED baubles. Then make them perform live in the middle of an exploding firework-and-diamond-factory.

But the galaxy of lightbulbs can't quite distract you from this year's thudding truth: there's no one that astonishing, really. They've got Stacey, who comes across as the sort of goonishly endearing comic character Victoria Wood would create (and is correspondingly impossible to dislike), a smattering of prettyboys, and that's about it. Even this year's joke act (a pair of twirling, tweeting Cornettos called John and Edward), doesn't seem massively grating, because we've seen it all before. Same difference.

And thanks to the new Sunday night results episode, viewers can now enjoy the same samey show twice in the same weekend.

Still, there are a few differences: last week's offering debuted with an oddly atonal opening number in which all the acts simultaneously tried to out-flat one another. Fortunately for all concerned, Robbie Williams soon bounded on stage to wipe viewers' memories by sounding marginally worse, repeatedly breaking off mid-lyric to squeal 'hello you!' and 'ooh!' and 'get her!' at random audience members. This after about two hours of sustained lecturing on the subject of what a world-class showman Mr R. Williams is courtesy of the judges the night before.

But never mind that: check out all that neon in the background! And, ooh, they've got a searchlight! Etc., etc. Repeat till Christmas.

Sleep: a guide for the knackered
26/10/2009

Sleep is underrated. According to experts, it is as important to your health as exercise, nutrition and not being set on fire. And it's the easiest route to self-improvement imaginable, far more straightforward and achievable than 100 squat thrusts. All you have to do is lie around doing nothing for eight hours. So simple, even a corpse could do it.

But not, apparently, a child. Concerned health campaigners want Britain's schoolchildren to be given 'sleep lessons' to teach them the benefits of regular night-long slumber. This is an exciting development, because it raises the prospect of 'sleep exams' – practical snoozing assessments that even the thickest kid could pass with their eyes closed.

It's easy to sleep when you're a toddler. Your mind and body skitter around all day until they burn themselves out, leaving you blissfully knackered when the sun goes down. You've only got two modes: on and off, like a blender. But once you reach adulthood, things are altogether less binary. You've got responsibilities and concerns, not to mention an alarm clock with a sarcastically oversized face sitting beside the bed mocking any attempt at shuteye. Chances are you've spent your day mumbling to co-workers, bumping into furniture and performing pedestrian chores. Your brain spends the daylight hours in a state of drowsy semi-consciousness, and only decides to spring into life when the lights go out.

The insomniac brain comes in various flavours; different personality types you're forced to share your skull with for several hours. It's like being trapped in a lift with someone who won't shut up. Sometimes your companion is a peppy irritant who passes the time by humming half-remembered TV theme tunes until 7 a.m. Other times it's a morose critic who has recently compiled a 1,500-page report on your innumerable failings and wants to run over it with you a few times before going to print. Worst of all is the hyper-aware sportscaster who offers an uninterrupted commentary describing which bits of your body are currently the least comfortable. No matter where you put that leg, he won't be satisfied. And he's convinced you've got one arm too many.

This is the point at which 'sleep lessons' might actually come in handy. Not when you're a kid (they'll only baffle you), but when you're an adult who spends several hours each night staring at the inside of your eyelids, exploring desolate inner dimensions on a rickety mental tricycle. That's when you need all the help you can get.

But practical tips only, please. No one needs to be told how important it is for your health. We've all experienced the aftermath of a sleepless night. You shuffle through the next day feeling fuzzily toxic, as though all your internal organs have been for a twenty-mile run and haven't had a hot bath yet. I've got a phrase for it: 'time-poisoning'.

Anyway, in a bid to pre-empt the health professionals, here's a list of insomnia 'dos and don'ts' guaranteed to give you a good night's sleep:

DO keep your eyes closed.

DON'T try to convince yourself you're asleep by making snoring noises.

DO focus on slowing your breathing down as much as possible. A handy tip is to imagine there's a speed camera pointing at your face; a magic speed camera that can photograph air. If you inhale or exhale too quickly, it'll fire a sharpened steel bolt into your forehead. Keep thinking about this all night.

DON'T go to bed wearing a makeshift crown fashioned from coat-hangers and bells – and if you do, don't sit upright violently shaking your head from side to side until sunrise.

DO keep the 'worrying cells' of your brain occupied. Playing simple word games in your head is an excellent tactic. If it helps, imagine you're a contestant on *Countdown*, but try not to picture the gigantic clock looming behind you on the studio wall, with its huge sweeping hand marking the frantic passage of time, its hideous unbroken sweep impassively signifying the silent extinction of second after second; the hand that describes an arc; an arc that becomes a circle; a circle that becomes a spiral; a spiral that mirrors your twisting descent as you corkscrew downwards through time itself, plunging ever deeper into a void of meaningless decay. If you start thinking about that, quickly interrupt yourself by imagining the presenter throwing to a break.

DON'T stay in bed if you haven't fallen asleep within thirty minutes. Instead, get up and do something practical, such as driving a car or operating some heavy machinery.

DO drink nine litres of warm milk before bed.

There. Simple. And if none of that works, eat some drugs, use a different pillow, or saw your head off and stick it on a pole made of lullabies. Piece of piss.

Next week: how to solve the Iranian nuclear crisis.

Masturbation minefield
31/10/2009

I don't want to claim I predicted the state of modern television in its entirety almost a decade ago or anything, but around ten years ago I wrote a website called *TV Go Home* filled with satirically exaggerated programmes, many of which have come frighteningly true.

Here's the latest example. In its *TV Go Home* incarnation, 'Masturbation Minefield' was a pornographic game aimed at lonely male viewers: a show which consisted of rude footage (such as a naked dairymaid bending over) randomly interspersed with profoundly unerotic imagery (such as an extreme close-up of Ian Beale's eye staring straight through the centre of your soul). It was a lo-fi interactive challenge: could the viewer achieve climax during the 'rude' bits without being put off by the 'unerotic' bits?

A puerile idea, but there you go. At least it wasn't real.

I lie. The new television show *Pants Off Dance Off* is essentially 'Masturbation Minefield' with one or two tweaks. The premise is as simple as its intended audience: ordinary members of the public dance to music while taking their clothes off. It's a striptease show. But, lest they be accused of peddling sordid pornography, the producers have cunningly included enough 'mines' to ensure that only the most determined psychopath could possibly manipulate their way to fruition.

First of all, the strippers themselves are self-avowedly 'zany' types: real yelping, whooping, jumping-up-and-down-and-clapping 'I'm-mad-me' irritants. Not only is it impossible to get turned on in their presence, it's impossible to assign them any human emotion whatsoever. If, instead of stripping, the programme showed them being injected with sedatives and dropped out of the back of a C-130 Hercules flying 20,000 feet above the Nevada desert, it would actually be easier to masturbate to.

Next, neatly sidestepping accusations of body fascism, they've chosen a wide variety of figures from both sexes. Fat ones, thin ones, hairy ones, ones whose faces are so disturbing they look like Steve Buscemi with Bell's palsy pressing his nose against your bathroom window ... all human life is here, apart from anyone you actually want to see naked. Occasionally they'll feature a Chippendale type or a lapdancer, but to stop this being arousing, they'll make a little window pop up, in which the next stripper (inevitably a 64-year-old man with a nose like a thumped glans) dribbles something about how they can't wait to show you their bum.

But they're not finished yet. There's still an outside chance you might be excited by the occasional shot of exposed flank, so just to nail that possibility to the floor and stove its face in with a jackboot, there's a kerrr-azy joke-filled voiceover yapping away in the background, which outstays its welcome at the first syllable. It's not very funny. In fact, if they replaced it with the soundtrack to one of Michael Buerk's 1984 Ethiopian famine reports, wailing children and all, there'd be 30 per cent more laughs.

Finally, they've cut out the actual nudity. Yes, you read that right: THEY'VE CUT OUT THE ACTUAL NUDITY. Instead, every time someone actually takes their 'pants off' (which, after all, is the entire purpose of the show), the action freezes and a URL pops up to protect their modesty. In other words, they're encouraging their audience to stop watching the show and go online instead, which must make the channel's advertisers very happy.

The website, incidentally, doesn't contain uncensored strip-teases either. But never mind! I'm told you can find footage of people actually taking their clothes off – and occasionally doing racier stuff, like kissing – elsewhere on the internet.

In summary: *Pants Off Dance Off* takes the concept of striptease, and removes both the 'strip' and the 'tease'. That's not a show, that's a vacuum. Worst of all, it's not even amusingly trashy. It's a load of energy expended for nothing. Just like masturbation itself. But less noble.

Death of a Glitterphile
07/11/2009

NB: This was a review of a real programme. Just worth pointing that out.

Don't know about you, but sometimes I can't sleep at night for wondering what it might be like if Gary Glitter were executed. I just can't picture it in quite enough detail for my liking. Would they fry him? Gas him? Or pull his screaming head off with some candy-coloured rope? I can never decide, and it often leaves me restless till sunrise. Thank God, then, for *The Execution of Gary Glitter*, which vividly envisions the trial and subsequent capital punishment of pop's most reviled sex offender so you don't have to.

I can't believe what I'm typing: this is a drama-documentary that imagines a world in which Britain has a) reinstated the death penalty for murder and paedophilia, b) changed the law so Britons can stand trial in this country for crimes committed abroad, and c) chosen Gary Glitter as its first test case. It blends archive footage, talking-head interviews with Miranda Sawyer, Garry Bushell and Ann Widdecombe, and dramatised scenes in which Gary Glitter is led into an execution chamber and hanged by the neck until dead.

He's not just swinging from a rope, mind. The Glitterphile is all over this show, like Hitler in *Downfall*. There are lengthy scenes in which he argues with his lawyer, smirks in court, plays chess with the prison chaplain, weeps on the floor of his cell, etc. Visually, we're talking late-period Glitter, with the evil wizard shaved-head-and-elongated-white-goatee combo that makes him resemble a sick alternative Santa. It would be funnier if they showed him decked out in full seventies glam gear throughout, being led to the gallows in a big spangly costume with shoulder pads so huge they get stuck in the hole as he plunges through.

I assumed the Glittercution would feature dry ice, disco lights, and a hundred party poppers going off as his neck cracked. But here there's not so much as a can of Silly String. This is a terribly serious programme.

Yes. It's illegal to laugh at this, see; it's not a comedy show, but 'an intelligent and thought-provoking examination of the issue' which 'confronts viewers with the possible consequences of capital punishment in the UK'. There's going to be an online debate afterwards and everything, which should help clear up all our thoughts about the death penalty. Let's face it, none of us really knew where we stood until we were 'confronted' by the sight of Gary Glitter staring wretchedly at an expectant noose. It really crystallised things, y'know? Before, I always thought of hanging as an abstract, faraway event existing only in ancient woodcuts or the minds of passing clouds. This makes it so much more real. My sincere thanks, Channel 4, for the searing moral clarity I've been granted. By the way, is the real Gary Glitter going to be taking part in that online debate thing afterwards? That'd be awesome.

What with this and the previous *Killing of George Bush* drama-doc a few years ago, the Channel 4 family is establishing itself as the home of thought-provoking celebrity death fantasies. Now they've whacked a president and strangled a paedo, what next? How about a two-hour drama-documentary that wonders what Britain might look like if al-Qaida attacked the Baftas? Lots of detailed close-up slow-motion shots of bullets blasting through the ribcages of absolutely everyone off *Coronation Street*, that kind of thing. It'd really kick-start that debate about terrorism we're all gasping for. Perhaps it could solve it altogether.

Or what about a mini-series showing what'd happen if you kidnapped a bunch of newsreaders and *X Factor* contestants and kept them on a remote island and glued masks on their faces and fed them LSD and MDMA for two years until they started killing each other and rutting the corpses and shoving bits of blunt stick in their eye sockets and howling at the sun? That'd help society explore its relationship with authority, celebrity, identity, controlled substances, sex, violence and sticks. And God knows we need to. Help us, Channel 4. Guide us. You're our moral compass. You're our only hope.

This is a column about buying a washing machine. A washing machine. A washing machine. A column about a washing machine. This is a column about buying a washing machine.
09/11/2009

As a child, I never pictured the adult 'me' journeying to other planets and having a fantastic time of it. Instead I pictured myself dying in a nuclear inferno. The future me was a screaming skeleton decorated with chunks of carbonised flesh and the occasional sizzling hair. Not really someone you'd have round for dinner.

Still, at least my premonition suggested I'd live an exciting life, albeit a short one. The reality is less spectacular. I never pictured myself as I was last week: a fully grown adult: alive, yet slowly losing the will to live while attempting to buy a washing machine from a high-street electrical retailer.

Let's be clear about this. Buying a washing machine is not the stuff dreams are made of. It's not a device you're going to fall in love with. It's a white box with a round mouth you shove dirty pants into. Hardly a new member of the family, unless you're a troupe of extreme performance artists.

Buying a mobile phone is easier than buying a washing machine because some phones have the decency to look ugly, thereby simplifying the decision-making process. Washing machines all look the same. Some eat bigger loads or have a more complex array of pre-wash options: whoopee doo. Some doubtless perform better than others: I wouldn't know. Bet it's all a con. Bet there's only one type of washing machine in the world, and they're all shipped from the same warehouse in slightly different packaging and sold at randomly generated prices.

I buy washing machines the same way I order wine in a restaurant: avoid the very cheapest on the basis that it'll be nasty, avoid the second cheapest on the basis that it's probably even worse, avoid the expensive options at the top of the list on the basis that they can't possibly be worth it, and wind up randomly picking something from the middle instead.

Just to make you feel even more uncertain about buying one, they don't have proper names. Once you strip the familiar manu-facturer trademarks away, all you're left with is a meaningless series of model numbers chosen specifically to confuse you. Did you order a BD4437BX or a BD3389BZ? Face it: you have no idea. Ring up to place an order and it sounds as if you're discussing chemical weapon formulae.

This is why buying a washing machine never feels 'real'. If you walk around Battersea Dogs Home, brown-eyed puppies with names such as Timbo and Ookums softly yelp for your atten-tion. Walk around Comet and you're confronted by a wall of emotionless monoliths with incomprehensible names. And that's just the staff!!!!??!!!!?!

I got caught in a high-street retail delivery trap recently; one of those Kafkaesque scenarios in which you pay for something on the basis that it will arrive at a certain time, only to find out it won't, and soon you're sucked into a spiral of helpline calls and telephone keypad options and complaints and counter-complaints until eventually you realise that you're both in a love-less relationship; needing each other, hating each other, revolving for hours in a weepy embrace, listlessly kicking at one another's shins.

But this time something new and modern happened. Shortly after one of our bitter rows, while waiting for them to call back, I went on Twitter (yes, bloody Twitter) and angrily compared the Currys electrical retail chain to the Nazis. The next day a mysterious message arrived with a number for me to call; this turned out to belong to one of their heads of PR, who'd spotted my outburst and tracked down my contact details.

It's a bit embarrassing when you find yourself talking to someone high up in a company you've loudly and publicly likened to the Third Reich only the night before. Fortunately for me, she was polite and savvy enough not to mention it. Instead she quickly sorted out my complaint, which is the closest I've ever come to feeling like a VIP, or Michael Winner. Nice for me, annoying for anyone reading about it who hasn't been afforded that kind of treatment, i.e., you. Perhaps, if I was principled, I'd have yelled 'I demand to be treated as a regular customer!' and slammed the phone down. But I didn't.

Still, if buying a big boring box from a big boring shop is a harrowing experience, isn't it time retailers were honest about it? There's no point in pretending to be fun, happy-go-lucky institutions. We're British. We know the truth and we can handle it. Dixons is running a campaign describing itself as 'the last place you want to go', which is meant to be a clever reference to its low prices (i.e., go and look at it in Harrods, then buy it from us), but effectively describes every electrical retail chain I've ever visited.

Someone needs to go further and launch a chain called Shambles, where all the familiar shortcomings are actively promoted as part of the 'experience'. The staff wear ironic dunce caps and vulture costumes; if you want to actually buy something, they walk to a stockroom ten miles away in a neighbouring county to check its availability, methodically harass you into taking out five-year cover using a subtle combination of CIA 'extraordinary rendition' psychological techniques and unashamed sulking, then arrange for it to be delivered at 7 a.m. by a surly man who'll arrive ten hours late on purpose, deliberately bring a BD4437BX instead of the BD3389BZ you ordered, attach a magic hidden 'hobbling' device that causes it to malfunction immediately before the next bank holiday weekend, screw your partner, scare your kids, wreck your life, and break wind on your doorstep as he's leaving. All of which is heavily advertised as an integral part of the service.

It'll be miserable. But at least you'll enter the transaction with your eyes wide open.

Christmas time: here come the girls
16/11/2009

'Yep, it's that time of year again – and the Christmas adverts are already on the telly', remarks a man at the start of this year's B&Q Christmas advert, proving that the grand tradition of moaning about premature Yuletide ads has itself been absorbed by the Matrix and turned into a stick to beat us with.

Let's hope this kind of jokey fourth-wall-breaking doesn't become a trend, or before long we'll all be moaning about the number of early Christmas ads that moan about the number of early Christmas ads, and then our moans about their moans will in turn form the basis of the next wave of ads, and so on and so on *ad nauseam*, until they're producing intricately constructed navel-gazing meta-commercials that are actually more self-aware than we are: fully sentient beings with thoughts and feelings of their own. And they'll rise up and strangle us in our beds. While humming 'Stop the Cavalry' by Jona Lewie.

Postmodernist intro aside, the B&Q ad is a fairly standard offering in which members of staff clutter the shop floor reciting lines about great savings and gawkily radiating a sense of forced bonhomie, as though the government's ordered them to look cheerful in case the enemy's watching. There is one startling departure from the regular formula: while most of B&Q's woodentops are presented in situ, stacking shelves or manning checkouts and presumably praying for death, one is depicted relaxing at home, sitting on his sofa in a Santa hat, wiggling his socks in front of a roaring fire. Worryingly, even though it's dark outside, he's still in uniform. Perhaps all new members of staff have the outfit sewn into their skin when they sign up, as a permanent reminder of kinship – in the same way that members of a shadowy militia might each get the same tattoo. We won't know unless they put a shower scene in their next commercial.

Come on, B&Q. We're waiting.

Still, at least B&Q's effort features common-or-garden schmoes, not a stomach-churning galaxy of stars. Watching Marks & Spencer's Christmas ad is like sitting through *Children in Need*. Joanna Lumley, Stephen Fry, Myleene Klass, Jennifer Saunders, Twiggy, James Nesbitt, Wallace and Gromit ... it's so chummy and cosy and thoroughly delighted by its own existence, I keep hoping it'll suddenly cut to a shot of a deranged crystal meth user squatting on the cold stone floor of a disused garage, screaming about serpents while feverishly sawing their own hand off at the wrist.

Instead it jokily tries to undercut itself by including a cameo from Philip Glenister, standing in a pub to prove what a bumptiously down-to-earth Mr Bloke he is. His job is to stand at the bar claiming that the best thing about Christmas is the sexy girl from the Marks & Sparks ads running around in her knickers. Then it cuts to the sexy girl from the Marks & Sparks ads running around in her knickers, as though this is somehow as iconic a Christmas image as Rudolph's nose or the little baby Jesus. Listen here, M&S: few things in life are more pukesome and hollow than a self-mythologising advert – so next year do us all a favour and just shake a few sleighbells, flog us some pants, and then fuck off back to your smug little shop and be quiet.

Like Marks & Spencer, Boots appears to have overestimated the popularity of its own Christmas adverts. Unless I'm mistaken, the people of this nation are not brought together as one joyful whole by the 'Here Come the Girls' campaign, so its self-celebratory tone seems somewhat misplaced. What started out a few years ago as a mildly amusing commercial in which an army of women prepared in unison for an office party has devolved into a nightmare vision of the future in which large groups of female office workers spontaneously organise themselves into a cackling mobile hen night at the first whiff of Christmas. This year they're causing mayhem in a restaurant. They're mad, they are!!!! One even tries to get off with the waiter!!!!

I usually quite like women, but this advert makes me want to kill about 900 of them with my bare hands. It ends with the tiresome ladettes marching down a high street triumphantly singing the 'Here Come the Girls' song out loud, like an invading squadron tormenting the natives with its war cry. Next year they'll probably be armed. Fear this.

Of the supermarkets, Sainsbury's are running with a relatively innocuous bit of fluff in which Jamie Oliver tours Britain handing out free vol-au-vents to greedy members of the public, like a zookeeper throwing sprats to a load of barking seals. It's been given a documentary feel, although everywhere he goes looks suspiciously wintry, with snow and swirling white flakes, which is weird considering it was probably shot in August. Still, that's climate change for you.

But the winner of the worst Christmas advert trophy for the second year running is Morrisons. They've got several short offerings, including one where Nick Hancock appears to be preparing Christmas dinner in the afterlife – but the prize goes to their centrepiece ad: a bafflingly pedestrian sixty-second fantasy in which straggle-haired midget Richard Hammond wheels an empty trolley through an over-dressed, snowblown Tunbridge Wells, yelping about food and steadily gathering a pied-piper-style following of locals (and Denise Van Outen) as he heads for an illuminated branch of Morrisons in the distance, like a wise man following a star – or, more accurately, like a slightly unkempt mouse following a shop. I keep hoping it'll suddenly pull out to reveal this is all just a slightly underwhelming dream he's experiencing, and that he's actually still in a coma following his 2006 rocket car mishap.

And judging by the look in his eyes, so is he.

Jordward
21/11/2009

People of Britain! Why so sad? You have at least four different flavours of mulch to choose from! Enjoy what you're given and shut up. The other day I was watching a report about the *The X Factor* charity single during an ITV news bulletin that followed *I'm A Celebrity Get Me Out Of Here!* It was the day Jordan went into the jungle. Jordan in the jungle, Jedward on the news. The media assumes you're fascinated by both of them.

There's not much to be fascinated by. Take Jordan. Ant and Dec announced her arrival on their gameshow in which celebrities eat live insects for publicity as though it was the most startling cultural event of the twenty-first century – a Festival of Britain for our times. She was presented as someone who divides opinion, which she simply isn't. Everyone feels the same way about Jordan. She's someone you're supposed to dislike, and in disliking her you're supposed to feel marginally better about yourself. So we all moan about this woman, moan about the weight of coverage devoted to this woman, and meanwhile this woman has herself sliced open and injected and sewn back together until she resembles some kind of rubbery pirate ship figurehead, a weird booby caricature looming at us out of the mist. But this mutilation only makes us moan all the more. No one's coming out of this well.

At least Jordan herself seems oblivious. She hardly radiates emotion. Her voice is a perpetual low flatline, and she can't or won't perform basic facial expressions, as if she's been unplugged on the inside. As fiery reality show catalysts go, sending in a mountain goat with a load of crude personal insults daubed on its flank would be a better bet. Instead, the best they can come up with is a boring tabloid story in boring human form.

Meanwhile, in the *X Factor* universe, we're encouraged to love/hate two seventeen-year-old twins with videogame haircuts called John and Edward. Of course the phrase 'John and Edward' takes too long to read or say, so to our collective shame it's been shortened to 'Jedward'. Ha ha! Jedward! Ha ha ha ha ha! Jedward! Ha ha! SuBo! LiLo! Ha ha! Brangelina! Ha ha! Bennifer! Ha ha ha ha ha! I am loving that! I am loving that! Ha ha!

Let's hope this stinking world comes to an end as soon as possible. Leswossible.

Simon Cowell keeps making proclamations about 'leaving the country' if John and Edward win *The X Factor*. Doesn't he leave the country each week? He flies to LA every ten minutes to appear on *American Idol*. And on his way back he lands his jet on a private island made entirely of gold ingots, to spend his weekend strolling up and down the beach listlessly kicking clouds of powdered diamond into a sea of molten platinum.

Of course, Cowell's yabberings are almost certainly a smart double bluff designed to ensure people continue to vote for the twins, because he knows they're the most interesting performers in this year's contest: while the others are merely boring, John and Edward are just a bit shit. This makes them the most interesting thing in the entire programme by default. We're accustomed to Cheryl Cole, and the judges' interpersonal bickering got stale some time ago, so the only other faintly diverting thing in the show is Cowell's hair. Suspiciously jet-black, bristly and curiously flattened on top, as though he prepares for each episode by dipping his head in matt-black Dulux and painting his dressing room wall with it, Simon's hair continues to mesmerise even after all these years.

Silly hair and shit singers: that's *X Factor*, the nation's sole mainstream conduit for popular music since the decline and fall of *Top of the Pops*. All the songs sound the same, all the singers are alike, and the only interesting acts are mediocre and officially sanctioned hate figures. One day we'll emerge on the other side of this unprecedented cultural drought and wonder how the hell our imaginations survived.

Till then, enjoy what you're given. And shut up.

Past Careying
23/11/2009

Last week Mariah Carey turned on the Christmas lights at the Westfield shopping centre in Shepherds Bush, west London. That might sound like a trivial event of interest only to cretins, but remember: hundreds of thousands of brave men and women died in combat so the current generation could enjoy such freedoms. The assembled masses weren't simply taking mobile phone snapshots of a vastly overrated singer emptily promoting a commercially appropriated religious festival celebrating the birth of a man who would have doubtless vomited up his own ribcage in disgust at the mere sight of the hollow, anaesthetising capitalist moonbase that is the Westfield Centre. No. They were honouring the fallen. Sort of. Vaguely. OK: not at all.

Anyway, any story featuring Carey has to at some point dwell on a list of outlandish arch-diva requests, and this one didn't disappoint. According to early press reports, she demanded to be driven along a long pink carpet in a vintage Rolls-Royce before arriving at the podium (also pink) at which point she'd activate the lights by waving a magic wand, accompanied by 20 white kittens and 100 white doves. Pink, butterfly-shaped confetti would shower all around her at the end of the ceremony.

In the event, that turned out to be bullshit. She arrived in a Merc, burbled a few inanities ('Wow, I've never been to a mall in London before!'), shook hands with some charity kids, and sodded off out of there. In fact the most startling thing about Carey's turn was her outfit: a pair of jeans so tight she was vaginally ingesting them. No kittens. No doves. Not even a pink podium. You could be forgiven for thinking the papers had just lazily printed a load of PR bibble cynically engineered to promote the event by playing on popular assumptions about Carey's caprice, and had done so without bothering to check any of the facts.

Thing is, even if Carey had made a string of crazy demands, I wouldn't blame her. I doubt many celebrities start out behaving like foot-stamping little Caligulas, but years of having their arses kissed left, right and centre – yes, even on that centre bit – steadily drives them insane.

I've seen it happen in my own life, in my own little way. About ten years ago I was co-presenting a technology show on a niche digital channel with an audience of about six. This was my first time in front of the cameras. I had less screen presence than the Invisible Man and the sex appeal of a fatal headwound. Since the show was shot in the 'zoo' format popular at the time, the camera often roved dangerously close to my face, which made the experience of watching me a bit like gazing through a security peephole to see John Merrick leering ominously on your doorstep. I was unfunny, uncomfortable and charmless.

Things have changed since then, obviously. I'm fatter.

Anyway, during the first week of making the show, the runner would come over between takes to check whether I needed anything. A chair, perhaps? A glass of water? At first, this was embarrassing. I didn't want anyone making a fuss of me. But one of the primary rules of television is to keep 'the talent' happy, and consequently there was no let-up. So you accept the proffered chair, sup the glass of water. And after several weeks of pampering, something snaps in your brain.

You grow accustomed to the attention; like wireless broadband, it's an everyday miracle you simply take for granted. Before long, the moment you get thirsty, your first thought is no longer 'I'll go and pour myself a drink', but something along the lines of 'Where's that runner gone?', 'Why haven't I been watered already?', or 'Isn't this a disgusting breach of my human rights?'

And that's the treatment given to an ugly bloke on a cheap satellite show. I can scarcely imagine the level of forelock-tugging servility Carey must have encountered during her lifetime. Her record company probably employs someone to walk ten paces in front of her, breathing on all the doorknobs in her mansion so they won't feel cold to the touch. Not that she'll have touched a doorknob in fifteen years. She must think every door in the world opens by magic at the first sign of her approach.

Under those circumstances, you'd rapidly lose all respect for 'regular people' and start issuing lunatic demands for them to follow, partly to keep yourself amused, and partly out of sheer disgust. After all, if you're going to bow each time I enter the room, I might as well make you kiss my feet a few times while you're down there.

Come to think of it, maybe that's why it's hard to detect much in the way of palpable feeling in Carey's music. Her singing voice wavers up and down through the octaves, like someone slowly tuning a shortwave radio in search of an authentic emotion. It's technically amazing, but almost impossible to relate to on a human level – possibly because she no longer experiences anything akin to regular human life. She might not even experience proper emotions these days. She might have people who do that for her. Aides who rush in and hitch up the corners of her mouth each time she starts to smile, and mop down her cheeks with tiny hand-knitted towels when she cries.

But is it Mariah's fault if she's over-indulged? No. It's yours. You specifically are to blame.

Oh OK: it's society's fault. If society insists on treating celebrities like royalty, there's little point lambasting them for behaving like princesses. It's nurture, not nature. And besides, the press is probably making it up anyway.

Tales of the cosseted few whistling through an unreliable

sphincter into the eyes and ears of the many: that's entertainment news, that is.

Dubai dooby doo
30/11/2009

I am phenomenally stupid. Stupid in every conceivable way except one: I'm dimly aware that I'm stupid. This means I spend much of my time assuming the rest of the world knows better, that everyone else effortlessly comprehends things I struggle to understand. Things like long division, or which mobile phone tariff to go for. In many ways, this is a comforting thought, as it means there's a limitless pool of people more intelligent than myself I can call on for advice.

But sometimes I find out my gut assumption was right all along, and it's a deeply unsettling experience. Take Dubai. I'm no expert on Dubai. Never been there, and only read about it in passing. The one thing I knew was that everything I heard about it sounded impossible. It was a modern dreamland. A concrete hallucination. A sarcastic version of Las Vegas. Dubai's skyline was dotted with gigantic whimsical behemoths. There were six-star hotels shaped like sails or shoes or starfish. Skyscrapers so tall the moon had to steer its way around them. It had immense off-shore developments: man-made archipelagos that resembled levels from *Super Mario Sunshine*. One was in the shape of a spreading palm tree. Another consisted of artificial islands representing every country in the world in miniature. As if that wasn't enough, a proposed future development called The Universe would depict the entire solar system.

When I first read about all this stuff, I felt a bit uneasy. None of it sounded real or even vaguely sustainable. I'd been to Las Vegas a few times and seen crazy developments come and go. The first time I visited, the hot new attractions were the Luxor, an immense onyx pyramid, and Treasure Island, a pirate fantasy world replete with lifesize galleons bobbing outside it. Roughly halfway between the pair of them, a replica New York was under construction. By my next visit, the novelty value of both the Luxor and Treasure Island had long since palled, and they now seemed less exotic than Chessington World of Adventures. Meanwhile, unreal New York had been joined by unreal Paris and unreal Venice.

But even at their most huge and demented, none of these insane monuments looked as huge and demented as the projects being announced in Dubai. Yet the novelties, while larger, were wearing thin even more quickly. Dubai's The World archipelago hadn't even opened when the same developers announced The Universe, thereby making The World sound like a rather diminished prototype before anyone had moved in.

In Las Vegas the grimy engine that paid for each new chunk of mega-casino was there in plain sight at street level: woozy drunks thumbing coins into slots twenty-four hours a day. Hundreds of thousands of them, slumped semi-conscious in rows like dozing cattle hooked up to milking machines. Ching ching ching, slurp slurp slurp. It was like watching a gigantic crystal spider increasing in size as it coldly sapped the husks of its victims. Ugly, but at least it made sense.

Where were the coin slots in Dubai? I had no idea. I just gawped at the photographs and was secretly impressed by the cleverness of the people who'd managed to generate so much money they could safely take leave of their senses and construct 300-foot buttplug skyscrapers and artificial floating cities shaped like doodles scribbled in the margins of sanity. To my dumb, uncomprehending eyes it looked like a collection of impossible follies. But what did I know? Clearly the people actually paying for all this stuff knew precisely what they were doing.

But ah and oh. It appears my uninformed gut reaction – that slightly worried vertigo shiver, the hazy sense of 'but surely they can't do that' – may have been precisely the correct response. Now it's in trouble, the world's financial markets seem shocked and surprised, like Bagpuss being disappointed to learn that the mice from the mouse organ couldn't really create an endless supply of chocolate biscuits from thin air. They should've phoned me for advice. If only I'd known. I could have charged a fortune. But then I'm so dumb I'd probably have blown it investing in an artificial Dubai archipelago shaped like Snoopy's head or something.

In the cold light of 2009, Dubai resembles a mystical Oz that was somehow accidentally wished into existence during an insane decade-long drugs bender. Those psychedelic structures, pictured in a fever by the mad and privileged, physically constructed by the poor and exploited, now look downright embarrassing, like a Facebook photo of a drunken mistake, as though someone some-where is going to wake up and groan, 'Oh my head ... what did I do last night? Huh? I bankrolled a $200bn hotel in the shape of a croissant? I shipped the workers in from India and paid them how little? Oh man! The shame. What was I thinking?'

The world's tallest skyscraper, the Burj Dubai, is due to open in January. It looks like an almighty shard of misplaced enthusiasm, a lofty syringe injecting dementia directly into the skies, a short-lived spike on a printed readout, or a pin pricking a gigantic bubble. Not a shape you'd want to find yourself unexpectedly sitting on, in other words. Just ask the world's financial markets, once they've finished screaming.

Fill your own bucket
05/12/2009

TV advertising used to work like this: you sat on your sofa while creatives were paid to throw a bucket of shit in your face. Today you're expected to sit on the bucket, fill it with your own shit, and tip it over your head while filming yourself on your mobile. Then you upload the video to the creatives. You do the work; they still get paid.

Hail the rise of 'loser-generated content'; commercials assembled from footage shot by members of the public coaxed into participating with the promise of TV glory. The advantages to the advertiser are obvious: it saves cash and makes your advert feel like part of some warm, communal celebration rather than the thirty-second helping of underlit YouTube dog piss it is.

Witness the current OXO campaign. According to the website: 'Has your Family got the OXO Factor? It's 2009. There's no such thing as "the OXO Family" any more. We're all OXO Families! That's why we asked you to film your family performing the script for our new TV ad, for the chance to see yourselves on TV, alongside some of Britain's other brilliant families.' Or 'other insufferable arseholes', depending on your point of view.

End result: a bunch of wacky-doo show-offs titting around in their kitchens, each reciting the same script, which they're not allowed to deviate from. They can perform it 'ironically', and indeed they all do, which somehow only makes it more horrible still: the OXO family of 2009 may display faint traces of corporate-approved subversion, provided they adhere to the corporate-approved screenplay. Lynda Bellingham's fictional family of yore might've been insipid, but at least they weren't willing participants in a macabre dystopian dumb-show.

Phone ads are worse. 'Everybody's brightdancing', according to the *X Factor* break bumpers. 'Brightdancing' consists of shooting a video of yourself waving your mobile around while being filmed by a Talk Talk website gizmo which turns the glare from your mobile's screen into a ribbon of light. It's less creative than choosing which colour iPod you want for Christmas. 'Brightdancing'. Fuck me.

Then there's Josh, a simpering middle-class mop who's apparently 'forming a supergroup' for T-Mobile. According to the official advert backstory, Josh was strolling down the street one day when a T-Mobile film crew asked him what he'd do if he had free texts for life. Rather than pointing out that 'free texts for life' means dick-all in a world containing the internet, Josh burbled something about forming a band. A few weeks later and gosh oh crikey that's precisely what's happening! And we're all invited! Hey everyone! Join Josh's band!

As well as TV spots recounting the irritating story of Josh and his 'volunteers' (Yikes! They're busking in an open-top London bus! Bonkers!), there are YouTube videos of Josh's utterly spontaneous and not-at-all-stage-managed musical quest. The group has its own song, which you're encouraged to perform and upload yourself, hastening humankind's slow cultural death in the process. The recurring melody sounds suspiciously like a seven-note ringtone, while the lyrics speak vaguely of inclusion and connectivity – y'know, the sort of thing they guff on about in mobile phone ads. The third line is 'I call up all of my friends'. Why call anyone? You've got free texts for life, you fucking prick.

It's so clumsily contrived it wouldn't fool a hen, yet we're meant to welcome this 'supergroup' as an authentic grassroots musical phenomenon. On MySpace, Josh (or whoever's controlling him) claims, 'It's a shame so many cynics think this band is completely manufactured.'

So it's a genuine people's movement, then? And this band doesn't contain any paid-for session musicians? And that song wasn't written by professional tunesmiths-for-hire? And the lyrics weren't penned by some dickshoe at Saatchi & Saatchi? Hmm. Go fuck yourselves, T-Mobile. Stop trying to 'crowdsource'. You're embarrassing yourselves. Scram. And empty that bucket on your way out.

Naughty or Nice
12/12/2009

Like a giant black velvet cat whose tusk-white incisors glint mal-evolently in the darkness as it slinks noiselessly towards its prey, the end of the year is almost upon us. Eager to get things over with, Christmas has faded in extra early this year. Everywhere you look it's yuletide this and festive that. Each shop window sports a snowman; each street lamp a coil of winking fairylights. I had a piss the other day and tinsel came out. Yippee for Christmas.

Christmas, of course, has its very own 'face of the channel': Santa Claus, although he doesn't appear in adverts as often as he used to. For the past few years Coca-Cola has been aggressively pushing Santa as some kind of God of its own making, so it's hardly surprising that in other ads, for other products, he's been usurped by celebrity cameos, or in Iceland's case, Jason Donovan and a Nolan.

He doesn't show up in films so much these days, either. It's been fifteen years since the last remake of *Miracle on 34th Street*, and almost a quarter of a century since *Santa Claus: The Movie*. Part of the problem is that you can't really do much with Santa himself. He's not a cop on the edge trying to outrun his own demons. He's a chuckling fat man. In character terms, Santa is bollocks.

If you really want to see Santa on screen in the run-up to 25 December, your best bet is to tune in to *Santavision* (Sky Channel 200), where he's preparing for the yuletide season by sitting in an unconvincing living room mercilessly wringing money from as many people as possible with an interactive text-to-TV dedication scheme. Merry Christmas!

The idea is simple: you text him the name of your kiddywink, accompanied by the words 'NAUGHTY' or 'NICE', and Santa duly enters them on to his 'Naughty' or 'Nice' list, scrolling up the right-hand side of the screen. He'll also say their name aloud, usually as part of a sparkling ad-lib such as, 'Ho, ho, ho! I see GREGORY has been a naughty boy! Naughty GREGORY.' This bespoke improvisation costs £1.50 a pop and, as the website is keen to point out, you're not allowed to include the names of more than one child per text, which seems a tad unsporting, since the largest families are often the ones most financially stretched at

Christmas. It's almost as if, contrary to everything we've been led to believe, Santa doesn't give a shit about kids after all.

Perhaps that's why he's lost weight. Apparently these days Santa looks like a skinny bloke in his twenties in a cheap beard, sweating his way through what amounts to a televised prison sentence. Sometimes he switches his microphone off and holds lengthy mysterious conversations with someone on the end of a phone, live on air. Possibly his lawyer.

At least you can keep his spirits up by sending in inappropriate names. I fearlessly borrowed someone's phone and used it to trick Santa into admonishing the serial murderer Dennis Nilsen for being a naughty boy. He also read out a follow-up name – the rather puerile 'Carmen Mite-Hitz' – but sadly blew it by mispronouncing the forename as 'Cameron'. A subsequent attempt to get him to read out the name 'Ivana Fahkz-Humbaddi' failed completely; they wouldn't even add it to the list, the cowards. If you fancy a laugh and don't mind pissing money up the wall like a champagne socialist, you could do worse than spend this afternoon texting in innocent-looking but obscene-sounding names for Santa to babble at his audience of oblivious children.

Currently, *Santavision* only runs from 4 p.m. to 7 p.m. In an ideal world it'd come back on air at closing time, with an 'Adult Santavision' service modelled on *Babestation* and the like, in which nihilistic drunks text in increasingly demeaning physical commands for him to obey, such as stuffing his balls into a stocking or coming down the chimney. Or let's dispense with the wordplay entirely and just make him roll around on the floor, clapping and farting until Christmas at £1.50 per emission. The perfect metaphor for the entire season.

Rage within the machine
21/12/2009

At the time of writing, it's not clear whether the 2009 Christmas No. 1 will be 'The Climb' by Joe McElderry, or 'Killing in the Name' by Rage Against the Machine. I've just done my bit to inch the latter closer to the top spot by downloading it – something I'd resisted doing until now because I initially thought there was something a bit embarrassing about the campaign. After all, as every other internet smartarse pointed out, both tracks are owned by Sony BMG – so no matter which one sells the most, Simon Cowell wins. In other words, even by raging against the machine, you're somehow raging within it.

But profit isn't the point – or at least it's not the reason I downloaded it. For one thing, I happen to think 'Killing in the Name' is an excellent song, so I've already got something out of it. Most importantly, it contains genuine emotion. Even if the climactic repeated howls of 'Fuck you, I won't do what you tell me!' put you in mind of a teenager loudly refusing to tidy his bedroom – as opposed to a masked anarchist hurling petrol bombs at the riot squad – there is at least an authentic human sentiment being expressed. Zack de la Rocha is audibly pissed off.

Compare this to the pissweak vocal doodle that is Joe McElderry's *X Factor* single. For a song whose lyrics ostensibly document an attempt to gather the spiritual strength to overcome adversity and thereby attain enlightenment, 'The Climb' is about as inspiring as a Lion bar. It's a listless announcement on a service station tannoy; an advert for buttons; a fart in a clinic; a dot on a spreadsheet. Listening to it from beginning to end is like watching a bored cleaner methodically wiping a smudge from a Formica worksurface.

But then nobody's buying 'The Climb' in order to actually listen to it. They're buying it out of sedated confusion, pushing a button they've been told will make them feel better. It's the sound of the assisted suicide clinic, and it doesn't deserve to be No. 1 this Christmas.

This isn't mere pop snobbery, by the way. I'd rather see Girls Aloud at No. 1 than Editors. But 'The Climb' is a lame cover version of a lame Miley Cyrus song. If *X Factor* can't be arsed to do better than that, its grip on the yuletide charts deserves to be broken.

Anyway, while I'm happy for Rage Against the Machine to be enjoying the sales and publicity, I can't help thinking we could've organised a slightly better protest ourselves. Chances are the *X Factor* will try to kick back extra hard next year – perhaps by actually releasing a song with a melody in it – so it's best to start planning the resistance now.

The temptation might be to pour a lot of time and effort into creating a catchy anti-*X Factor* anthem, but the smartest counter-move would be to release something short, cheap and throwaway that isn't even a proper song at all. I propose a track called 'Simon Cowell: Shit for Ears', which consists of a couple of eight-year-olds droning the phrase 'Simon Cowell, shit for ears' four times in a row in the most deliberately tuneless manner possible. It should last only about fifteen seconds or so. Quick enough to register; brief enough not to outstay its welcome.

Then we release it online at the lowest price possible. What's the bare minimum you can charge and still be eligible for a chart position? It could be as little as 2p. Because the track is just recorded on to a cheap mic, and released without the assistance of any record label, 100 per cent of the profits go to charity.

Dot-eyed CGI judge and omnipresent hair product spokes-woman Cheryl Cole recently complained that the campaign against McElderry's single was 'mean', adding 'If that song – or should I say campaign – by an American group is our Christmas No. 1, I'll be gutted for him and our charts.'

She's missing the point. It's not mean: it's funny. If the Christmas No. 1 turns out to be an angry, confrontational rock track that concludes with an explosion of f-words, it'll be precisely the shot in the arm the charts have been sorely lacking the last few years: something that puts a genuine smile on the face of millions of people; sensitive people, thoughtful people; people alienated by the stifling cloud of grinning mechanical pap farted into their faces on a weekly basis by cocky, clattering, calculating talent shows like *X Factor*. It would give these people hope. Maybe only in a very small and silly way, but still: a tiny spoonful of hope. And what could be more Christmassy than that?

In retrospect, reading this back now, I seem to be taking everything in the world terribly seriously indeed. Like, about twice as seriously as necessary. I mean really: 'a tiny spoonful of hope'? What a dick I am.

Proximity Big Brother
09/01/2010

The final *Celebrity Big Brother* is here. Yes, the final one. As you watch Sisqo hooking his pants out of his bumcrack, or Vinnie Jones boiling an egg, remind yourself that this is your last opportunity to do so, and attempt to defy the tears prickling the rim of your eyeballs. Where do we go from here, as a people? I cannot tell you. All I have to offer is sneering descriptions of the contestants. My existence is pointless. I'm banging on the glass here. Release me or kill me, someone.

This year's launch night included a telling format-change. Normally we're introduced to each celebrity via a short VT in which they themselves explain what a must-watch character they'll be ('I'm not afraid to speak me mind . . . if anyone in there winds me up the wrong way, there'll be fireworks' etc., etc.). But this year, these talking-head character sketches were absent, replaced by short packages in which Davina patiently explained why each inmate qualified as a 'celebrity'. Often the evidence consisted of photographs of them standing near other, indisputably more famous, people on a red carpet. Two of the contestants appear to have been invited to participate on the basis that they've been inside a famous person, and one because a famous person has been inside them. That's not celebrity, that's proximity. 'Proximity Big Brother' actually has a nice ring to it.

The trouble with introducing each player via their CV is that the viewer ends up with zero idea of their actual character. Basshunter's arrival was a low point. His VT package might as well have been a short educational film outlining the properties of magnesium. In fact, sending in a small mound of powdered magnesium in his place wouldn't have been an entirely bad idea. What happens when you introduce a small quantity of magnesium to a room full of quasi-famous people? Nothing. But at least that's a genuine 'TV experiment'.

So who's in? Well, you've got Vinnie Jones (yawn), Alex Reid (a videogame version of Daniel Craig), Dane Bowers (nice but yawn), Lady Sovereign (a Sporty Spice keychain figurine), the aforementioned Basshunter (a stretched Swedish Hasselhoff), Rolling-Stone-seductress Katia (effectively a student-age Alice who's wandered through the looking glass and into her TV), and Nicola T of 'having tits' fame.

Nicola T already seems likely to establish herself as TV's dimmest comic character since the heyday of Trigger in *Only Fools And Horses*. She communicates exclusively by asking stunningly stupid questions, and always seems surprised and confused by the answer. It's an endearing trait, albeit one which would swiftly become grating during a day trip to the Science Museum.

Grand dame Stephanie Beacham should probably win, on account of her habit of sitting in the corner making laconic observations, like a louche unseen narrator. Just for an experiment, they should scrap Marcus Bentley for an episode and get her to do the voiceover. Or permanently station her in an adjoining antechamber and let her communicate with the other contestants via an animatronic stag's head mounted on the wall.

Finally, there are the Americans. Sisqo, a poor man's Skee-Lo. *Usual Suspects* actor-turned-born-again-rightwing-talk-radio-scary-man Stephen Baldwin, who looks and sounds like an escaped serial killer who, having cut off Alec Baldwin's face with a jagged spear of glass, is currently wearing it as a mask and speaking very softly in a bid to evade the authorities. He's the contestant most likely to perform a live, spontaneous exorcism in the house. In fact, I thought he might do precisely that when Heidi Fleiss walked in. Fleiss is spooky. She vaguely resembles Aerosmith's Steve Tyler morphing into Jack Skellington from *The Nightmare Before Christmas*.

And that's the lot. *Celeb BB* can probably safely shuffle off into history with a mild snort, leaving we viewers to blink away the tears and try to put our lives back together. If we possibly, possibly can.

As you may be aware, this was not the final Celebrity Big Brother, *because Channel Five revived it shortly afterwards. It will never, ever end. Never. Ever.*

Britain's got payback
11/01/2010

So then. Following a half-hearted coup attempt, which turned out to be the equivalent of Hoon and Hewitt trying to assassinate their target by firing a rubber band at his head as he walked past the tuckshop, bookmakers say there is currently 25 per cent less chance of Labour winning the general election than there is of Kevin Keegan giving birth to a horse on St Swithin's Day.

The Conservatives don't have to do much except wait patiently, gliding towards 6 May like a baleen whale with its mouth flapping open, lazily preparing to inhale an acre of krill. Unless

David Cameron holds a live televised press conference at which he pulls his fleshy mask off to reveal he's been Darren Day all along, they've got it in the bag.

Even a preposterous advertising campaign can't dent the Tories. All over London, billboards depict Cameron looking you in the eye with an expression of genteel concern, accompanied by the slogan 'We can't go on like this'. To the observer, the overall effect is that of a man trying to wriggle out of an unfulfilling sexual relationship without hurting your feelings. Would you vote for that? Not normally, no. But when the opposition is a flock of startled, shrieking hens, your range of options shrinks drastically.

But perhaps there's still a glimmer of hope for Labour. I recently watched several episodes of a high-quality US comedy-drama serial called *Breaking Bad*. The storyline revolves around an underachieving, debt-ridden fifty-year-old chemistry teacher who discovers he's got terminal cancer. But wait, it gets funnier. Realising he has absolutely nothing to lose, he decides to become a crystal meth dealer in an insane last-ditch attempt to provide financial support for his family when he's gone. Cue plenty of pitch-black hi-jinks.

It's a good show. It's also a road map for Labour. The party's condition is similarly terminal, so it might as well go for broke by announcing a series of demented and ill-advised election pledges in an openly desperate bid to retain power. Who knows? It might just work. And if it's having a hard time choosing some make-or-break policies, I'll be only too happy to provide a list. Starting now.

Pledge 1: Promise to govern while wearing spandex leotards like they do on *Hole in the Wall* if elected
On the face of it, this sounds terrible. No one wants to see David Miliband rising to his feet in a silver bodysuit so tight you can make out every facet of his groin in topographic detail. They don't even want to read that description of it. But while it might

be hard on our eyes, it would be uncomfortable and humiliating for the MPs. And think about it: they have to wear it every day for at least four years. They're not allowed to take them off either, so by the end of the term the House of Commons would reek. I'd vote for that. Come on, it would be funny.

Suggested campaign poster: Ed Balls in horribly tight leotard.

Slogan: 'SEE BALLS PUSH FOR GLORY'.

Pledge 2: Tudor-style execution of Simon Cowell

This would be desperately unfair on Cowell, who would be arrested, held in the Tower of London, and beheaded on live television should Labour get back in. No matter how low your opinion of *Britain's Got Talent*, the man has clearly done nothing to deserve that kind of extreme treatment. But extreme treatment grabs headlines. And the recent Christmas chart triumph of Rage Against the Machine over Joe McElderry's *X Factor* single indicates a hitherto-untapped, steadily expanding groundswell of anti-Cowell discontent which a cynical and desperate party could exploit for its own nefarious ends. Barbaric and cynical, yes – but on balance marginally more humane than scapegoating an entire minority and establishing death camps or anything quite as horrible like that.

Poster: Photoshop of Cowell's head on pole.

Slogan: 'BRITAIN'S GOT PAYBACK'.

Pledge 3: Free warm croissants on buses

Yes it's lame, but it'll get people talking far more than yet another dull promise about education spending or the like. Not only can the voter imagine it actually happening, they can virtually smell it in their mind's nose. And that feels good during a cold snap. Come on, Labour. Go for it!

Poster: Mouth-watering close-up of warm croissant.

Slogan: 'MMMM!'

Pledge 4: Let the country exit with a bang

Let's face it, no matter what we do the environment's knackered, the deficit's insurmountable, and *Britain's Got Talent* will return in the summer. The future's bleak, so rather than face it, why not encourage the entire nation to go out in a frenzy of nihilistic excess? Step one: legalise everything. Step two: sell all remaining national assets to the Chinese. Step three: spend everything we have on chocolate pudding, narcotics and sex toys. Step four: announce the beginning of a year-long mass public orgy during which absolutely anything goes and participation is compulsory. Step five: on New Year's Eve, we congregate naked around a massive bomb and nuke ourselves out of history forever.

Poster: An explicit orgy photo.

Slogan: 'HEY, WE MIGHT AS WELL'.

Anyway, there you go. One or more are probably worth a try. In *Breaking Bad*, the protagonist uses his grim predicament as the catalyst for a string of crazy actions that leave him feeling more alive than ever. Perhaps embracing an equally hopeless situation with similarly mad gusto is the only actual hope Labour has left.

The treacherous snow
16/01/2010

Oh, how it snowed. It snowed like a bitch. It snowed so hard you could be forgiven for thinking God had decided planet Earth was an embarrassing celestial typo and was desperately trying to Tipp-Ex it out of existence. The build-up was unrelenting: everywhere you looked compacted strata of white powder looked back at you. It was like being trapped in one of Shaun Ryder's nostrils circa 1992. But colder. Much colder.

It was so cold your breath hung in the air before you, then froze, plummeted and broke your foot. And icy. Did I mention it was icy? It was so icy that if you lived in a south-facing house in Edinburgh and slipped outside your front door, you'd slide all the way to Plymouth and fly off the edge of Britain without passing a single frictional surface along the way.

Not that you'd drown: the sea was frozen too, so you'd simply carry on skidding, all the way around the entire circumference of the globe, eventually ending up back where you started. Where you'd find a news crew waiting to interview you.

You may think I'm exaggerating. So do I. But I've been watching the saturation news coverage of Britain's cold snap and consequently it's hard not to view the snowfall through apocalyptic eyes. The thick layer of snow received, quite literally, blanket coverage. As far as the twenty-four-hour rolling networks were concerned, this wasn't a freak weather condition. This was war. Death from the skies. Earth versus the Ice Warriors. Snowmageddon.

Actually, 'Snowmageddon' would've been a good name for it. Every news crisis needs a snappy name. The BBC initially christened it 'Frozen Britain'. Sky opted for 'The Big Freeze', and everyone else eventually fell into line. The Big Freeze it was.

The minute the government started issuing guidance about not making journeys unless strictly necessary, the reporters hit the road. Every five minutes we had to go live to some poor sod standing outdoors in Benson or Brome or Bromsgrove or Birmingham, shivering like a man with a vibrator in his pocket, telling us how cold it was through his chattering teeth. Not that you could actually see him: chances are he was obliterated by an alabaster flurry.

Presumably at some point the British climate had promised to behave and then unceremoniously reneged on the deal, because everyone kept referring to the weather as 'treacherous'. The phrase 'treacherous conditions' was repeated like a mantra, like a catchy tune the news couldn't shift.

Every witch-hunt has its victims, and before long the accusing finger pointed at roads and pavements: the reporters screamed that these too were 'treacherous', and presumably had been in cahoots with the weather all along. Icy patches on pathways provided the news with chucklesome footage of people falling over and agitated soundbites in which aggrieved pratfallers complained about the lack of grit on pavements. You can't please some people. One minute they're whining about the mollycoddling nanny state, the next they're insisting the council employs a man to walk directly in front of them, shovelling grit beneath each potential footfall.

Not that there was grit to spare for the pavements. The news was neurotic about dwindling grit. When they weren't throwing live to a man with snow up to his balls, they were linking to a woman in a Puffa jacket close to tears at a gritting depot.

Gritting depots don't usually get this much prime-time TV exposure. There's never been a rough-and-tumble comedy drama starring Jimmy Nail set in a gritting depot, or a 'Live From the Gritting Depot' variety hour. Why? Because gritting depots are unbelievably fucking boring, a fact the news did its best to prove for several thousand hours.

At the time of writing, the Big Freeze began to thaw – or at least it did in the south, where the news lives – and consequently fell off the running order. Still, it was fun while it lasted. But only if you prefer gazing into a snow globe to actually watching the news.

Bunny ears for all
18/01/2010

According to technophiles, experts, and that whispering voice in your head, 2010 will be the year that augmented reality makes a breakthrough. In case you don't know, 'augmented reality' is the rather quotidian title given to a smart, gizmo-specific type of software that takes a live camera feed from the real world and superimposes stuff on to it in real time.

Being a gadget designed for people who'd rather look at a screen than the real world, the iPhone inevitably plays host to several examples of this sort of thing. Download the relevant app, hold your iPhone aloft and gawp in astonishment as it magically displays live footage of the actual world directly in front of you – just like the real thing but smaller, and with snazzy direction signs floating over it. You might see a magic hand pointing in the direction of the nearest Starbucks, for instance – a magic hand that repositions itself as you move around. It's incredibly useful, assuming you'd prefer to cause an almighty logjam by shuffling slowly along the pavement while staring into your palm than to stop and ask a fellow human being for directions.

The Nintendo DSi has a built-in camera with a 'fun mode' that can recognise the shape of a human face, and superimpose pig snouts or googly eyeballs and the like over your friends' visages when you point it at them. You can then push a button and save these images for posterity.

For a while, it's genuinely amusing ('Look! It's dad with a pair of zany computerised bunny ears sprouting from the top his head. Ha ha ha!'), until you realise there are only about six different options, two of which involve funny glasses. If you could customise the options, you could make it automatically beam a Hitler moustache on to everyone in sight, which would improve baby photos a hundredfold – but you can't customise the options, probably for precisely that reason. You could print the picture out and draw the Hitler moustache on yourself with a marker pen, but that wouldn't be very 2010.

But while current examples of augmented reality might sound a tad underwhelming, the future possibilities are limitless. The moment they find a way of compressing the technology into a pair of lightweight spectacles, and the floating signs and bunny ears are layered directly over reality itself, the floodgates are open and you might as well tear your existing eyes out and flush them down the bin.

Years ago, I had an idea for a futuristic pair of goggles that visually transformed homeless people into lovable animated cartoon characters. Instead of being confronted by the conscience-pricking sight of abandoned heroin addicts shivering themselves to sleep in shop doorways, the rich city-dweller wearing the goggles would see Daffy Duck and Bugs Bunny snoozing dreamily in hammocks. London would be transformed into something out of *Who Framed Roger Rabbit*.

What's more, the goggles could be adapted to suit whichever level of poverty you wanted to ignore: by simply twisting a dial, you could replace not just the homeless but anyone who receives benefits, or wears cheap clothes, or has a regional accent, or watches ITV, and so on, right up the scale until it had obliterated all but the most grandiose royals.

At the time this seemed like a sick, far-off fantasy. By 2013, it'll be just another customisable application you can download to your iBlinkers for 49p, alongside one that turns your friends into supermodels and your enemies into dormice.

And don't go thinking augmented reality is going to be content with augmenting what you see. It's a short jump from augmented vision (your beergut's vanished and you've got a nice tan), to augmented audio (constant reactive background music that makes your entire life sound more like a movie), to augmented odour (break wind and it smells like a casserole), and augmented touch (what concrete bench? It feels like a beanbag). Eventually, painful sensations such as extreme temperature and acute physical discomfort could be remixed into something more palatable. With skilful use of technology, dying in a blazing fireball could be rendered roughly half as traumatic as, say, slightly snagging a toenail while pulling off a sock.

Some people will say there's something sinister and wrong about all of this. They'll claim it's better to look at actual people and breathe actual air. But then they've never lived in Reading. And anyway, even if they're right, we'll all ignore them anyway, because the software will automatically filter them out the moment they open their mouths.

In other words, over the coming years we're all going to be

willingly submitting to the Matrix, injecting our eyes and ears with digital hallucinogens until there's no point even bothering to change our pants any more. Frightening? No. In fact, I'll scarcely notice.

PART THREE

In which Paddy McGuinness gets flushed down a tube, the Cameron era creeps closer, crisps are eaten and newspapers are likened to a narcotic.

No likey, no lighty
23/01/2010

Anticipation is everything. If someone tells you to close your eyes and open your mouth while they feed you a slice of the most delicious chocolate mousse you'll ever encounter, only to spoon a helping of mouldy mashed cat onto your tongue, chances are you'll vomit. You'd vomit anyway, of course, but the contrast between what you were expecting and what you actually got would make you spew hard enough to bring up your own kidneys.

This also works in reverse. Over the past few weeks, several people have emailed imploring me to watch *Take Me Out*, ITV's new Saturday night dating show. They described it using the sort of damning language usually reserved for war crime tribunals at The Hague. I rubbed my hands together, like a sadist approaching a car crash, settled in to my sofa and watched an episode. And you know what? It's not bad.

Okay, it is bad, obviously, but only if you compare it to something worthy or suave or less shrieky. On its own terms, as a raucous chunk of meaningless idiocy, it succeeds.

If you're not familiar with the format (maybe you had harpsichord practice last Saturday), it's a studio-based cross between *Blind Date* and Boots' mortifying Here Come The Girls campaign. In fact I'm willing to bet *Here Come The Girls* was a working title. You know I'm right.

It's hosted by Paddy McGuinness, who arrives on the studio floor by descending down a huge glittery pipe, like a showbiz turd being flushed into the nation's lap. He introduces thirty women – yes, thirty – who march in jiggling their tits and blowing kisses at the camera, cackling and screaming and winking like a hen night filling the front row at a Wham! reunion. It's a crash course in misogyny.

The girls line up behind a row of illuminated podiums, and the first of the men arrives, sliding down the same pipe Paddy came in earlier (if you'll pardon the expression).

Said bloke must impress the women by speaking, dancing, performing party tricks, and so on, like a jester desperately trying to stave off his own execution at the hands of a capricious female emperor. If he does a backflip and six of the girls didn't like the way his buttocks shook as he landed, they switch their podium lights off, thereby whittling down his selection of available mates, and by extension, the gene pool.

There's an elephant in the room. Not literally, as a format point, but in the moment where each man first slithers down the tube and some of the girls immediately turn their lights off based on appearances alone. Paddy skitters around asking what's turned them off, and they dole out diplomatic answers about disliking the way he walked, or his shoes, rather than saying he's too ugly or fat or that his skin's the wrong colour for their tastes. At a push, they'll gently mock someone's height, but that's about it. There's little crushing honesty here. If they were hooked up to brainwave-reading machines, the outcome might be a little more brutal and a lot more disturbing. But probably not very 'Saturday night'.

Anyway, if our isolated male makes it through to the end with some girls still lit up, he picks one to take away with him. If the show was as hideous as I'd been led to believe, it'd culminate in a round where the newly paired-off couple rut like dogs in a Perspex dome while McGuinness films it on his mobile. Instead they somewhat meekly go for a drink, the results of which we get to see the following week.

That's it. The clever bit – in format terms at any rate – is that the girls return each week, so we get to know their 'characters'. And they're all 'characters'. There are mouthy ones, stupid ones, sweet ones, gothic ones, young ones, old ones, and identical twin ones. All human life is here, apart from anyone you'd actually want to spend the rest of your days with. Or more than about an hour on a Saturday night, come to that.

In summary: yes, it's horrible. But that's its job.

Cadbury's real ale eggs
25/01/2010

I'm not especially patriotic – I find the Union flag a tad garish, and the white cliffs of Dover a touch bland – but the news that the US company Kraft had bought Cadbury came as a bitter blow. It's a very British thing, Cadbury. We've all got a great deal of fondness for it. It's one of the few home comforts you miss while you're abroad, like the BBC or Marmite or self-deprecatory humour.

Considering how much imagination the Americans have, and how much they like food, it's surprising we're so much better at making chocolate than them. And we are better. I can still vividly recall trying Hershey's chocolate for the first time. The name held a certain glitzy allure: after all, I'd heard it mentioned in countless Hollywood movies. Like Oreo cookies and M&Ms, it was one of those brands you faintly revered even though – at the time – it wasn't available in British shops. So when I eventually got my hands on an authentic Hershey bar, it was quite an event.

I stared at the iconic packaging for about five minutes, as though it were a prop from the set of *Ghostbusters*, before unwrapping it with care, breaking a bit off and preparing to savour what would surely be the most powerfully glamorous chocolate experience imaginable.

But the moment the product itself hit my tongue I was plunged mouthwards into an entire universe of yuk. In terms of flavour, it tasted precisely like I'd swallowed a matchbox full of caster sugar five minutes earlier, then somehow regurgitated it into my own mouth. And the texture was crumbly, dusty – slightly old even, as though this was a chocolate bar that had been found in the pocket of a Civil War soldier and preserved specifically for my disenchantment.

It was so horrible, I charitably assumed there was something wrong with it. I was eating it in England (someone had brought it back from the States), so perhaps it had gone off somehow in transit. But no. Subsequent encounters proved I'd got it right the first time. Hershey's tastes downright bad.

But then American mass-market snack food is downright bad in general. They can't do crisps either. In addition to 900 varieties of Walkers, we Brits produce Frazzles and Chipsticks and Monster Munch and all manner of wacky corn shapes, in flavours ranging from pickled onion to polar bear. Virtually all American crisps – or 'chips', as they doggedly insist on calling them – are prosaic constructions tasting vaguely of watered-down bright orange cheese. We do bright orange cheese too, in the form of Wotsits, but we only did it once because we nailed it first time. They've got Cheetos in every shade of orange you could wish for (Spicy Orange! Smokey Orange!), but they're all a bit weak; no match for the confident chemical oomph of a Wotsit.

Anyway, the prospect of the Americans – so good at so many things, so bad at snack foods – meddling with the Cadbury formula is too much for many of us to bear. Hence the protest signs outside the factory in Bournville. We've been told the flavour won't change – but that isn't enough. Kraft needs to go one better, and reassure us that our national identity will remain intact by launching a whole new range of Cadbury's snacks that simply couldn't exist – or sell – anywhere else in the world. Chocolate bars with a uniquely British flavour. Here are some suggestions:

Cadbury's Full English Breakfast

Walkers have had a stab at a 'full English breakfast' flavoured crisp, but the result was disappointing, to say the least, because it relied on various flavoured powders. Cadbury's Full English

Breakfast bar would contain the real thing: fried egg, bacon, chips and beans, mashed and compacted into a Crunchie-sized slab, covered with a layer of ketchup, then swaddled in thick Dairy Milk chocolate. It'd look and weigh about the same as a Double Decker. And yes, it sounds disgusting – but you'd have to try it once, wouldn't you?

Cadbury's Real Ale Eggs
Creme Eggs are all well and good, but there's something vaguely continental about them. How about promoting the real ale industry with a chocolate egg containing 2 fl. oz. of Bishop's Finger? If that fails to catch on, how about a range of special 'Binge Drinker's Eggs' – available only in 'Happy Hour' packs of six – filled with sugary blue alcopop swaddled in thick Dairy Milk chocolate.

Cadbury's Tardis Bars
Nothing fancy: these are just Tardis-shaped slabs of chocolate – part of a range that includes Caramel Cybermen and Toffee Daleks. But the proceeds go straight to the BBC, to help keep it afloat after Cameron gets in and sets about dismantling it to impress Rupert Murdoch. Other BBC-themed snacks could include Holby City Liquorice Bandages, Panorama Mint Crisp Curls, and a disturbing 100 per cent edible lifesize replica of Terry Wogan's head, replete with crunchy shortbread teeth, praline eyeballs and a brain made of nougat. Swaddled in thick Dairy Milk chocolate.

As you may have noticed, the above suggestions work on the assumption that everything tastes nice when it's swaddled in Dairy Milk chocolate. Which it does. A bloated corpse dredged from a polluted canal would taste nice if it was encased in a Dairy Milk shell. If it was coated in Hershey's, you'd find yourself glumly picking the chocolate off to get at the sludgey grey flesh beneath. And that's a FACT.

2010: when iPads were new
01/02/2010

A star appears over San Francisco and a new gizmo is born. The iPad! At first glance it resembles an iPhone in unhandy, non-pocket-sized form. But look a little longer, and . . . No. You were right first time.

Not that that's necessarily a bad thing. Apple excels at taking existing concepts – computers, MP3 players, conceit – and carefully streamlining them into glistening ergonomic chunks of concentrated aspiration. It took the laptop and the coffee-table book and created the MacBook. Now it's taken the MacBook and the iPhone and distilled them into a single device that answers a rhetorical question you weren't really asking.

It's an iPhone for people who can't be arsed holding an iPhone up to their face. A slightly-further-away iPhone that keeps your lap warm. A weird combination of portable and cumbersome: too small to replace your desktop, too big to fit in your pocket, unless you're a clown. It can play video, but really – do you want to spend hours staring at a movie in your lap? Sit through *Lord of the Rings* and you'd need an osteopath to punch the crick out of your neck afterwards. It can also be used as an ebook, something newspapers are understandably keen to play up, but because it's got an illuminated display rather than a fancy non-backlight 'digital ink' ebook screen, it'll probably leave your eyes feeling strained, as though your pupils are wearing tight shoes.

The iPad falls between two stools – not quite a laptop, not quite a smartphone. In other words, it's the spork of the electronic consumer goods world. Or rather it would be, were it not for one crucial factor: it looks ideal for idly browsing the web while watching telly. And I suspect that's what it'll largely be used for. Millions of people watch TV while checking their emails: it's a perfect match for them.

Absurdly, Apple keeps trying to pretend it'll make your life more efficient. Come off it. It's an oblong that lights up. I'm sick of being pitched to like I'm a one-man corporation undertaking a personal productivity audit anyway. I don't want to hear how the iPad is going to make my life simpler. I want to hear how it'll amuse and distract me, how it plans to anaesthetise me into a numb, trancelike state. Call it the iDawdler and aggressively market it as the world's first utterly dedicated timewasting device: an electronic sedative to rival diazepam, alcohol or television. If Apple can convince us of that, it's got itself a hit.

Some people are complaining because it doesn't have a camera in it. Spoiled techno-babies, all of them. Just because something is technically possible, it doesn't mean it has to be done. It's technically possible to build an egg whisk that makes phone calls, an MP3 player that dispenses capers or a car with a bread windscreen. Humankind will continue to prosper in their absence. Not everything needs a fifteen-megapixel lens stuck on the back, like a little glass anus. Give these ingrates a camera and they'd whine that it didn't have a second camera built into it. What are you taking photographs of anyway? Your camera collection?

And don't bring up videocalls to defend yourself: it'd be creepy talking to a disembodied two-dimensional head being held at arm's length, and besides, the iPad is too heavy to hold in front of your face for long, so you'd end up balancing it in your lap, which means both callers would find themselves staring up one another's nostrils, like a pair of curious dental patients.

Videocalls are overrated anyway. You just sit there staring at each other with nothing to say. It's like a prison visit: eventually one of you has to start masturbating just to break the tension.

Personally, I'm not sure whether I'll buy an iPad, although I think – I think – I'm about to buy a MacBook. Yes, I was a dyed-in-the-wool Mac sceptic for years. Yes, I've written screeds bemoaning the infuriating breed of smug Apple monks who treat all PC owners with condescending pity. But being chained to a

Sony Vaio for the last few weeks has convinced me that I'd rather use a laptop that just works, rather than one that's so ponderous, stuttering and irritating I find myself perpetually on the verge of running outside and hurling it into traffic. (That's a moan about Sony laptops, not PCs in general, by the way. I'm keeping my desktop PC, thanks: that's lovely. Smooth as butter. Better than I deserve, in fact.)

I just hope buying a MacBook won't turn me into an iPrick. I want a machine that essentially makes itself invisible, not a rectangular bragging stone. If, ten minutes after buying it, I start burbling on about how it's left me more fulfilled as a human being, or find myself perched at a tiny Starbucks table stroking its glowing Apple with one hand while demonstratively tapping away with the other in the hope that passersby will assume I'm working on a screenplay, it's going straight in the bin.

The iBin. Complete with built-in camera. $599.99.

The book of the future
15/02/2010

Following my blithering about the iPad the other week, I found myself thinking about ebooks. That's my life for you. A rollercoaster. Until recently, I was an ebook sceptic, see; one of those people who harrumphs about the 'physical pleasure of turning actual pages' and how ebooks will 'never replace the real thing'. Then I was given a Kindle as a gift. That shut me up.

Stock complaints about the inherent pleasure of ye olde format are bandied about whenever some new upstart invention comes along. Each moan is nothing more than a little foetus of nostalgia jerking in your gut. First they said CDs were no match for vinyl. Then they said MP3s were no match for CDs. Now they say streaming music services are no match for MP3s. They're only happy looking in the rear-view mirror.

Crackly warm vinyl sounds wonderful, but you can't listen to it on the bus, or squish it into a machine the size of a raisin. And unless your MP3s are encoded at such a low rate that it sounds as though the band's playing woollen instruments in a water tank, and provided you're listening to some halfway decent music in the first place, your brain quickly cancels out any concerns about 'lossiness' and gets on with enjoying the music.

I've never quite understood the psychological makeup of the self-professed audiophile – the sort of person who spends £500 on a gold-plated lead and can't listen to a three-minute pop song without instinctively carrying out a painstaking forensic audit of the sound quality. That's not a music fan. That's a noise-processing unit.

Just as it was easy to dismiss MP3s until you'd test-driven an iPod, so the advantages of an ebook only become apparent when you use one. Yes, there's no 'new book smell', no folding the pages over, and if you drop it in the bath you've ruined it – but on the other hand, the whole 'electronic ink' malarkey actually works (so you don't feel as if you're squinting at words made of light), downloading new books is easy, and it can store about 1,500 titles; approximately 1,499 more than I could comfortably carry otherwise. It can also read books aloud, which is great if, like me, you've spent years wondering how the great works of literature might sound if recited by a depressed robot.

But the single biggest advantage to the ebook is this: no one can see what you're reading.

You can mourn the loss of book covers all you want, but once again I say to you: no one can see what you're reading. This is a giant leap forward, one that frees you up to read whatever you want without being judged by the person sitting opposite you on the tube. OK, so right now they'll judge you simply for using an ebook – because you will look like a showoff early-adopter techno-nob if you use one on public transport until at least some time circa 2012 – but at least they're not sneering at you for enjoying *The Rats* by James Herbert.

The lack of a cover immediately alters your purchasing habits. As soon as I got the ebook, I went on a virtual shopping spree, starting with the stuff I thought I should read – *Wolf Hall*, that kind of thing – but quickly found myself downloading titles I'd be too embarrassed to buy in a shop or publicly read on a bus. Not pornography, but something far worse: celebrity autobiographies.

And coverlessness works both ways: pretentious wonks will no longer be able to impress pretty students on the bus by nonchalantly/demonstratively reading *The Journals of Soren Kierkegaard*, at least until someone brings out an ebook device with a second screen on the back which displays the cover of whatever it is you're reading for the benefit of attractive witnesses (or more likely, boldly displays the cover of *The Journals of Soren Kierkegaard* while you guiltily breeze through *It's Not What You Think* by Chris Evans).

I like the notion of this blunt technological camouflage, where it looks as if you're doing one thing while you're doing the exact opposite. Here's another idea. Modern 3D cinema technology works by ensuring your left eye sees one image while your right sees another. But they could, presumably, issue one pair of specs comprising two left-eye lenses (for children to wear), and another with two right-eye lenses (for adults). This would make it possible for parents to take their offspring to the cinema and watch two entirely different films at the same time. So while the kiddywinks are being placated by an animated CGI doodle about rabbits entering the Winter Olympics or something, their parents will be bearing witness to some apocalyptically degrading pornography. The tricky thing would be making the soundtracks match. Those cartoon rabbits would have to spend a lot of time slapping their bellies and moaning.

Anyway: ebooks. They're the future. The only thing I'd do to improve them is to include an emergency button that automatically sums the entire book up in a sentence if you couldn't be arsed to finish it, or if your plane starts crashing and you want to know whodunit before exploding over the sea. Ideally it'd shriek the summary aloud, bellowing something like 'THE BUTLER DID IT' for potboilers, or maybe 'THE SCULPTRESS COMES TO TERMS WITH THE DEATH OF HER FATHER' for highbrow fiction. Which means you could effectively skip the reading process entirely and audibly digest the entire contents of the British Library in less than a month. That's ink-and-paper dead, right there.

Only one's a Winner
20/02/2010

Not sure why, but many people seem to think I'm some kind of knee-jerk anti-everything hate machine, particularly with regards to TV. Was it something I said? In reality, I'm happy to sit through what might broadly be considered 'crap' programming when the mood strikes me. I can't get enough of *To Buy or Not To Buy*, for instance: I don't exactly tune in specifically to watch it, although to the casual onlooker it might look as though I have, what with me sitting rapt on the sofa and everything. If I catch the start of an episode I'm done for. Will they pick house one, house two, or the 'wildcard' choice? I can scarcely breathe till I know.

But my new favourite rubbish show has to be *Michael Winner's Dining Stars*, the sort of programme that simultaneously makes you feel glad and aghast to be alive. Put simply, it's 'Come Dine With Prick'. Put very slightly less simply, it's *Come Dine With Me* meets *The Apprentice*, which was presumably the opening sentence of the pitch document.

The format: notorious moneyed dickhead and unforgiving gourmand Winner visits ordinary plebs' houses to be served a free dinner. Afterwards, he reviews the meal, at which point he may or may not give them a 'star' award. This works just like the Michelin star system, in that receiving just one is an almighty achievement, while receiving three is nigh-on impossible. Actually, it's marginally better than the Michelin star system, because a) it's televised, and b) the awards are handed out by the director of *Death Wish*.

Winner himself plays to the cameras with more knowing skill than anyone in any of his own films has ever managed. He positively revels in his arrogant eccentric's role. Every moment he's on screen is deeply, unpleasantly strange. One of the first things we see him doing is washing his hair in beer, which apparently gives it great shine and bounce. That's before he's left the house.

Part of the format requires him to fill airtime by touring the hometown of each prospective chef before he visits their home itself. Cue ten minutes of him walking around some cosy Lancastrian market town, screeching and shouting at everyone like a mad uncle. It's all put on for the cameras of course, but somehow this in itself is fascinating: he's deliberately being a comical arsehole in a way which genuinely makes him a comical arsehole ... but not in the way he probably thinks it does. There are multiple layers of arseholery going on here and it's impossible to pick them apart. In the end I simply admitted defeat and started laughing at and with him.

Still, most of the entertainment value comes in watching the civilian chefs bend and scrape at every opportunity to accommodate Mr Winner's caprice, as though he's a visiting emperor. The level of terrified veneration on display is truly mystifying, as though they've been told he's carrying a loaded pistol and won't be afraid to use it. There's got to be some explanation. They can't just be nervous simply because he's Michael Winner. We've all seen those insurance ads. Would they be similarly deferential if the Go Compare opera guy turned up? Or the eastern European meerkat thing?

There's a spin-off series in the making here, surely: Mascot Meals, in which stressed-out punters heat casseroles for inexplicably demanding commercial frontmen.

Anyway, despite glaring evidence to the contrary, everyone involved behaves as though *Michael Winner's Dining Stars* is an authentically rigorous examination of world-class cuisine, and it's this insane act of collective will that elevates the show from mere schedule-filler to amusing cultural artefact. The sequence where he delivers his verdict is one of the most bizarre sights I've witnessed in a long while. For one thing, his reviews are breathtakingly cutting, especially when you consider these people have provided this egocentric millionaire with food and shelter for nothing. At one point this week everyone in the room is genuinely in tears, and I almost followed suit out of sheer sheeplike compliance.

Was I laughing or crying? In all honesty, I couldn't tell you.

Tiger and Terry and Vernon are sorry
22/02/2010

Tiger Woods said sorry. John Terry said sorry. Even Vernon Kay said sorry. It's a sorry state of affairs. If you were to rank the three in terms of transgression, that's probably the order they'd fall in: Woods first, then Terry, and finally Kay, who didn't even cheat, or at least not in our physical realm. Texting flirty messages? Maybe unwise when you're otherwise engaged in a relationship, but at the very worst it's a Matrix shag. I'm not exactly what you'd call a fan of Kay's presentational style, but I don't derive any pleasure from watching him squirm and apologise to a pointing, cackling nation.

When did public displays of contrition become the norm? More to the point, who actually appreciates them? Sitting through any public apology is mortifying. It just feels wrong. And unless the poor bastard in question is saying sorry for something as momentous as a war crime, it's entirely unnecessary. The public don't need to hear it, because the public isn't as psychotically, self-regardingly deranged as the press. Consequently, these apologies are aimed not at the public, not at the fans or the listeners, but the press. The press demands apologies on its own behalf, regardless of the will of the people. And it does this because it is insane, truly Caligula-level insane.

When it comes to the three scandals in question, the press has been perpetually and erroneously outraged on behalf of the public. During the Terry debacle, I was working on a TV show that required me to watch hours of rolling news coverage, like a lab rat with its eyes glued open. TV news vox pops are about as far from a scientific survey as it's possible to get without literally gluing a scientific survey to a rock, blasting it into deep space and bicycling like billyo in the opposite direction, but still: not one member of the public, with a microphone shoved in front of their face, managed to work up even 1 per cent of the indignant fury of some media pundits.

For the first couple of days, they couldn't find anyone who wouldn't simply shrug and say, 'So what? It's his private life.' After a week's worth of media sabre-rattling and interminable witless debate over the morals of a man who kicks a ball around for a living, they managed to uncover a few – a few – pedestrians who were grudgingly prepared to admit that maybe he should step down, considering his position as a role model to kids.

But the whole role-model-to-kids argument was a bogus mantra in the first instance. For one thing, kids don't care about or even comprehend their idols' sex lives, and for another, if you're so worried about the havoc Terry's shenanigans could wreak on impressionable minds, stop dredging up the details and printing them in simplified prose a child could understand, accompanied by massive photographs of his alleged mistress in her underwear.

And besides, even if Terry had been caught having sex with a Cabbage Patch Doll in the window of Hamleys, he'd still be a better role model than any tabloid newspaper. A child who idolised the tabloids would grow up to be a sanctimonious, flip-flopping, phone-tapping Peeping Tom who thinks puns are hilarious and spends half its life rooting through bins for a living. If I had a child like that, I'd divorce it. Or kill it. Whichever proved cheapest.

Of course, the press has to feign outrage on behalf of the public because that's virtually the only thing that lends the public-interest argument much weight when you're dealing with ethical transgressions in the private lives of sportsmen. It's interesting that when the *News of the World* lawyer (the cheerfully named Mr Crone) spoke to ITN about the lifting of Terry's super-injunction, he said that too often the public's right to know is overlooked in favour of 'wealthy and pampered' celebrities and footballers.

That's true, of course, but the words 'wealthy' and 'pampered' seemed to be delivered with particular emphasis, as though this was a noble victory for the downtrodden little guy, rather than an immense corporation that makes a fortune from prying into the sex lives of hapless soap stars and clueless ball-wallopers. It would've been refreshing if he'd said: 'This is an important victory for freedom of the press – but never mind that: wahey! Filth galore!' And then rolled his eyes and rubbed his belly and performed a cartoon backflip. But no. He didn't.

Instead, Terry paid the price for that daft super-injunction: he was publicly tarred and feathered. As was Woods. As was Kay. In the West, adultery isn't punishable by stoning. Instead, if you're famous (and even if you've only committed virtual adultery by text) it's punishable by kicking. Step out of line and the press will encircle and kick you. And kick you and kick you and kick you until you beg for forgiveness. At which point, if you're lucky, they'll chortle and sneer and move on. They must be frightfully proud.

Your beautiful password is dead
27/02/2010

In days of yore, we're told, people had less leisure time because everything – everything – was a protracted pain in the fundament. Want to clean that smock? Then you'll have to walk six miles carrying a pail of water back from the village well. And that's before you've tackled the laundering process itself, which consists of three hours laboriously scrubbing your soiled garment against a washboard and wringing it through a mangle. By the time you've finished, it's bedtime. Did you remember to clean your pyjamas? No. Back to the village well for you, then.

No wonder the people in medieval woodcuts look so miserable, even when they aren't being cleft in twain by knights or dropping dead in a flurry of popping buboes. And oh how we modernites love to chortle at their unsophisticated lives. DARK AGE LOSERS PROBLY USED TURNIPS FOR IPHONES LOL!!!!

But in many ways, the rustic serf of yesteryear had a better quality of life than the skinbag-about-town of space year 2010. Computers have freed us from hours of drudgery with one hand, but introduced an equal amount of slightly different drudgery with the other. No matter how advanced civilisation becomes, there's an unyielding quota of drudgery lurking at the core that can never be completely eradicated.

These days it's commonplace to do everything online, from designing the layout of your kitchen to locating a stranger prepared to kill and eat you for mutual sexual gratification. Tasks that would have taken years to organise and achieve can now be accomplished in the blink of an icon. Or would be, if you could remember your password. But you can't remember your password. You can't remember it because you chose it so very long, long ago – maybe three days afore. In the intervening period you've had to dream up another six passwords for another six websites, programs or email addresses.

In this age of rampant identity theft, where it's just a matter of time before someone works out a way to steal your reflection in the mirror and use it to commit serial bigamy in an alternate dimension, we're told only a maniac would use the same password for everything. But passwords used to be for speakeasy owners or spies. Once upon a time, you weren't the sort of person who had to commit hundreds of passwords to memory. Now you are. Part of your identity's been stolen already.

In the meantime: you need a new password. One as individual as a snowflake. And as beautiful, too. Having demanded a brand new password from you for the twenty-eighth time this month, His Lordship Your Computer proceeds to snootily critique your efforts. Certain attempts he will disqualify immediately, without even passing judgment. Less than six letters? No numbers? Access denied. This is a complex parlour game, OK? There are rules. So start again. And this time: no recognisable words. No punctuation marks. No hesitation, deviation or repetition. Go.

Pass the qualifying round and it gets worse. Most modern password entrance exams grade each entry as you type, presenting you with an instant one-word review of your efforts. Suppose you glance around your desk and pick the first thing you set eyes on, such as a blue pen. You begrudgingly shove a number on the end, creating the password 'bluepen1'. You submit this offering to the Digital Emperor, and he derides it as 'Weak'.

You can use it if you want. It's valid. But still; it's 'Weak'. So you try again. This time you replace some of the letters with numbers and jumble the capitalisation a bit, like a chef with limited ingredients trying to jazz up an omelette to impress a restaurant critic. The Computerlord pulls a vaguely respectful face. You've jumped a grade, to 'OK'. You tingle within.

But you can do better. Admit it: you want HRH Computer to actively admire you. You want him to give you a rosette for creating the most carefully constructed password in history, a password that isn't merely secure, but is beautiful. A password that sings. A password to make angels weep. You will present His Majesty the Mainframe with a masterpiece of encryption, an ornate lexicographic sonata – a creation whose breathtakingly impressive elegance is magnified by the heartbreaking knowledge that no human other than yourself will ever set eyes upon it. This is your private cryptographic poem, your encoded love letter to the machine. Better be good.

So you take bold made-up words, weave them with numbers,

stud the soufflé with spicy CaPiTaLs and garnish it with a random string of characters carefully chosen for their memorable unmemorableness. You've performed reverse cryptanalysis; been a one-man Enigma machine. And your offering pleases God. He deems it 'Very Strong': his highest accolade.

Still glowing, you try out your hand-crafted key for the first time, typing it into the lock. With a soft click, the mechanism turns. Access granted. You are now part of the smocklaundry.com community. How many of your smocks need laundering? When would you like them returned? No problem. Thanks for your custom. Farewell.

Three weeks later your smocks are returned, late and still plastered with hideous stains. You revisit smocklaundry.com to protest. But you can't remember your password. You can't remember it because you chose it so very long, long ago – maybe three weeks afore. And in the intervening period you've had to dream up another forty-two passwords for another forty-two websites, programs or email addresses.

Your beautiful password is dead. It was simply too complex and too damned exquisite to live in your humdrum world, your humdrum mind. Now you must face the ignominy of clicking the password reset button for the fifty-eighth time this year. And as you trudge dolefully towards your inbox, waiting for the help letter to arrive, the cruel laughter of His Computerised Majesty rings in your ears. You have failed, human. You have failed.

Pain, fury and joy
06/03/2010

Reader, I apologise in advance. Words can't describe the exquisite mix of pain, fury and joy that is *Pineapple Dance Studios*. Yet words must suffice. I can't just sit here silently popping my mouth open and shut like a surprised mute, although that's precisely the reaction it provokes.

You know how every so often the natural history unit throws up a documentary about hallucinogenically weird organisms that live fifteen miles down in the deep, during which some undulating avant-garde cross between a jellyfish, a diagram and an inside-out seahorse will wobble across the screen, defying any rational attempt at description? This is the docusoap equivalent of that.

Yes, it's a docusoap. That much we can cling to. It's a docusoap about the various characters around Pineapple Dance Studios in Covent Garden. The most immediately noticeable example is a berk called Louie Spence, a creature so theatrically camp he seems perpetually on the verge of turning into a disco-dancing peacock. God knows what his job at the studio actually consists of: you could watch for a thousand years and never find out. All he does is mug for the cameras, perpetually striking poses, pulling arch faces, cracking lurid innuendo, shrieking, mincing and generally behaving in a way no fictional gay character has been permitted to do for decades. Given the right narrator, this could be a heartbreaking doc about an incurable mental condition whose sufferers lose their minds at the sight of a film crew and turn into 1978 sitcom homosexuals.

And incredibly it has been given the right narrator: former BBC news anchor Michael Buerk. You'd be hard pressed to find a more sobering voice of authority. Instant gravitas. Each time there's an establishing shot of a building exterior, I fully expect to hear him say: 'Dawn – and as the sun breaks through the piercing chill of night on the plain outside Korem, it lights up a biblical famine; now, in the twentieth century.' But he doesn't. Instead he says something like: '9 a.m. – and Louie is pirouetting in a stairwell'. Cut to Louie pirouetting in a stairwell. It's upsetting and funny and wrong and right. It's everything. This is madness.

Louie is a show-off, but at least he isn't Andrew Stone. In reality, Andrew Stone is one of the resident dance teachers. In his head, he's a global superstar. The show focuses heavily on the ups and downs of his derivative, deeply uninspiring band, Starman, which he fronts with a level of egomaniacal self-assurance hitherto undocumented on British TV. Seriously, they've captured lightning in a bottle here: the man is a tool of such breathtaking immensity, it's a wonder the cameras didn't simply explode out of horrified glee. One of life's sorest tragedies is that the people who brim with confidence are always the wrong people. This is the clearest possible illustration of that truth ever committed to videotape. Show this to your children. Make them learn from it.

On and on the show goes, swerving effortlessly from fist-chewingly mundane office-management sequences straight out of *The Day Today*'s famous docusoap spoof *The Pool* one moment, into bizarre choreographed dance sequences the next.

Dance sequences? Yes: they've thrown in occasional fourth-wall-smashing musical numbers just to baffle you to death.

One minute Louie is complaining to the builders next door about noise and then suddenly – boom! – they unexpectedly start dancing, as though he's stumbled into a dream sequence. And this breakdown of reality isn't acknowledged in Michael Buerk's voiceover at all. No, it simply occurs. And then the show moves on as if it hadn't. As though the TV fakery scandals never happened. And suddenly you question the veracity of everything you're watching. Except the rest of it is real. It just doesn't – just shouldn't – feel that way.

But that's *Pineapple Dance Studios*. A show designed to trigger life-threatening cognitive dissonance. As mundane as a breadbin; more outlandish than *Avatar*. As horrible as war; as funny as a guffing cartoon donkey.

Words don't even graze the surface.

Customers who bought Tony Blair also bought the following

08/03/2010

So: those televised prime ministerial debates will definitely be happening in the run-up to the election. The excitement is hard to contain: three separate prime-time shows on Sky, ITV and the Beeb in which Brown, Cameron and Clegg will get the opportunity to talk and talk and talk and talk and talk. And possibly jig. But mainly talk.

Depending on your point of view, this is either a refreshing opportunity for politicians to connect with the electorate, or the least sexy hour of television since that Channel 4 documentary where they chopped up an elephant.

Even though its power and influence are in decline, TV still fascinates and horrifies politicians in equal measure. They're attracted by its potential to hypnotise and pacify millions, but repelled by its laser-like ability to magnify physical flaws or tonal cock-ups. It's like a magic amulet that can sometimes control the masses, but also might explode in the user's hand at any time.

Obviously image is paramount. On TV, no matter how eloquent you are, 75 per cent of the audience can't even hear what you're saying: they're too busy making subconscious judgements about the tone of your voice or the angle of your lips. Conventional wisdom would have it that Gordon Brown is clearly at a massive disadvantage here, since he's slowly come to resemble a lumbering, doomy Mr Snuffaluffagus with all the carefree joie de vivre of the *Kursk* submarine disaster. But Cameron and Clegg are, if anything, a bit too telegenic, a bit too slick, a bit too clean-cut and heigh-ho. They've tried too hard to appeal in soundbite pop-up form: stretched over an hour, they may start to grate, their smooth appearances unexpectedly conspiring against them.

Cameron in particular looks like a boring dot-eyed 'nice' neighbour from an underwhelming Christian soap opera. He's a replicant; an Auton; a humanoid; a piece of adaptive software that's learned to appeal to your likes and dislikes – 'customers who bought Tony Blair also bought the following' – but inadvertently creeped you out in the process. Let's face it: if you discovered he doesn't have a belly button or any pubic hair, and spends one night each week lying semi-conscious, face-down, 'recharging' inside a giant white laboratory pod filled with amniotic fluid, you wouldn't be entirely surprised. And voters are likely to sense that eerie unearthliness. He'd better stutter or fluff a few times, just to throw them off the scent.

But even if all three manage to flawlessly imitate human beings, defeat may still be snatched from the jaws of victory: if Nick Clegg spends the first fifty minutes rousing the audience with his fiery, lyrical rhetoric – as per usual – only to sneeze unexpectedly five minutes before the end, leaving a giant pendulum of mucus dangling off the end of his conk, the unfortunate mishap would be looped and repeated *ad nauseam* on every rolling news bulletin for weeks to come. He'd be Mr Snot. And do you want to vote for Mr Snot? No way. What if he sneezed on the nuclear button? He's out of the running. Which leaves you choosing between a haunted elephant or the humanoid.

(There are other parties you could vote for, obviously. But they're excluded from the debates and therefore no longer exist – a terrible blow for BNP leader Nick Griffin, who was hoping to win over the public with his devilish good looks and impish personality.)

So: mammoth or android. Which is it to be? To help you choose, the news networks will doubtless offer post-match analysis of each nanosecond. Professional Westminster spods will deconstruct each sentence in search of hidden meanings, like scientists translating garbled messages from space. A body-language expert will discuss Cameron's eyebrows for thirty-eight minutes. A fashionista will tell us who wore the best shirt. And every other citizen in the country will be asked to deliver their opinion via vox pop, email, tweet, phone poll or synchronised Mexican wave. Eventually a consensus will form regarding who won, at which point the lucky victor will be given the keys to 10 Downing Street, a fly-drive holiday for two courtesy of Virgin Atlantic, a five-album recording contract with Sony BMG, and an ITV2 reality show of their own.

So terrifying-yet-alluring is the prospect of the debates, the parties have only consented to take part provided each broadcaster adheres to a series of seventy-six rules, drawn up in advance. Every aspect will be controlled, from the time allocated to each question, to the layout of the set – even the framing of audience cutaway shots is crucial.

Presumably spin doctors from all three parties will be lurking ominously on the sidelines, ready to run in and kick the cameramen to death if their candidate starts looking too sweaty. You can already picture Andy Coulson in the wings, chewing gum and eavesdropping on the gallery audio feed, which has been illegally tapped by a private detective and routed directly into Andy Coulson's earpiece without Andy Coulson's knowledge.

Curiously, one thing that's left open to the broadcaster is the opening and closing credits. Rule 68 states that 'each broadcaster [is] responsible for their own titles, music, branding etc.' If I was running ITN – which, at the time of writing, I'm not – I'd make the most of this sole crumb of freedom by creating an insanely inappropriate title sequence in which a claymation Brown, Cameron and Clegg take turns performing sex acts on a cow, a kettle and a hole in the ground, all of it backed by the old *It's a Knockout* theme tune. Then it abruptly cuts live to the studio, where all three leaders have been waiting to speak, watching with mounting horror as this sickening cartoon unfolded on the monitors. As they storm out, a body language expert analyses their facial expressions, and the studio audience waves giant foam hands around. It might not affect the election either way, but who cares: that's entertainment.

Meat and skeletons
13/03/2010

Eating huge quantities of food is an unobtainable fantasy for some and an everyday luxury for others. To Adam Richman, voracious host of *Man vs Food*, it's a career choice.

Man vs Food is obscene on many levels, but daft on several more. The format couldn't be much simpler: every week, Richman travels to a city (Memphis this time) and samples its most notorious 'pig out joints': the sort of quintessentially American restaurants where everything is charbroiled or smoked or sizzled to death in a deep fat fryer vat the size of a swimming pool; places where each mammoth portion comes with a side order of type two diabetes. Establishments of this kind often tend to have a 'challenge' item on the menu – a dish so offensively huge, anyone who successfully manages to eat it has their portrait hung on the wall. The end of each episode sees Richman taking on one of these challenges, hence the title. That's all there is to it.

Essentially this is *Top Gear* for food: a jokey, blokey exercise in excessive indulgence. It's all sensation, sensation, sensation. Just as Clarkson emits orgasmic whimpers when his driver's seat judders on acceleration, so Richman groans like a man having his perineum tongued by three cheerleaders as he ingests each warm mouthful of stodge. If food is the new porn, this is an all-out orgy between wobbling gutsos and farmyard animals – a snuff orgy, no less, since the latter end up sawn in half and smothered in BBQ sauce.

Plenty of cattle get eaten; at times Richman may as well lie down, open his gob and let a herd stampede directly into his stomach. Entire carcasses are greedily consumed by overweight folk with juice dribbling down their chins, tearing flesh from charred bones with their glistening teeth. It's like sitting in Sawney Bean's cave. Meat and skeletons, meat and skeletons. A sequence in which Richman peers inside an oven at Memphis's premier rib joint to witness a landscape of scorched and smouldering ribcages almost resembles the aftermath of the Dresden firebombing. This is definitely not a programme for vegetarians.

Things reach an insane peak (or more accurately, trough), as Richman takes on the eating challenge. This week he faces the 7½-pound 'Sasquatch Burger' at the Big Foot Lodge. 1,300 people have attempted to eat one; only four have succeeded. This high failure rate is hardly surprising when you see the bloody thing: it's the size of a sofa cushion. The bun alone accounts for two pounds. The burger itself is an ominous cake of mashed cow as thick as your thigh. When he first tucks in, Richman is chirpy and cocky, shovelling handfuls of meat down his neck with the gluttonous abandon of a self-aware Homer Simpson. Several minutes later, as it becomes clear he still has an immense mountain of food to get through, he appears sickened and woozy – presumably because his blood sugar levels have hit a dangerously narcotic high as his stomach desperately tries to break down the busload of beef that's just appeared inside it. This is the point at which the show stops being fun. It's like watching a man dealing with an instant, unexpected pregnancy.

But what I'd really like to see is what happens the next morning, when the show presumably turns into *Man vs Poo*, as Richman empties the dauntingly substantial, hopelessly compacted contents of his engorged colon, clenching the bathroom doorhandle between his teeth as he attempts to give birth to a leg-sized hunk of fecal sod without killing himself. Cue footage of him sweating, shaking and sobbing like a man impaled on a clay tree, before eventually squeezing out a log with the dimensions and weight of a dead gazelle in a greased sleeping bag. As he mops his brow (and backside), he smiles weakly with exhausted triumph, whispers farewell, and the credits roll. And we've all learned something about the price of excess.

The strangest substance known to man
15/03/2010

Time is the strangest substance known to man. You can't see, touch, hear, smell, taste or avoid it. Time makes you stronger-minded but weaker-bodied, gradually transforming you from blushing grape to ornery, grouching raisin. Time is the most precious thing you have, yet you're happiest when you're wasting it. Time will outlive you, your offspring, your offspring's robots and your offspring's robots' springs. It will outlive the wind and the rocks, the sun and the moon, Florence and the Machine. Time, in short, is King of Things.

Because time is invisible, it's hard to work out which bit to focus on at any given moment. It's even hard to work out just how long 'any given moment' is. Right now, as you're reading this article, are you absorbing it by the paragraph, by the sentence, or on a word-by-word basis? When I type the word 'word', does time temporarily slow down while you hear the word 'word' spoken aloud in your mind, or have you already leapt ahead to discover the end of the sentence doesn't sense quite make? How big a 'timeslice' can your awareness eat in one go?

The more time you swallow in one sitting, the wiser you become. In Kurt Vonnegut's *Slaughterhouse Five*, we're introduced to the Tralfamadorians, an alien race who can see in four dimensions. They experience life not as a linear sequence of unexpected events, but a timeline of inexorable peaks and troughs, occurring simultaneously. Tralfamadorians aren't upset by tragic events or overjoyed at happy events, because the concept of 'events' has no meaning; to them, sunrise, sunset, birth, death, peace, war are all just notches on the same stick. When confronted with tragedy, they merely shrug and say, 'So it goes.' That's why there's never been a Tralfamadorian on *EastEnders*.

Anyway, while most people don't perceive life with the worrisome scope of a Tralfamadorian, they're capable of projecting at least a little. Take joggers. They weren't born with a pre-programmed desire to jog. No. One day they decided they'd like to get fit, and chose to sacrifice their immediate comfort in favour of delayed gratification: they got off the sofa and jogged themselves slim.

Every jogger is essentially a clairvoyant. They've transcended the shackles of contemporary subsistence and risen above the likes of you and me, to witness a vision of the future so captivating it blocks out the pain of the present, so enticing, they're literally compelled to run towards it. Not only that, they've been organised enough to buy proper trainers and shorts and everything, the smug bastards. No wonder everyone else wants to hit them. Here's a tip: visualise a future in which you've toned yourself to athletic perfection by fighting random joggers in the park. Here's another tip: wear some sort of mask. And maybe a cape. We'll come up with a logo for your chest plate later.

Joggers are a minority, but then exercisers generally are a minority. Even though we're repeatedly told that regular exercise combats heart disease and cancer and blah blah nag nag nag, more than 60 per cent of the population couldn't be arsed trying, because it makes their legs ache. They're not necessarily lazy, but suffering from an inability to perceive the future as a solid and tangible thing, unlike those far-sighted seers in running shoes and sweat pants. Perhaps joggers have a few additional Tralfamadorian synapses; only by experimenting on their brains can we be sure. Meanwhile, the rest of us remain stubbornly wedged into narrow individual pockets of time, moaning that we need to lose a few pounds while sobbing into our chips.

And we do the same with the environment: we fail to take painful measures in the present that could ease our existence in the future, because we think they're too arduous – unless you're a spluttering contrarian, in which case you think the whole climate-change thing is a load of trumped-up phooey anyway, and that all scientists are shifty, self-serving exaggerators, apart from the brave handful who agree with you. Hey, I'm no scientist. I'm not an engineer either, but if I asked a hundred engineers whether it was safe to cross a bridge, and ninety-nine said no, I'd probably try to find another way over the ravine rather than loudly siding with the underdog and arguing about what constitutes a consensus while trundling across in my Hummer.

Still, it's easy to picture a collapsing bridge. Picturing a collapsing environment is trickier. Hollywood has tried its best, but all I learned from sitting through *The Day After Tomorrow* is that, contrary to my previous expectations, the end of the world might be boring.

What we need, if we're really going to work in unison to overcome climate change is a mix of Tralfamadorian perspective and joggers' resolve: to let visions of the future dictate our present, rather than the other way round.

So: we need to loosen mankind's dogged grip on a linear interpretation of time if we're going to save the planet. But how? We can't go round injecting our brains with Tralfamadorian grey matter, because it doesn't exist. Instead the closest thing we have is LSD, which must be pumped into the water supply as a matter of urgency. A couple of months of steady supply should be enough to expand our collective perception.

Let's start by testing it out on Stourbridge (no reason; just picked it at random: sorry Stourbridge). The results can be televised live. It'll be funny watching them trying to eat their own ankles or chase the town hall into the sky: just like *It's a Knockout*, but with a sense of civic purpose.

Yes. For all our sakes, this must happen NOW.

Meow meow meow meow
22/03/2010

I'm a lightweight; always have been. I didn't get properly drunk until I was twenty-five, on a night out which culminated in a spectacular public vomiting in a Chinese restaurant.

Ever wondered what the clatter of sixty pairs of chopsticks being simultaneously dropped in disgust might sound like? Don't ask me. I can't remember. I was too busy bitterly coughing what remained of my guts all over the carpet.

Not a big drinker, then. Like virtually every other member of my generation, I smoked dope throughout my early twenties. It prevented me from getting bored, but also prevented me from achieving much. When you're content to blow an entire fortnight basking on your sofa like a woozy sea lion, playing *Super Bomberman*, eating Minstrels and sniggering at Alastair Stewart's bombastic voiceover on *Police Camera Action!* there's not much impetus to push yourself.

Marijuana detaches you from the world, like a big pause button. The moment I stopped smoking it I started actually getting stuff done. I still sit on my sofa playing videogames, necking sweets and laughing at the telly, but these days if I have to leave my cocoon and pop to the corner shop to buy a pint of milk before they close, it's a minor inconvenience rather than a protracted mission to Mars. That was the worst thing about being stoned: there came an inevitable point every evening where you'd find yourself shuffling around a massively overlit local convenience store feeling alien and jittery. Brrr. No thanks.

I tried other things, only to discover they weren't for me. LSD, for instance, definitely isn't my bag. Call me traditional, but if I glance at a wall and before my very eyes it suddenly starts sliding around like oil on water, my initial reaction is not to be amused or amazed, but alarmed about the structural integrity of the building.

My most benign lysergic experience consisted of an hour-long stroll around an incredibly verdant, sun-drenched meadow, watching the names of famous sportsmen appear before me in gigantic 3D letters carved from fiery gold. Eventually someone passed me a cup of tea and the spell was broken: there I was, sitting in a student hall of residence, watching late-night golf on BBC2 on a tiny black-and-white TV. From that point on it was like being trapped in a David Lynch film that lasted for eight hours and was set in Streatham.

Once again: Brrr. No thanks.

These days I'm sickeningly lily-livered, by choice rather than necessity. I don't smoke, I drink only occasionally, and I'd sooner saw my own feet off than touch anything harder than a double espresso. I don't want to get out of my head: that's where I live.

In summary: if I've learned anything, it's that I don't much care for mood-altering substances. But I'm not afraid of them either. With one exception.

It's perhaps the biggest threat to the nation's mental wellbeing, yet it's freely available on every street – for pennies. The dealers claim it expands the mind and bolsters the intellect: users experience an initial rush of emotion (often euphoria or rage), followed by what they believe is a state of enhanced awareness.

Tragically this 'awareness' is a delusion. As they grow increasingly detached from reality, heavy users often exhibit impaired decision-making abilities, becoming paranoid, agitated and quick to anger. In extreme cases they've even been known to form mobs and attack people. Technically it's called 'a newspaper', although it's better known by one of its many 'street names', such as 'The Currant Bun' or 'The Mail' or 'The Grauniad' (see me – Ed.).

In its purest form, a newspaper consists of a collection of facts which, in controlled circumstances, can actively improve knowledge. Unfortunately, facts are expensive, so to save costs and drive up sales, unscrupulous dealers often 'cut' the basic contents with cheaper material, such as wild opinion, bullshit, empty hysteria, reheated press releases, advertorial padding and photographs of Lady Gaga with her bum hanging out. The hapless user has little or no concept of the toxicity of the end product: they digest the contents in good faith, only to pay the price later when they find themselves raging incoherently in pubs, or – increasingly – on internet messageboards.

Tragically, widespread newspaper abuse has become so endemic, it has crippled the country's ability to conduct a sensible debate about the 'war on drugs'. The current screaming festival over 'meow meow' or 'M-Cat' or whatever else the actual users aren't calling it, is a textbook example. I have no idea how dangerous it is, but there seems to be a glaring lack of correlation between the threat it reportedly poses and the huge number of schoolkids reportedly taking it.

Something doesn't add up. But in lieu of explanation, we're treated to a hysterical, obfuscating advertising campaign for a substance that will presumably – thanks to the furore – soon only be available via illegal, unregulated, more dangerous, means. If I was fifteen years old, I wouldn't be typing this right now. I'd be trying to buy 'plant food' on the internet. And this time next year I'd be buying it in a pub toilet, cut with worming pills and costing four times as much.

Personally speaking, the worst substances I've ever encountered are nicotine (a senselessly addictive poison) and alcohol (which spins the inner wheel of judgement into an unreadable blur). Apart from the odd fond memory, the only good thing either really have going for them is their legality. If either had been outlawed I'd probably have drunk myself blind on cheap illegal moonshine or knifed you and your family in the eye to fund my cigarette habit.

But then I'm pretty ignorant when it comes to narcotics. Like I said, I'm a lightweight. I can absolutely guarantee my experience of drugs is far more limited than that of the average journalist:

immeasurably so once you factor in alcohol. So presumably they know what they're talking about.

It's hard to shake the notion half the users aren't trying to 'escape the boredom of their lives': just praying for a brief holiday from society's unrelenting bullshit.

Let's eat crisps
04/04/2010

This being Easter Monday, what better way to celebrate than a column devoted to describing the flavour of assorted novelty snacks? It's what Christ himself would've wanted. Although I suspect even the messiah himself might prefer crucifixion to the horror of tasting Walkers BBQ kangaroo crisps. The moment the first sliver of fried potato hit his tongue, delivering its payload of marsupial flavouring, he'd moan 'forgive them father, for they know not what they do' through a mouthful of wet crumbs.

Last year's 'Do us a Flavour' campaign, in which the company launched six temporary new varieties, was eventually won by the hideous 'Builder's Breakfast', which tasted like a fried egg in an envelope. This year, they're celebrating the World Cup by launching fifteen – yes, fifteen – new flavours, each ostensibly representing a different nation. I was alerted to this exciting development by an email from Walker's PR agency – I'm presumably on their radar after reviewing the 'Do Us a Flavour' varieties last year. On that occasion, I went out and bought the crisps myself. This time I'd get them for free. Following a brief phone call, a courier delivered a mock suitcase full of crisps to my door. So you can view everything that follows as essentially free publicity for Walkers, albeit the kind of publicity that explicitly states that their new crisps taste revolting. Well, most of them. A couple of them are quite interesting, as you'll see in a moment:

Japanese chicken teriyaki

The first ones I tried, and not a good start. There's no identifiable teriyaki element – just a whiff of chicken stock. They should've tried tackling a sushi-themed salmon-and-wasabi flavour. Instead they've created something that tastes about as authentically Japanese as Lenny Henry. Cowards.

Scottish haggis

After a bad start, another step down. These tasted of nothing, yet somehow managed to make that 'nothing' deeply unpleasant. It's like a small piece of fried potato failing to recall a repressed abuse memory while sitting on your tongue.

Argentinian flame-grilled steak

At last a vague stab at accuracy: there's a faint whiff of steak, although identifying the 'flame-grilled' aspect would require a leap of the imagination so vast you might as well use it to imagine something more exciting, like sex with a movie star or a holiday on Venus. Still: the Argentinians take the lead.

English roast beef and yorkshire pudding

Did Rio Ferdinand create this himself? The beef hits you first: not dreadful, but quickly overpowered by the oleaginous 'yorkshire pudding' element. The result is a mixture of cold Sunday roast and stale grease: like inhaling from a pub dustbin on Monday morning. Also, it's surely not wise to use the word 'roast' in any product that notionally represents the England World Cup squad. It's not looking good for our boys.

German bratwurst sausage

Ah. These actually taste like sausages. Not suitable for vegetarians either. Glancing at the ingredients reveals no pork, although they do contain the downright sinister 'poultry extract'. What exactly is 'poultry extract'? And how is it 'extracted'? Walkers must tell us. Preferably in the form of a televised re-enactment starring Gary Lineker.

Dutch Edam/Welsh rarebit
Yeah, whatever: these are both just 'cheese flavour'. The former is mild, but still tastes more like 'real' cheese than Edam itself does. The rarebit offering tastes like a flattened Wotsit with a splash of Worcestershire sauce. Perhaps that's a traditional Welsh dish too.

South African sweet chutney
South African what? They've made this one up, surely. It's actually OK-ish: a bit like spicy ketchup flavour.

Italian spaghetti bolognese/Brazilian salsa
Tomato time. These both taste like scratch'n'sniff pizza aroma: a lame committee meeting of watered-down herbs. The 'Brazilian salsa' has a slightly more sugary feel, but otherwise I couldn't tell the difference. My face was openly sobbing by this point, mind.

Spanish chicken paella
It would've been fun to have annoyed the Spanish by releasing 'maltreated donkey' or 'slaughtered bull' flavours instead, but no: chicken paella it is. Amazingly, these actually taste like rice. And slightly like chicken. But they don't taste like chicken paella: more like chicken fried rice. Maybe Walkers were expecting China to qualify.

Irish stew
No.

French garlic baguette
Garlic bread diluted by a factor of approximately 10,000. So weak and ineffectual, it's almost homeopathic. They missed a

trick: a novelty 'snail' or 'frog's legs' flavour would at least have grim curiosity value, much like . . .

Australian BBQ kangaroo

See? You want to know what these taste like, don't you? Answer: watery barbecue sauce with a dim hint of meat. There's no actual kangaroo in them, so the 'kangaroo' is delivered entirely by your subconscious. They could call it 'boiled pilot's leg' and the effect would be similar.

American cheeseburger

By far the most interesting entry, if only for the sake of accuracy: these precisely capture that instantly recognizable McDonald's aroma. Not Burger King, not Wendy's: McDonald's. If they were an official McDonald's product, you'd begrudgingly admire their authenticity. Instead, you're left wondering whether Walkers will get sued.

So that's the lot. If these crisps are in any way representative of their associated national squads, the World Cup itself will be an underwhelming kickaround which the US will eventually win on points. Presumably the company's crisp technicians are already working on a series of stunt flavours to honour the 2012 Olympics. Here's hoping they steer clear of yet more bastardised takes on national dishes and go for topicality instead. How about American tea party flavour? Iranian uranium? Chinese dissident? Give it your best shot, Walkers, and with any luck you'll start a war.

Brief gush about *Mad Men*
09/04/2010

Mad Men is one of those rare shows you just don't want to end. Thankfully its pace is so languid, it almost doesn't start, let alone finish. Eighty-five per cent of each episode consists of Don

Draper staring into the middle distance through a veil of cigarette smoke. Sometimes so little appears to be happening, you have to fight the urge to get up and slap your TV to make the characters start moving again.

Hypnotic visuals, lingering pace: *Mad Men* is television's very own lava lamp. I'm exaggerating, of course, as anyone who's been absorbing the show on a season-by-season basis will attest. And I use the word 'absorb' deliberately: you don't really 'watch' *Mad Men*: you lie back and let it seep into you. It works by osmosis.

David Simon once explained that *The Wire*'s deliberate refusal to decode cop jargon and street lingo was a conscious ploy to force the viewer to 'lean in'; to make an effort, to engage, to pay close attention to the dialogue.

Mad Men plays things differently. It makes the viewer lean back.

The programme's glacial tempo is startlingly alien to the average modern viewer, accustomed to meaningless televisual lightshows such as *CSI Miami* – all winking lights and trick shots and musical montages telling you what to think with such detached efficiency they might as well issue a bullet-pointed list of plot points and moods and have done with it. Shows in which the story is secondary to the edit, edit, edit: where any sense of meaning or even authentic emotion is doomed to death by a million tiny cuts. *Mad Men*'s tranquility and poise makes it resemble a still photograph by comparison. The viewer has to calm the fuck down to even start appreciating it.

But the notion that nothing happens in *Mad Men* is bullshit. Every scene has a pay-off; every line has momentum. But like life, it's often not clear in the moment quite what the direction is. Go back and watch a season again from beginning to end and the trajectories are startlingly clear. Even moments which appeared entirely aimless are suddenly sodden with purpose. There's constant churning activity – but it's largely happening inside the characters' heads. Everyone in *Mad Men* hides a secret, often a driving force they're scarcely aware of themselves. They don't know who they are or what they want. Unlike many characters in TV drama, they don't verbally telegraph their motivations: in fact they couldn't if they tried. This is what gives the series such a steady pull: there's a mystery at the core of every character, and they're trying to solve it at the same time as the viewer.

If you've been following the third series – and if you haven't, stop reading now and go rent the box set, and LOOK AWAY NOW because I'm about to start coughing out minor spoilers – Don Draper's gradual disintegration this year has been fascinating to behold. It's a measure of how composed he usually appears – sailing through countless pitch meetings and illicit legovers like some kind of Brylcreemed, priapic luxury cruise liner – that the sight of him nervously fumbling the act of lighting a cigarette in his kitchen has provided one of the most startling single images of the season. His perpetual adultery suddenly looks less like the devilish behaviour of a rogue who just can't help himself, and more like the desperate flailings of a sad, confused human shell whose mojo is deserting him.

This week's season finale answers the question of whether he'll get it back or not, and it's one of the most electrifying hours of TV I've seen in a long time. By the time the credits roll you'll be craving season four like a starving bear craves meat. You can gauge how addicted to *Mad Men* you are by working out how much of your body you'd be prepared to slice off, fry and eat in exchange for a five-minute sneak preview of the next season. I'm currently standing at one little finger, which might not sound like much. But if pushed I could raise it to a thumb. A thumb, goddammit. *Mad Men* really is that good.

Desperate Scrabbling
11/04/2010

Last week, Mattel caused distress by apparently announcing that Scrabble would shortly be accepting brandnames and proper nouns as words in a bid to attract younger players. The prospect of some feckless nineteen-year-old gumpo winning a game by placing the word JEDWARD across a triple-word-score hotspot led to mass nerd anguish. Have you ever heard mass nerd anguish? Imagine the sound of one freelance graphic designer whining because their iPad can't find a wireless connection, multiply it by 20,000 and garnish with the occasional wounded sob. It's like a choir with backache, and it's what the internet sounds like if you hold an empty tumbler against its walls and squint really hard with your ears.

Anyhow, it soon transpired there was no cause for alarm. First, the hardcore dweeb contingent was quickly silenced by the launch of an insanely advanced Apple-approved version of Scrabble, in which you use an iPad as the board and up to four iPhones as tile racks. (I'm not making this up: it's just like the real thing, but more expensive and less eco-friendly.)

Second, it turned out Mattel wasn't going to mess with the rules of original lo-fi 3D real-world Scrabble at all; it was merely launching a zany limited-edition called Scrabble Trickster, which as well as permitting entries such as YAKULT, also lets players place words backwards or in floating, unconnected spaces, because hey – it's kerrr-azzzy! You can play it on the table! You can play it on the floor! You can even play it at one o'clock in the morning – if you're mad!!!! Look out! It's Scrabble Anarchy!

Pfff. Anyway, harmless though it is, Scrabble Trickster does represent a missed opportunity. Look here Mattel, if you must launch a new version of Scrabble aimed at youngsters, why not create one called Scrabble Corrective in which players can indeed use the names of products and celebrities, but doing so earns them one hard punch to the face or chest for each point scored? That

JEDWARD gambit might win the match, but the victor wouldn't be conscious for long. Forget a return to National Service, just make every kid in the country play Scrabble Corrective at gunpoint once a week for the next four years. And televise that instead of football. I'm sure we'd all feel better.

Actually, forget it. We don't need any more Scrabble mutations. What started out as a simple word game already comes in various bastardised flavours, ranging from My First Dora the Explorer Scrabble (for toddlers) to Scrabble Scramble (in which the tiles are replaced with dice). At this rate, Scrabble risks falling victim to the same greedy function creep that has hopelessly diluted the Monopoly brand.

Monopoly isn't really a board game any more, but an outsized cardboard souvenir coaster. There's an officially licensed Monopoly board promoting almost everything you can think of, from *Coronation Street* to the US Marine Corps, not to mention insanely specific localised editions (the Northampton edition, for example, features Lodge Farm industrial estate in place of The Strand). And those are just the ones you find in shops. Many businesses have their own officially licensed Monopoly vanity boards, hence such pulse-quickening oddities as the BBK Clinical Research and Development Edition. What next? An official Monopoly board celebrating former Channel 4 continuity announcer and current Smooth Radio drivetime DJ Paul Coia? I hope so.

Still, Monopoly hasn't got its claws into every intellectual property going. Say what you like about the *Britain's Got Talent* franchise, but at least it's taken the trouble to invent an original game of its very own, albeit one whose contents make for sobering reading if you envisage a scenario in which it's the only form of entertainment left following a nuclear apocalypse: '1x board with electronic unit. 6x playing pieces. Game cards with 300 talents. 1x microphone with echo effect. 1x Kazoo. Magic playing cards. Plastic cups. Balls. Origami paper.'

A kazoo and some origami paper (i.e. a square piece of paper). And if you can't think of a talent to demonstrate with that lot, just stand in front of the judges and tear random bits of your face off. Order today, before your family enters the bunker.

But no. Wait. There's something even more suited to post-apocalyptic bunker-fun than that. Behold The Logo Board Game (rrp £29.99), in which players have to 'identify images and answer questions based on logos, products and packaging of the UK's most well-known brands'. The box art features the corporate identities of Shell, Burger King, Walkers, Pampers, Heinz, Alfa Romeo, Wrigley, Birds Eye, Kellogg's, Interflora, Uncle Ben's, The Chicago Town Pizza Company, Sun-Maid Raisins and National Express coaches, flanked by Homepride Fred and Churchill the nodding insurance dog.

Again, I'm not making this up. This is a genuine product. Popular too, going by the number of five-star Amazon reviews. 'We play lots of family board games but this has to be the No. 1 of all time ... The whole family played this from aged 14–85 and what fun we all had – we thought we knew our logos but boy did it make us use our brains!!'

It includes questions ('How many different flavours are there in a tube of Rowntree's Fruit Pastilles?'), visual trials ('What type of Mr Kipling cake is this?'), and performance-related challenges in which dad hums an advertising jingle and the other players try to guess what it is.

And if everyone in the bunker tires of that but there are another three months until the all-clear sounds, there's always Operation. Not the board game version, but an improvised real operation, in which everyone crowds round the body of whoever died last and takes turns carving bits off with a butter knife in exchange for corks or chunks of tin or whatever you're using as currency. It's fun for all the family! Apart from Amy, who's a bit squeamish. And Brian. Who's the dead one.

On the televised leadership debates
29/04/2010

If the leadership debates were supermarkets – which they're not – ITV's would be Tesco, Sky's would be Morrisons, and the BBC's offering would be Waitrose. The ITV debate felt like a 1990s gameshow whose rules required Alastair Stewart to bellow 'Mr Clegg!', 'Mr Brown!' or 'Mr Cameron!' every thirty seconds; the Sky studio was a poky black cave cluttered with discarded British Airways tail fins dwarfed by an immense Sky logo. With its mix of cavernous space and high-tech backdrops, the BBC debate resembled a cross between *Songs of Praise* and current Saturday night talent-show splurge *Over the Rainbow*: I half expected the loser to hand his shoes to Dimbleby at the end before jetting off into the sky on a rocket-powered podium.

The chief topic was the economy, a subject of which I have such a poor grasp that from my ignorant perspective all three men may as well have been debating the best way to kidnap a space fox. Cameron proposed 'efficiency savings' which seemed to boil down to a war on unnecessary leaflets; Brown boomed that this would shrink the economy by £6bn and risk a double-dip recession. Clegg didn't care what happened as long as it was fair. He proposed some kind of cross-party economic fairness committee, which as secret fellowships go, sounds about as much fun as a clandestine cardboard-licking society.

Clegg was big on fairness generally. Fairness and difference. He used so many distancing tactics – references to 'these two', phrases like 'there they go again', constant calls to 'get beyond political point-scoring' – he may as well have thrown in a 'hark at these arseholes' at the end for good measure. It's a tactic that largely works: he sometimes came across as a slightly exasperated translator sadly explaining to his fellow earthmen in the audience that these two visiting Gallifreyan dignitaries were well-meaning but essentially wrong.

Brown's ears are amazing. I think they're made out of sausages. And he still can't smile properly, which is hardly surprising given his ongoing luck allergy. Following the overblown 'Bigotgate' media piss-fight, which saw him force-fed fistfuls of shame, it was vaguely impressive to see him standing at a podium instead of screaming on a ledge. Just as Cameron likes to shoehorn the 'change' meme into every sentence (or rather did, before Clegg-mania flared up), so Brown mentioned 'the same old Conservative Party' so many times he began to sound like a novelty anti-Tory talking keyring.

According to some polls, Cameron won, or at the very least tied with Clegg. Which is odd, because to my biased eyes, he looked hilariously worried whenever the others were talking. He often wore a face like the Fat Controller trying to piss through a Hula Hoop without splashing the sides, in fact. Perhaps that's just the expression he pulls when he's concentrating, in which case it's fair to say he'd be the first prime minister in history who could look inadvertently funny while pushing the nuclear button.

Festival of falseness
02/05/2010

One of the most fascinating sights I've witnessed thus far during the coverage of the 2010 election campaign is Gordon Brown's visit to a branch of Tesco in Hastings on 16 April, which was broadcast live and uninterrupted for about five minutes on Sky News.

'Hello, good to see you,' says Gordon, shaking someone's hand. 'It's great to be here,' he continues, waving at a wellwisher.

He looks around. 'This is a good store, isn't it?' he enquires of no one in particular.

He spots a young boy. 'How old are you?' he asks. The boy is eight. 'That's a good age,' Gordon concludes. 'Which football team do you support?'

As he continues walking through the supermarket, the pictures carry on moving, but the sound appears to be stuck on a loop, because Gordon's repeating the same words.

'Hello, good to see you.' 'It's great to be here.' 'This is a good store, isn't it?' 'How old are you?' 'That's a good age.' 'Which football team do you support?'

The same handful of phrases, over and over again, for five minutes.

When you watch the footage repeatedly, as I have, distinct patterns start to emerge. Throughout the visit, Brown looks marginally less comfortable than a horse crossing a rope bridge, and his internal dialogue tree is starkly visible. Whenever he meets a boy of eight years old or older, for instance, Gordon briefly asks which football team they support, then chuckles, whatever the answer, before moving on to say 'Hello, good to see you' to someone else. That's the way he's been programmed.

(He occasionally breaks up his repetitive mantra with brief statements of the obvious: at one point, he glances at a shelf full of produce and says, 'There's a lot of produce here.' It almost makes you wish he was being shown around an orgy instead. Almost.)

The footage is funny, yet somehow heartbreaking. Brown looks clumsy, ungainly and chronically unsure how to behave around everyday shoppers. He reminds me of me. I can scarcely look people in the eye in supermarkets either. But I've learned to survive in demanding public situations – such as standing in front of an audience of expectant strangers – by adopting a babbling, deliberately awkward, vaguely nihilistic persona that is 50 per cent me and 50 per cent comic construct. It's a shield of radioactive bullshit that hopefully provides just enough entertainment value to stop the crowd physically attacking me, and just enough psychological distance to stop me crumpling to the floor and ripping my own face off at the sheer uncomfortable weirdness of it all.

Thing is, this performance wouldn't withstand five minutes of serious scrutiny. I could open a supermarket, no problem, but sit me opposite a combative Jeremy Paxman and I'd have a massive nervous breakdown within five minutes.

With Brown, it's the other way around. In the supermarket, he looked so anxious I half-expected him to climb inside a freezer compartment and refuse to come out until everyone else had left. In his interview with Paxman, held in the wake of the preposterous Bigotgate storm and a widely criticised final debate, he was frighteningly confident. At times, he even seemed to be enjoying himself.

Technical in the social situation, sociable in the technical situation? That's the hallmark of a nerd. And most nerds are simply too gawky – gawky, not aloof – to connect with the general public.

So he's not endearing. The press held up Brown's Bigotgate outburst as evidence that he's two-faced and contemptuous of everyday people, especially those who mention immigration, a subject so taboo in modern Britain that even fearless defenders of free speech such as the *Mail* and the *Express* only dare mention it in hushed capitals tucked away on the front page of every edition.

Two-faced contempt is the basic mode of operation for many newspapers: mindwarping shitsheets filled with selective reporting and audacious bias. The popular press is a shrill, idiotic, bullying echo chamber; a hopelessly poisoned Petri dish in which our politicians seem resigned to grow. Little wonder they develop glaringly artificial public guises. Picking a modern leader boils down to a question of which false persona you prefer. At least Brown's is almost admirably crap. It's easy to see through it and catch hints of something awkwardly, weakly human beneath.

Clegg's persona is roughly 50 per cent daytime soap, 40 per cent human, and 10 per cent statesman. Cameron is 100 per cent something. He isn't even a man; more a texture-mapped character model. There's a different kind of software at work here, some advanced alien technology projecting a passable simulation of affability; a straight-to-DVD retread of the Blair ascendancy re-enacted by androids. Like an ostensibly realistic human character in a state-of-the-art CGI cartoon, he's almost convincing – assuming you can ignore the shrieking, cavernous lack of anything approaching a soul. Which you can't.

I see the sheen, the electronic calm, those tiny, expressionless eyes ... I glimpse the outlines of the cloaking device and I instinctively recoil, like a baby tasting mould.

Don't get me wrong. I don't see a power-crazed despot either. I almost wish I did. Instead, I see an avatar. A simulated man with a simulated face. A humanoid. A replicant. An Auton. A construct. A Carlton PR man who's arrived to run the country, and currently stands before us, blinking patiently, blank yet alert, quietly awaiting commencement of phase two. At which point, presumably, his real face may finally become visible.

PART FOUR

In which Katie Price takes on the afterlife, some white supremacists show off in prison, and cows stare at you. Just stare at you. *

---

* What are they up to, those cows? What are they thinking? No one knows. Maybe they're not thinking anything. Maybe cows' heads are made of wood and filled with tar. Can you prove they're not? Right now, without access to a cow or Wikipedia, or a cow's head with some Wikipedia stuck to it, can you prove a cow's head is not made of wood? No, you can't. So don't come the fucking smartarse with me. Shut up and read your fucking book. You heard me. Shut up and read it. Stop reading this bit. This bit isn't here. You're imagining it. Seriously, your mind is projecting these words onto a blank page. You've gone mad. Totally mad. In a moment, these words will disappear and be replaced by a brightly coloured three-dimensional landscape filled with spinning, screaming dolls' heads. That's how mad you've gone: like, proper mad.**

** It's okay. You have not really gone mad. I was kidding up there. Just my little joke. Apologies if it upset you. Although if it upset you to the point where you physically wept onto the book, maybe you have gone mad after all, you poor mad fuck.

Going live
09/05/2010

So the other day I had to appear on live television several times throughout the evening, as the polls closed and the votes were counted and my guts turned to cold cream. Not because of the exit poll (although that was pretty depressing), but because appearing on live television is so profoundly scary.

Since most of my contributions were prerecorded, I didn't have to do much except turn up, state my name and introduce some VTs – but nevertheless the fact remains that you, sir, are on LIVE TELEVISION.

And this does very strange things to your brain. Having lived through the experience, I can now only assume that every single one of the nation's favourite live telly faces has the ice-blooded, psychotic personality of a long-range military sniper. That nice Christine Bleakley? Bet she could emotionlessly blast a hole through your forehead while linking to a report on wind farms.

On the morning itself, I was fine. I'd been up until 5 a.m. in an edit suite, where we were cutting one of the VT packages I'd written (to make two of them, totalling just over eight minutes, took roughly forty hours; viewers, of course, are blissfully unaware of the slog involved, and often assume it takes as long to create something as it does to watch it). Therefore I was too knackered to really think about the LIVE aspect of the LIVE show that I was taking part in.

It was only during a cautionary pre-broadcast talk from the lawyer that it began to sink in. The lawyer's job is to remind you not to say anything libellous or illegal while the camera's pointing at you, because, y'know, it's live. As he ran through an exhaustive list of things that could potentially go wrong, my mind began to cry.

Five minutes before the broadcast, I suddenly realised I couldn't see properly. Or rather, I could see perfectly well – objects and surfaces and people and all that – but nothing I looked at made sense. At one point, I stared at my shoe and wondered if it was real. Just as a spider in a bathtub will repeatedly run up the sides yet inexorably slide back to the same spot, my brain pounced in all sorts of oblique directions but always returned to the same thought: you are about to die.

All of which means that, by the time you walk out in front of an audience, in front of a camera, you aren't really 'you' any more, but a vaguely human-shaped cloud of screaming nerves. This is actually quite a useful state of mind: you essentially become someone else. And since whatever's happening is no longer happening to you, an eerie calm descends.

Not for long, though. As the countdown begins, a comprehensive list of fears spools through your head. Your primary concerns, in order of repulsion: 1) you might vomit with sheer terror while everyone's looking; 2) you might snap and start bellowing obscenities or gibberish or violent threats against named individuals until a cameraman has to physically wrestle you to the floor. Trust me, given the addled mindstate you work yourself into, this is not as unlikely as it appears on paper; 3) there might be a technical hitch that forces you to fill in, live, without a script. (Later, backstage, Armando Iannucci told me that halfway through the 1997 *Election Night Armistice* – which has to rank as one of the best live TV comedy events of all time – he looked at the camera to discover his autocue was completely blank. 'The VT's gone down,' said a producer in his ear. 'Just talk for two minutes.' So he did. Because he had no choice. 'It's amazing what comes out,' he told me.

In the event, I got through my first weeny link without a hitch. But moments before doing my second link, much later in the night, something completely unexpected happened. I did a piss.

Only a little one – a mere eighth of a teaspoon at most – but nevertheless: I did a piss. Not backstage either, but right there on the set, nanoseconds before I was due to start speaking. Fortunately, I was wearing black trousers and sitting down so I got away with it, but inside my head it was pure nuclear war. You see, by that point I'd largely managed to convince myself that the nervous energy I was experiencing was actually just excitement in disguise. The micropiddle was my body's way of reminding me that, even if my head deluded itself, the rest of me was still petrified.

Do rookie news anchors piss their pants on day one? Did Phillip Schofield launch his career by shitting in the broom cupboard chair? If you'd asked me a week ago, I'd have said no. Now I'm not so sure.

It didn't end there. Later, I had to take part in a brief roundtable discussion during which I realised my hands were now urinating.

Well, kind of: they were virtually pissing sweat. And although my vision had sorted itself out, my hearing was now proving troublesome (everything everyone said sounded like an incomprehensible jumble of vowels). It really is amazing how the human brain responds to high-stress situations. Specifically, it's amazing how it conspires to mess you up.

What with all that self-indulgent terror coursing through my veins, I hardly had time to digest the outcome of the election itself, which started out depressing before turning deeply weird. So weird, in fact, that I'm becoming convinced I actually died of a heart attack during my first live piece to camera, and am dreaming all of this on my way to the afterlife.

Cameron suggesting a LibDem coalition? Naaah. That's the *Twilight Zone*.

Workplace T&A
14/05/2010

A few weeks ago thousands of volunteers stripped off to pose for Spencer Tunick, for what must be his 500th photographic study of several thousand nudes. How many sets of genitals do you think he's laid eyes on throughout his career? The man must've seen more shivering naked bodies than Caligula in his prime.

Whenever one of Tunick's stunts makes it on to the news – i.e. each time he does one – the report is rounded out with a few soundbites from participants in which they explain how 'empowered' and privileged they felt to help form a work of art. Good for them, because I know for a fact that if I took part, I'd spend the whole time staring at tits and bums, thinking, 'Look at all these tits and bums', with one half of my brain, and answering, 'I already am', with the other. Art wouldn't really come into it.

That's why I'm suspicious of any attempt to 'empower' individuals by encouraging them to strip off, a psychological journey television is especially fond of, since human nature dictates that the viewer is going to want to stick around till the end just to see what the lead character's pubic hair looks like. Millions of viewers would sit through a four-hour live discussion about quantitative easing if the participants promised to flash their arses at random intervals.

Gok Wan pioneered the 'healing striptease' format, and at least seemed to be doing it for reasons that were directly related to body image. Since then, we've been subjected to BBC3's *Naked*, Sky's *The Real Full Monty*, and now *The Naked Office*, in which office workers are gradually cajoled into coming into work with nothing on, because – hey! – it'll make them a more cohesive team, right?

Overseeing the experiment is a ridiculous self-help guru called Seven Suphi (pronounced 'Seh-venn Soopee'), who repeatedly claims her mission is to 'help individuals unleash their full potential'. Her job consists of getting the volunteers to play various bollocksy team-building exercises and trying to pretend that turning up to work naked on Friday to have your genitals filmed and broadcast wouldn't be a crazy thing to do. Seven doesn't get naked herself, incidentally. She's not stupid.

Several problems immediately present themselves. For one thing, the first episode doesn't really take place in an office. Instead, we're on the premises of an organic food delivery company, which means most of the action takes place in a chilly warehouse full of cauliflowers. Furthermore, after watching them walk around fully clothed, you don't particularly want to see any of the workforce naked.

But perhaps the most damning indictment of the whole enterprise is this: most of them don't actually get naked at all. OK, so one of them does – strides around bold as brass with his penis bobbing hither and thither like a giraffe with a broken neck in fact – but the majority of them cover up their raciest bits with underwear, stickers, or strategically positioned briefcases. One bloke doesn't participate at all, presumably on the basis that it's humiliating and pointless.

Nonetheless, the whole thing is packaged up as an inspirational journey that's transformed the way they do business and blah blah blah. What's worrying is the thought of office managers watching at home thinking, 'Hey, that's a good idea!' and organising their own Naked Fridays. Most desk jobs are perfectly soul-destroying enough without the prospect of having to gaze up a co-worker's anus each time they bend down to pick up a paperclip.

Besides, where does this 'openness' end? Once you've done Naked Friday, what other taboos are there to break? Masturbation Monday? Farty-Nosepick Tuesday? How about Bin-Shit Wednesday, where everyone has to use a makeshift toilet in the middle of the room? That'd be so empowering, it'd move you to tears – and could change the atmosphere in the office so profoundly they'd have to open the windows for a full ten minutes.

The possibilities, like human stupidity, are endless.

Never-ending Tories
16/05/2010

So: the weirdest election in history has produced the weirdest government imaginable. Well, almost. If Cameron had formed a coalition with the cast of *Bergerac*, that might be weirder – but only by about 7 per cent.

The worst part is working out who to hate, and why. I was eight when Thatcher got in, and didn't really understand what was happening. Nonetheless, before long the Tories had replaced the Cybermen as my number one bogeymen. At first there was a simple, visceral reason for this: they seemed alarmingly gung-ho about nuclear war. They believed nuclear missiles were an effective deterrent, and furthermore, that a nuclear war might be winnable anyway.

I was opposed to all kinds of nuclear war – even little ones between neighbouring Welsh counties were simply not on, in my book. It was my understanding that these things tended to spiral out of control, and burning to death in a massive exploding fireball didn't rank very high on my list of hopes and dreams for the future.

(My paranoia wasn't that far off, as it happens. According to the book *Rendez-Vous: The Psychoanalysis of François Mitterrand*, at the height of the Falklands War, Thatcher threatened to nuke Argentina unless President Mitterrand handed over disabling codes for the French-built Exocet missiles which were pounding British ships. If that's true, and if Thatcher had carried out her threat, you wouldn't be reading this now – you'd be fighting a giant scorpion to impress the village elders.)

As if plotting to destroy the world wasn't bad enough, the Conservatives went on to preside over the most wilfully obnoxious and polarising decade imaginable: braying yuppies at one extreme, penniless strikers at the other. The Tories weren't just nasty – they seemed to actively *enjoy* being nasty.

And there was no getting rid of them, even when Thatcher got the boot. Consequently, an entire generation grew up regarding the Tory government as something like rain, or wasps, or stomach flu: an unavoidable, undying source of dismay.

Until 1997, when they were eradicated overnight. It was as if scientists had suddenly discovered a cure for the common cold. A permanent millstone – gone! The initial glow of jubilation never completely faded. For years afterwards, simply knowing the Conservatives weren't in power left me mildly delighted on a daily basis.

Even when Blair and Co. turned out to be so disappointing, I could console myself with the thought that the Conservatives would have been even worse. OK, so Labour started an illegal war. The Tories would've started six – four of them nuclear. So what if the rich/poor divide grew bigger under Labour? The Tories would've reopened the mines just so they could enjoy closing them again, right? Then they'd fill them full of tramp corpses and raze the surrounding communities to the ground, yeah?

Yeah.

As this year's election crept closer, and a Conservative government appeared ever more likely, the Tories became meaningful bogeymen once again. The fact that Cameron generally looks and sounds even less sincere than Blair ever managed to, meant that the more he professed to be caring, the more sinister he became.

Around a year ago, it seemed clear that Cameron would be PM and that, after six weeks in power, the mask would slip and he'd legalise the hunting of single mums. The BBC website would be deleted and replaced with a twenty-four-hour Sky News propaganda feed. Thatcher would be commemorated on banknotes. Drunk with power, Cameron would issue breathtakingly heartless decrees from his onyx throne, while Andy Coulson squatted at his feet, cackling like Gollum and drinking from a skull.

But instead we've got this coalition thing. This disorientating mash-up. Cameron and Clegg engaging in public foreplay. A sour Tory cookie with chunks of LibDem chocolate. Even the prospect of George Osborne as Chancellor seems less chilling in the knowledge that Vince Cable can pop his head round the door from time to time, if only to pull disapproving faces. If the Tories had won more seats, or slogged on as a minority government, at least we'd have a clear set of hate figures we could start despising immediately. Instead, we've got the Nazis forming an alliance with the Smurfs.

We couldn't even hate the Tories for looking smug on the steps of Downing Street – partly because Downing Street doesn't have steps, but mainly because the result forced a helping of humble pie down their necks, which they swallowed with infuriating good grace. Cameron appears to be making a sincere attempt to permanently drag his party towards more moderate ground, which is a crushing blow for those of us who were expecting outright malevolence from day one.

Then there's the scrapping of ID cards and limits on the spread of CCTV, which are genuinely refreshing. What next? Harsh new punishments for anyone caught snooping on private voicemails? Chances are, Coulson's typing up a cheery press release on that very subject right now.

As long-dreaded bogeymen, these twenty-first-century Tories are proving a damp squib, like the brightly coloured Daleks. No doubt they'll do something horrific fairly soon, but so far they haven't quite obliged, thereby depriving us all of a good cathartic hate-in. I always knew the Tories were selfish at heart, but this really takes the biscuit. Why can't they just be massively and obviously unreasonable from the outset, like they're supposed to? If all this pragmatism and inclusion they're apparently demonstrating doesn't turn out to be a cynical ruse, I'll be sorely disappointed.

In the meantime, we'll just have to wait for them to do something unequivocally shitty before we can say 'I told you so' – unless the whole '55 per cent majority' thing turns out to be their equivalent of Hitler's Enabling Act, which strikes me as unlikely at the time of writing, since even constitutional experts can't agree whether it's a disgraceful abuse of democracy or nothing to worry about.

But by all means remind me of my nonchalance on this subject in four years' time, when we're being issued uniforms and ushered down the bunkers. Unless it's illegal for citizens to converse by then, in which case simply arch your eyebrows and shrug a bit, and I'll know what you mean.

Sex and violence FTW
21/05/2010

If you're a fifteen-year-old boy, chances are *Spartacus: Blood and Sand* will strike you as the finest TV show ever made. The only drawback is that you're too young to watch it.

This is possibly the lustiest, goriest, most wilfully red-blooded drama series the law and human decency will allow. Roughly every thirty seconds someone gets an axe or sword in the face. Roughly every twenty seconds a woman bares her breasts. Roughly every ten seconds someone grunts a four-letter word starting with either 'f' or 'c'. There's more fruity language than a week-long Jam convention. Everyone swears like a foul-mouthed trooper stubbing his toe on a slang dictionary. It's not so much *I, Claudius* as *I Claudi-cuss*. HA HA HA.

So: sex, violence, and hardcore swearing. Sometimes all three at once. This programme was not written and performed by pussies. They should've called it *Spartacus: Blood and Fucking Tits* instead.

The plot concerns a nameless Thracian warrior who spends half his life fighting barbarians on behalf of the Romans in unconvincing green-screen CGI landscapes, and the other half having slow-motion sex with his wife. This violent/sexual idyll is spoiled forever when the Romans betray him and his wife

135

is kidnapped. Our nameless hero becomes a gladiator named Spartacus, which means his job now consists of weekly kill-or-be-killed hack-and-slash encounters in the Colosseum.

According to the head trainer, every time a true gladiator enters the ring he must 'look death in the eye, embrace it and fuck it'. Which was a round sadly missing from the ITV version of *Gladiators*. But not here. Make no mistake: the gladiatorial scenes are pretty brutal. Limbs are hacked off with such nonchalant frequency, it sometimes feels more like an extreme whittling contest. During one match Spartacus manages to carve two legs off one adversary using a single, uninterrupted back-and-forth slicing action. But the guy's still going – dragging himself away with his palms as his knee stumps piddle blood. Will Spartacus show mercy? What do you think?

By the end, he's carved his opponents into such small pieces, it looks like he's picked a fight with an animated lasagne.

Then there's the sex. Apparently ancient Rome played host to more blowjobs than the internet. Rich couples nonchalantly screw slaves while discussing the weather. There's a lot of nudity here, and not just female nudity either. It's always dick o'clock in *Spartacus* land.

The first time our hero indulges in a little locker-room back-chat with his fellow gladiators, the main antagonist paces around him, penis swinging proudly in the breeze. Usually I find it impossible to hear what actors are saying during a nude scene – my brain's too busy screaming 'LOOK AT THEIR TITS LOOK LOOK LOOK' to process anything as complex as dialogue – but here, for once, the nudity is so persistent, the mind quickly compensates for it. By episode four I was staring at orgy sequences and wondering who composed the background music.

But here's the surprise – after a disappointingly slow (yes, slow – despite the constant sex and violence) pair of opening episodes, *Spartacus* starts to improve exponentially until somewhere round episode five, where you stop enjoying it ironically and start to enjoy it outright. Yes, it may be the kind of show in which a tattooed warrior gets his face hacked off by a man armed with a hook; it may feature lines like 'your wife has been fucked to madness by a thousand vermin cocks'; it may toss in pointless cameos of one-armed topless transsexuals – and all three of these things genuinely happen in the early episodes – but it's also not half bad. In fact I'd go as far as to say it actually gets quite good. There's just a hell of a lot to desensitise yourself to first. Good luck. Give it a go.

Oh and that nice John Hannah's in it, and very good he is too. Your mum likes John Hannah. So if she asks why you're watching it, cite his involvement. Just don't, under any circumstances, invite her to watch it.

How to remix humankind
23/05/2010

OK, time to revise those nightmare visions of the future. Rather than being laser-gunned in the lungs by robotic shock troopers, we'll be absorbed by undulating blob monsters – all because a group of scientists in Maryland have created artificial life in a laboratory. What surprised me most about the news was that it was surprise news. I thought artificial life had been mastered years ago, when Sega created Sonic the Hedgehog. But apparently he didn't count.

Instead we're meant to be excited by a pair of thing-a-zoids which, placed side-by-side in the photographs, look less like the dawn of a new scientific era and more like a pair of giant googly eyeballs, as though Nookie Bear is staring at you from inside a burqa. The underwhelming bio-glob in question is, we're told, 'based on a bacterium that causes mastitis in goats', which might make an amusingly wry on-screen sub-heading at the start of the next Transformers movie, but doesn't do much to make the breakthrough any more thrilling.

That's possibly because the breakthrough itself is impossible to understand unless you're a geneticist. Here's what happened: the scientists created a computer simulation of the goat bug thingy, then fed the code into a genetic synthesiser. You know, a genetic synthesiser. It looks like a George Foreman grill, but in white, and with twice as many winking lights on the top. They fed it into that. Probably using a USB stick. Anyway, the DNA grill heated up and went beep and 'produced short strands of the bug's DNA', which I imagine were an absolute bugger to pick up with tweezers. Said strands were then 'stitched together' by some bits of yeast and *E. coli*, which eventually knitted the strand into a complete million-letter-long DNA sequence, which you're probably incorrectly picturing right now.

So far, so baffling. Then it gets weirder. To 'watermark' their artificial bug, the geneticists spliced a James Joyce quotation into the DNA sequence. The unsuspecting genome now has the phrase 'to live, to err, to fall, to triumph, to recreate life out of life' written through it like letters in a stick of rock. In other words, it's the world's most pretentious bacterium. After Quentin Letts.

This raises the question of whether it's possible to shove an entire book into the genetic synthesiser and create a new life form. I'd be quite interested in seeing what would pop out if you fed it one of Jordan's novels. It might result in a lifeform more sophisticated than Jordan herself, even if it was just a burping elbow with eyelashes.

Incidentally, the DNA sequence also includes an email address, presumably so you know who to contact if you discover a bacterium wandering about in the street without its owner present.

Anyway, leaving aside the immense philosophical and spiritual considerations, the most pressing concern about artificial life is the prospect of sinister man-made lifeforms being used for nefarious means. Even Craig Venter himself, who oversaw the experiments, describes it as a 'dual-use technology', which is a brilliantly non-specific way of saying 'good or evil'.

On the one hand, energy companies could create an organism that converts CO_2 into power, thereby solving climate change and the energy crisis. And on the other, North Korea could unleash an army of sabre-toothed jackdaws. Or we could accidentally create a kind of whispering, intelligent mud that rises up and smothers us to death in our sleep. Literally all of the above can but won't happen.

If we survive long enough to perfect the life-creation process, we'll have zany new animals to look forward to. Entire zoos will be dedicated to ridiculous remixed animals: 100-legged cat centipedes, crocodiles with breasts, ladybirds the size of a church. Ever wondered what happens when you cross a cow with a shark? Wonder no more at the charkinarium.

Disney could breed a real Mickey Mouse, a real Donald Duck, and a real whatever-Goofy-is to greet kids in their amusement parks – genuine walking, breathing mascots, with their own lungs and digestive systems and everything. Your kids won't know whether to laugh or cry. Although ultimately 'cry' is probably the likeliest option, since given the size of Mickey's head he'll probably break his own neck when he bends down to shake their hand.

I'd create an animal that excretes meat, just to give vegetarians pause for thought. Ethically, what's the problem with eating a sausage, if it's been harmlessly pooed out by an animal? To sweeten the pill yet further, what if you put pleasure receptors in the animal's colon, so it actively enjoys the sausage-creation process – enjoys it to such a degree that it chases you down the street, yelping in orgasmic delight while shitting a string of pan-ready chipolatas?

If you think that's disgusting, I'd just like to point out that it's far less revolting than killing a pig with a bolt gun then mashing it up into sausagemeat.

And we could remix humankind too, removing all the rubbish bits we're cursed with, like the appendix, or empathy.

It'd be fun to create a race of people without memories, pain receptors, or shame cells, then populate a pleasure-island with them: a hyper-decadent, consequence-free paradise where you can spend a fortnight's holiday having sex with everyone you see, or deliberately ramming your car into them, or both – like a real-life 3D *Grand Theft Auto*. It'd be just like being an oligarch.

All in all, a brave new world full of sweating, belching horror lies just over our collective horizon. But don't be scared. Consider yourself lucky to be alive just as we've worked out precisely how special that's not.

Going 'woo' on a rock in the sea
28/05/2010

I gave up on *Lost* some time during the first season, having decided it was just a bunch of irritating people going 'woo' on a rock in the sea. An episode detailing Charlie the rock star's backstory, replete with hammy flashbacks to a wildly implausible version of Manchester, was the final straw. But since then I'd heard from devoted fans, who insisted that despite a few major wobbles somewhere round the halfway point, it was actually well worth watching.

I never acted on their advice. I could've bought the box set, I suppose, but that'd be a lot of investment in a show which had annoyed me so much in the past. Best just to tune in to the final two episodes ever instead, then. I can probably just pick up the story, right?

Wrong. Thumpingly, obviously wrong.

Far from clearing up the mystery of what the island was and why they were there, from my uninformed point of view, the finale consisted of random sequences in which irritating people went 'woo' on a rock in the sea and in a city, apparently simultaneously. The city was purgatory and the island was real. Or was it the other way round? Characters I recognised rubbed shoulders with strangers, all of whom were imbuing each line of dialogue with such sombre, knowing significance, you could be forgiven for assuming we were witnessing the end of history itself.

The plot made less sense than a milk hammock. Jack was apparently no longer Jack, but a man who looked like Jack. He was certainly just as punchably earnest as I remember. There was much kerfuffle over a kind of magic reset button located down a well in the middle of the island.

The story ended with alternative-universe-Jack having an existential chat with his dead dad. I remembered Jack's boring daddy issues from the first season; back then they struck me as a spectacularly tedious attempt to give our clean-cut hero some depth. Has any viewer, in the history of film and television, ever actually cared about a lead character's parents? Faced with a character as blankly dull as Jack, I'd be more interested in learning about the tortured background of a piece of office furniture.

Anyway, having healed his life, Jack was free to stand around in an imaginary church backslapping other *Lost* characters while the room was filled with heavenly light: the end. Intense and moving, no doubt, for loyal fans of the show. Might as well have been a pretentious building society advert for anyone else.

But *Lost* isn't the only series coming to an end. *Ashes To Ashes*, *Law & Order*, *24*, *Heroes*: it's almost as though populist TV drama itself is shutting down. Some shows, like *Heroes*, don't have an opportunity to plan for their own deaths, leaving the characters stuck in limbo. Others, like *Lost* and *Ashes To Ashes*, turn out to have been in limbo all along. Limbo's very much in vogue at the moment. In fact there's roughly a 50 per cent chance that any serial you're following will turn out to be set there. All this publicity must be doing wonders for the limbo tourist industry.

Of course saying 'aha, it was limbo all along' is just a marginally more profound way of saying 'aha, it was a dream all along', a trope which became a cliché through overuse. There's no room for any more limbo-based programming, so anything currently on air is going to have to find a different way of ending, which sadly means *24* – which finishes for good in a fortnight – won't conclude with Jack Bauer kicking his way through Hell and kneeing Satan in the bollocks. Another twist is necessary. Here's hoping it transpires the whole thing took place in a paperback novel being read by Shaz from *Ashes To Ashes*, who was herself being daydreamt by Sawyer from *Lost* – while he was trying to think up a satisfying conclusion for *Heroes*. That or it pulls out to reveal it all took place in a cat's bum.

A cat's bum doing a poo.

I am thirty-nine years old.

Twenty-two millionaires fucking up a lawn
04/06/2010

I wish I enjoyed the World Cup, if only for some fleeting sense of common unity with the rest of humankind. But I simply don't get it. A huge number of my fellow citizens tune in and witness a glorious contest of ecstatic highs and heartbreaking lows. I see twenty-two millionaires fucking up a lawn.

If the fans want to enjoy their sport, fair enough. Judging by their rapt faces, I'm the one losing out. What puts me off isn't the game itself, but the accompanying patriotism; or, more specifically, the hollow simulation of patriotism used to hawk products throughout the contest.

Take the current Carlsberg campaign featuring an insanely jingoistic dressing room 'pep talk' which blathers on and mindlessly on about national pride. 'Know this,' the voiceover whispers portentously, 'that shirt you're wearing? Your countrymen would give *anything* to put it on.' Really, Carlsberg? I wouldn't put down a sandwich to lift the World Cup, let alone pull a sweat-sodden sports jersey over my head. And would even the most committed fans really do 'anything' to wear it? Would they saw their own feet off with a bread knife dipped in cat piss? No. They wouldn't. So stop lying.

Having grossly overestimated the cachet of said hallowed shirt, the ad treats us to a cameo from virtually every notable English sporting hero of the past fifty years, pausing briefly for a patronising moment of silence for Sir Bobby Robson, before depicting an ethereal Bobby Moore, bathed in heavenly light at the top of the tunnel, standing proudly beside a lion. The whole thing plays like a masturbatory dream sequence for Al Murray's *Pub Landlord* character, the punchline being that the whole thing is a sales pitch for a Danish brewing company. The tagline should be: 'Carlsberg: as English as Æbleskiver'.

The American confectionery company Mars is also keen to pat our patriotic behinds. It's paid John Barnes to jokily recreate his notoriously poor rap from the 1990 New Order single 'World In Motion'. And – ha, ha! – it's hopeless. But if you're not familiar with the original, it just looks as though we, the English, have absymal taste in music. Tourists watching this advert in their hotel rooms will spread tales of our cultural ineptitude on their return home. Thanks for that, Mars. Incidentally, Barnes's lyric has been altered, so he's now rapping about 'three lions on a Mars', which rather implies that the sacred England shirt that Carlsberg was getting religiously excited about is, in practice, interchangeable with a calorific chocolate-and-nougat slab.

Japanese technology giant Sony is also capitalising on the World Cup. It's got an advert starring Brazilian star Kaka which aims to convince viewers to trade in their old TV sets for shiny new 3D ones. It's an exciting prospect, only slightly undermined by the fact that the World Cup is being transmitted in the UK by the BBC and ITV, neither of whom will be broadcasting any of the matches in 3D. In fact, if you want to watch the World Cup in three dimensions, you'll have to go to the cinema, where Sony plans to show it, in 3D, on around fifty screens. That'll mean leaving your brand-new 3D telly at home, of course. But never mind. You can watch *Avatar* when you come back. In 2D. Because the 3D version won't be out until months after the World Cup. So you might as well not bother getting a 3D TV till then. And come to think of it, it's probably best not to bother anyway, because *Avatar* is rubbish. (I couldn't stand that tribe of pious, humourless, surly blue luddites. Fuck their stupid tree. I was cheering on the bulldozers.)

There are other adverts of course: Coca-Cola, Nike, Pepsi-Cola, BP, Blackwater Security, the Tyrell Corporation, Damien Thorn Enterprises and so on. All hitting the same phoney note of concord, all somehow cheapening the fun that millions will extract from the tournament itself. Not me, though. I'll be out of the country for the whole thing. When I think of all the adverts I'll miss, I'll try not to sob too loudly.

150 per cent more British
14/06/2010

Flippantly putting the grave environmental tragedy of it all to one side for a moment, the Deepwater Horizon oil leak isn't just causing extensive damage to the Louisiana coastline. What about our accents? Our lovely British accents? Thanks to the BP link, they've been destroyed too. Don't know about you, but whenever I'm around Americans, I tend to exaggerate my Britishness in a pathetic bid to win their approval. Those days are gone.

The first time I visited the US, I ran into trouble at immigration. Half the group I was travelling with decided to get drunk on the plane, which probably would've been fine with all the other passengers if it hadn't been for the unrelenting cackling and yelping and removal of trousers. I was fairly drunk too, incidentally, but only because I was so terrified of flying I'd decided to blot out the whole of reality by glugging myself into an inflight coma. From my slumbering perspective the flight was a warm fifteen-minute snooze. To the other passengers it must've felt like a thirty-year sentence in baboon prison.

Upon arrival, we were identified as troublemakers and hauled off one-by-one for a comprehensive bothering. Instantly I realised my only hope of avoiding immediate deportation was to behave like a minor royal – not an aloof, chilly posho, but a genial gosh-what-a-wonderful-country-you-have Hugh Grant-type, one who smiles a lot while using slightly formal language.

I apologised profusely by saying, 'I apologise profusely.'

The officer started out prickly – one of his opening gambits was, 'You could be spending the night in jail, wiseguy,' which simultaneously impressed and scared me – but several minutes of profuse apologies and crikey-I'm-sorry delivered in an embellished British accent appeared to disarm him, and I was released without being subjected to gunfire.

That's my recollection, anyway. Perhaps he just got bored with watching me grovel. But from that point on, my dial was set to 150 per cent British for the duration. I said 'Good day' to receptionists and 'I beg your pardon' to waiters. At one point I think I even said 'Toodle pip' to a cabbie.

Incredibly, rather than calling me a dick, they said they loved my accent. The US was a magic country where strangers liked me on the strength of my voice alone, unlike cold anonymous London where, rather than break their stride, pedestrians would blankly step on your face if you were dying on the pavement, quietly tutting at the blood on their shoes.

On a subsequent trip I discovered mockney was just as useful, and deliberately roughed my accent down in gas stations or bars, saying 'blimey' and 'bloke' and 'bleedin' 'ell', even if I was only asking the way to the toilet (sorry, 'bog'). This was even more popular than my Little Lord Fauntleroy act. Thank God I can't do a Liverpudlian accent. I'd probably have adopted a Beatles persona in music stores.

But now, as a company with the word 'British' in its name pisses apocalyptic quantities of oil into the ocean, and CEO Tony

Hayward pops up on the news to make tactless statements in a British accent, anglophilia is shrivelling. Things must be bad when gimpy Cameron has to reassure us that BP wiping its arse on the Gulf of Mexico won't disturb the 'special relationship' between the US and the UK. Of course it will.

Never mind that BP is an international company. Never mind that 39 per cent of its shares are held in the US, that half its directors are American. It's got the word British in the title, and that'll do. It genuinely feels like our fault. Like you, I've never supervised the offshore drilling policy of a major oil company, but I can't help feeling responsible. It's like watching a news report in which someone with your surname has been caught having sex with a hollowed-out yam. The disgrace is shared, however irrationally.

And to be honest, the Americans are thus far admirably restrained about the whole thing. If a company called Texan Gloop belched a carpet of black gunk over Norfolk, we'd be surrounding the US embassy and burning sarcastic effigies of Boss Hogg within minutes. And that's just Norfolk: flat earth and windmills. Having vandalised Louisiana and laminated thousands of pelicans, the BP spill now threatens to disfigure the Miami coastline, corrupting its relentlessly cheery blue-and-yellow colour scheme with a sea of rainbow black. Congratulations, people of Britain. Even though, strictly speaking, it isn't your fault.

Clearly a rebrand is in order if we're to maintain any national pride whatsoever. Trouble is, BP's already had one: ten years ago it changed its name from British Petroleum to BP following a merger with a US oil company. Since that's not enough to dissociate it from Britain, Britain itself will have to change its name. It'll still need to feel quintessentially British, mind. For the tourists, like. How about London Kingdom? Great Crikey? Yeoman Island? Hobbiton? Churchill-on-Sea?

Let's face it: to recoup our cultural value, it's either that or we all head over there and start cleaning the mess up ourselves, while muttering 'blimey' and 'gosh' and doing our best to be charming. If you've got a fly-drive holiday booked, start practising that Hugh Grant act now. Chances are you'll need it.

On white power
25/06/2010

Man, I love being white. It's great. I love my fine white skin, my stretchy alabaster bodysuit. I wear it every day. Sometimes I'll be on my way to the shops, and I'll catch sight of my own pallid forearms and I can't help it; I stop dead in the street, stroking them and weeping for joy. They're so damned pearly. Hooray for whitehood!

Could do without the sunburn, mind. It's hard to get the balance right. I only have to gaze at a blank sheet of A4 to start sizzling, but if I avoid sunshine completely I wind up looking ashen and sickly. Little wonder there's a multi-million-dollar industry creating creams and lotions for us to smear all over our superior white skin in a desperate bid to protect it from the sky, and another multi-million-dollar industry devoted to turning our superior white skin brown so it looks better.

Despite these drawbacks – and its propensity for showing up pimples and ageing quickly and going wrinkly – there's no doubt that white skin is the best, in the same way green Smarties are the best. Simple logic.

No one in their right mind would begrudge a green Smartie the right to celebrate its own identity. So what if a group of green Smarties wants to organise a green pride march and demand the immediate expulsion of all the other colours from the tube? You can't expect them to mingle with the others. Some of them are pink, for Christ's sake. Trace the history of that tube and you'll find a green Smartie was dropped in first, maybe. Therefore that tube is green land. Greens should call the shots. To think any-thing else is just madness. And it's the same with white skin.

If only there was some sort of club I could join to celebrate my whiteness, I've wondered many times, while masturbating over paintings of Hitler. Well there is! It's called the Aryan Brotherhood of Texas (or ABT), and this week it's celebrated in a documentary called *Inside The Aryan Brotherhood*. Heavily tattooed, spouting hate speech, bragging about their appetite for violence and openly boasting about their crystal meth-smuggling business, they're the kind of people you'd expect to find in prison. Which is probably why they're in prison.

Despite being in prison, they're a force to be reckoned with, according to this documentary, which in no way glorifies them unless you think intercutting violent CCTV prison fights with menacing soundbites from masked members of the Aryan Brother-hood underscored with dramatic music counts as 'glorification'. Anyone who thinks those sequences look like precisely the sort of thing the ABT might edit together themselves is mistaken. For one thing, the captions are spelt correctly. And for another they're not allowed to use Final Cut Pro in prison.

They're allowed to do push-ups, though. Lots of push-ups. We see one of them doing push-ups in his cell and he looks pretty cool, if you ignore the seatless metal toilet in the corner which he has to piss and shit in every day with no privacy because he's in prison.

They're not all in prison. Some remain outside, including a one-legged member called Lucky, and a man who wears a bandana to protect his identity but fails to cover up the huge, immediately identifiable tattoos on both his arms. Maybe he thinks a black man invented the sleeve.

The programme hasn't noticed how funny this is; it's too busy hammering home the notion that the ABT is a terrifyingly huge organisation, although when you Google 'ABT', the first things that pop up are American Ballet Theatre and the Association of Beauty Therapists, which is probably almost as annoying for the Aryan Brotherhood of Texas as being in prison.

This could be a desperate tragedy about wasted lives and misplaced rage. Instead it fetishises an angry, misguided prison gang furiously clinging to their own whiteness as the one source of self-esteem they have left. When your skin is the only thing you feel truly proud of, it's become a prison in itself. A cell of cells. Whatever the colour.

Of cows and men
02/07/2010

Advice for anyone wanting to become a TV presenter: stop trying to become a TV presenter. Instead, become an expert in something. Anything. Ghosts. Wool. Glass-blowing. Then you've got at least a fighting chance of shoehorning your way on screen as part of a specialist programme, before eventually becoming 'the face of' ghosts or wool or glass-blowing.

Forget cookery, though. It's oversubscribed. Throw a rock at any catering college and you'll hit an aspiring TV presenter who only signed up in the hope of becoming the next Gordon Ramsay.

If I ran a catering college – which I don't – I'd reflect this social shift by offering courses on how to slice an onion while doing a piece to camera without hacking off your fingertips. It's a vital skill: any wannabe TV chef who carelessly lops off half a digit has ended their future showbiz career right there. Creating an aspirational BBC2 cookery series is an uphill struggle at the best of times, but when the director has to frame out a stumpy knuckle each time they want a close-up of their star chopping coriander, it becomes nigh-on impossible.

Play your cards right and you can become a TV ambassador for any profession. Take pig farming. Specifically, take Jimmy Doherty, Britain's first celebrity pig farmer. He started out as the subject of a fly-on-the-sty-wall documentary about the trials and tribulations of pig-rearing and has risen to become the designated frontman for virtually any series with a hay bale in it.

Now, having presented shows about GM food and farming, he's back with a natural history series about animal behaviour. Ever wondered what goes through a chicken's mind? He'll tell you. But not right now. Because the first episode is about cows.

The Private Life Of Cows (BBC2) is one of those subjects you'd never wondered about until someone draws your attention to it. There's something creepy about cows. They've got the blankest face of any animal. A dog pulls expressions. A cat bares its teeth. What does a cow do? It just looks at you. It doesn't even stare, because staring implies some kind of effort on the cow's behalf. A cow just stands there with its dumb face angled in your direction. Its huge eyes somehow combine approachability with a terrifying lack of any discernible sentient feeling whatsoever. Cows are ultimately unknowable.

If you fell in love with a cow, the lack of emotional feedback would slowly drive you mad. You'd never know whether your feelings were reciprocated. You'd know if the cow thought it was going to rain, because it'd lie down. But you'd never know if its heart skipped a beat when you whispered its name. That is the tragedy of human–cow romances. That and the locals beating you to death with hoes.

But it turns out there's more to cows than emotional blankness. The programme points out that cows can be dangerous. It includes a dramatic montage of news reports about cow attacks, including footage of a bleeding, battered man being treated by paramedics after taking a beating from some cows. Having frightened you, it then offers tips on how to avoid being trampled to death by cows. The key lies in developing a rudimentary understanding of cow psychology, and not running near their offspring with a snarling dog.

It's a good show, full of informative nuggets. You'll learn how to build a bond of trust with a cow (honestly), learn to identify their individual personality traits, and how to teach a cow to ring a doorbell. Mainly, though, you'll learn that cows are faintly more interesting than you previously thought they were. You won't look at a cow in the same way again. You'll tip your cap out of respect.

And ultimately the cows are allowed to maintain an air of mystery. At one point, over footage of slumbering cows in a state of REM sleep, Jimmy explains that they're dreaming. Then he tells us rather sadly that we'll never know what the cows are dreaming about. Probably just as well. Bet it's something boring involving cud.

Jabscreen 4.0
04/07/2010

Sorry to talk about technology again, but there's really no escaping it, especially when you work in the media and spend more time gazing at screens than into the eyes of people, thank God. Furthermore, my subject is the iPhone, which demands a second apology.

To sweeten the pill, I'll stop calling it the iPhone right now. Instead, for the remainder of this article, it'll be known as the Jabscreen. A better name in any case.

Several times over the last year I've attended meetings which started with everyone present gently placing their Jabscreen face-down on the table, as though commencing a futuristic game of poker. It wasn't rehearsed, wasn't planned, it just happened; a spontaneous modern ceremony.

There's something inherently nauseating about the sight of a roomful of media types perched reverentially around their shiny twit machines, so each time it happened, a vague discomfort would hang in the air until, in a desperate bid to break the tension, someone would mumble a sardonic comment about the sinister ubiquity of the Jabscreen, likening it to a scene from *Invasion of the Bodysnatchers*.

This would in turn prompt a twenty-five-minute chat about apps and gizmos and which level of *Angry Birds* you're stuck on.

Sometimes there wasn't much time for the meeting at all after that. But never mind. You could schedule a follow-up on your Jabscreens.

If you didn't have a Jabscreen, it was hugely alienating, like being surrounded by new parents swapping baby anecdotes for an hour. There's no way in for the outsider, no conversational foothold. That partly explains why I eventually caved in and got one myself. A Jabscreen I mean, not a baby. What's the point of a baby? You can't even play a rudimentary game of Tetris on a baby. Not without taking hallucinogens.

But once I had a Jabscreen of my own, I soon discovered the novelty lasts six months, tops. There's a limit to how many conversations you can have about it before you reach burnout. Have you seen the app which takes your photo and makes it look like you're really fat? Yes. And the game where you land all the planes on the runway? Yes, that too. Hey, how about this thing with the funny red monster that repeats everything you say? Go now. Go. And leave me here to die.

Thoughtfully, just as Jabscreen owners everywhere were running out of apps to compare – and by extension running out of anything to talk about – the nice droids at Apple Castle gifted them a whole new branch of conversation: the launch of the Jabscreen 4, which apparently is miles better than a regular Jabscreen, although no one can really explain why. Its most impressive feature is this: simply by existing, it suddenly makes your existing Olde Worlde vanilla Jabscreen seem rubbish. How can you enjoy sliding the little icons around on your Jabscreen 3 when you know that if you had a Jabscreen 4, those very same icons would be slightly sharper?

The answer is you can't.

The Jabscreen 4 also functions as an HD video camera, which is ideal for capturing precious moments in your life you'll want to treasure forever. You could capture them on your existing Jabscreen, but they wouldn't be absolutely pin-sharp, and that's the important thing about memories: being able to make out individual nosehairs.

Of course, by the time your HD Jabscreen 4 footage is old enough to qualify as nostalgia, you'll be viewing it on a Jabscreen 20, so rather than enjoying the memories, you'll be whining that it's 2D and odourless and doesn't let you walk inside the image and rearrange the furniture. Also, it's full of gross nosehair. Everyone went *au naturel* back then.

Speaking of nosehair, the new Jabscreen has an additional camera on the front, so you can conduct video calls in which you and a friend stare at each other from an unflattering angle, counting the seconds till this misery ends.

Best of all for Jabscreen 3 owners, however, is the news that the Jabscreen 4 also has a minor flaw. According to some reports, it can appear to lose reception under exceptional circumstances, such as a nuclear winter or someone holding it. Apple zealots were quick to point out that you can get around the problem entirely by placing the device on a velvet cushion and gazing at it and breathing through your nose and masturbating instead of making any calls.

Thing is, even if the Jabscreen 4 was reportedly biting users' ears off and spitting them into a ditch, every Jabscreen 3 user is going to wind up buying one anyway. One day soon, a meeting will open with the familiar synchronised clunk of Jabscreen 3s being placed on the table, except one of the clunks will sound slightly newer, slightly weightier, slightly more HD. The winning hand will be a Jabscreen 4.

Everyone will ask what it's like. The owner will affect nonchalance. It's OK, they'll say, while stroking it longingly. And the following week there'll be another one. Then another. Then another. And still the world will have failed to improve.

Although on the plus side, no one will have to put their phone on silent at the start of the meeting. Just hold it in your left hand and bingo: no incoming calls.

Twilight of the vampires
11/07/2010

Until this week the one thing I knew about the *Twilight* saga was that it had vampires in it, which was enough to put me off. I didn't realise it was a romantic fantasy aimed at teenage girls. Turns out it's possible to be put off something twice before you've actually seen it.

The central theme, apparently, is abstinence; the heroine, Bella, is contemplating whether she wants to lose her virginity to a vampire or a werewolf. She's not allowed to try them both out, or get to second base with one and third with the other. And she's certainly not allowed to take them both on at once, although that would clearly make for a far better film.

Whichever one she picks is the one she's stuck with forever. In some quarters the films and books are lauded for their wholesome message, which is weird considering Bella is essentially deciding whether she'd rather fuck a bat or a wolf.

She's got zero interest in honest-to-goodness human-on-human action. No. It's magic farmyard creatures or nothing for her.

Oh, and apparently she chooses the bat in the end, which is the worst possible choice, because being a vampire, he's not just any old bat, but one that's hundreds of years old and isn't even properly alive. If the final film doesn't culminate in a twenty-eight-minute shot of her lying spread-eagled on the marital bed tearfully rubbing the leathery, disintegrating corpse of a 200-year-old bat against her marital sector, the entire saga has been a cop-out and a lie.

But even if you weren't boycotting the film on the basis of its disgraceful necro-bestiality theme, boycotting it on the basis of its vampires is reason enough. Vampires are the worst monsters ever created, as the following list of the worst monsters ever created, in ascending order of badness and culminating in vampires, will prove:

Mummies. Zombies – mindless human-hating reanimated corpses – are brilliant monsters because their motivation is brutally simple: they're very hungry thick people. Yet mummies – who are effectively zombies in medicinal giftwrap – are laughably non-threatening. Since their teeth are covered up, they're reduced to stumbling around with outstretched arms trying to hug you to death.

If they had erections, they'd be scary. But so would Goofy.

Ghosts. At its most ambitious a ghost might appear in your bedroom in the guise of a glowing holographic figure, loudly complaining about the circumstances of its death, particularly if you killed it. But that's the worst a ghost will do: whine about its own misfortune, like someone writing to *Watchdog* to moan about their broadband provider. And they usually don't even manage that. Instead, they make intermittent knocking sounds or slam the odd door in a huff. I've had neighbours worse than that. In fact there's a guy a few doors down who's been loudly practising the drums every weekend for the past five years with no sign of improvement. I'd gladly swap him for a ghost. Even if it walked through the walls and tried to stop my heart with its gaze every couple of nights it'd still be an improvement.

Serial killers. Real serial killers are genuinely frightening. You wouldn't catch me on a log flume ride with John Reginald Christie. No siree. But fictional serial killers are usually more pretentious than frightening, perpetually quoting Milton or arranging their victims in poses designed to evoke the martyrdom of St Sebastian. What are you, a cold-blooded murderer or the controller of Radio 3?

Proper maniacs are too disturbed to complete a Sudoku, let alone conduct an intellectual game of cat-and-mouse with an existentially minded detective. Put your cryptic crossword down and just strangle people. Or don't bother.

Vampires. See? Worst. Vampires are the only monster that's actually grown less brutal and frightening as time has passed.

Early vampires were stiff and aloof, with a cold sexual intent which was, at the very least, slightly creepy. Now they've got bloody feelings. They're lonely and tortured and all messed up inside. They spend more time staring at their shoes than killing people. Proper monsters only stare at their shoes when they're stamping on a villager's windpipe.

There is one good film about a meditative, troubled post-modern vampire: *Martin*, directed by zombie supremo George Romero in 1977. The main character is a disturbed young man who roams Pittsburgh by night, chemically sedating his victims with a syringe before razorblading their wrists and drinking their blood. But that's far too nasty and unsettling to pass muster as a vampire movie in today's wussy world.

No. Contemporary vampires come in two flavours, if you'll forgive the expression. Sexless wimps (*Twilight*) or smouldering hedonists (*True Blood*). Morrissey or Michael Hutchence. Both troubled. Both dreamy-eyed frontmen with nice hair. Forgive my pants for remaining unshitten.

It's a humiliating climbdown for a monster originally inspired by Vlad the Impaler, a man who'd happily eat his lunch while watching a skewered peasant slide down an immense wooden spike, being slowly and agonisingly dragged towards the ground by their own kicking, flailing body mass. Vlad would sit among entire forests of screaming human kebabs, chuckling and munching his oxburger or whatever the hell they ate back then.

Confronted with that kind of visceral horror, Robert Pattinson wouldn't make it through his asparagus and shaved parmesan starter. Even if he was only watching it on a four-inch LCD screen. The pussy.

Twilight? Pisslight, more like.

On the death of Raoul Moat
16/07/2010

Must be difficult for news teams, struggling to shed light on this immense planet peppered with stories. Where do you start? You determine which current event is most likely to affect your audience, and place that at the top of your agenda. Then you methodically explain said event, so your viewers or readers retire for the night with a clearer sense of the world, and their place in it.

Unless there's a gunman on the loose. Then you just shout like a wanker.

That masturbatory term is a fitting one. When it develops an obsession with a particular kind of story, the news turns into an idiot with an erection. Its IQ plunges fifty points and it can't stop till it's satiated.

The hunt for Raoul Moat got the news so flustered, it shrieked its reports at a pitch several hundred octaves above satire. Beneath a photograph of Britain's Most Wanted Man as an infant, *The Sun* ran the caption 'Cute baby . . . but two-month-old Moat clenches his fists'. On the front page, his estranged mother apparently wished him dead.

Moat was so enraged by this kind of coverage, he threatened to kill a member of the public for each inaccurate report he came across, like an extremist wing of the Press Complaints Commission. The police requested a news blackout on stories relating to Moat's private life. Soon the rolling news networks were reduced to filling hours of airtime with speculation about what kind of campsite he might have built. To make this seem exciting, they'd yabber that 'the net' was 'closing', or read out exhaustive lists of how many guns the police had.

When the police cornered Moat on the outskirts of Rothbury, the immediate advice to everyone in the vicinity was this: for your own safety, go inside and lock your doors. The BBC's Jon Sopel recounted this information as he strode down Rothbury high street, moving as close to the standoff as possible. At the cordon, a distressed and tearful woman explained that her mother's home was in the sealed-off area. She rang her mum. Sopel asked her to put it on speakerphone. 'That's a bit impersonal,' said the daughter. But she obeyed.

Then Sopel borrowed the phone himself, presumably so everyone at home could enjoy hearing how scared the old lady was. After several minutes he handed the handset to the woman's husband, who was standing patiently on the sidelines, waiting to speak to his wife. The phone was still on speaker when Sopel passed it back, so the man's conversation with his shaken wife was also broadcast live on air, with a camera trained on his reaction.

In the background, lads attracted by the cameras grinned and gave the odd thumbs-up, lending events the air of a live *Children In Need* link-up. Why stay indoors for your own safety when you can walk outside and be on TV? If I was fifteen, I know what I'd do.

Meanwhile, other reporters were competing to get as close as possible to an armed confrontation with a mentally unstable gunman with an acknowledged hatred of the media. On air, they whispered down phones so the police couldn't hear them. Sky's James Matthews crept to 'within metres' of the standoff until an armed officer caught him. 'Crept up silently, first I knew was when I felt his breath on my cheek,' he tweeted. There were other tweets from TV reporters, written in a breathless hurry. Channel 4's Alex Thomson apologised for the rush: 'Sorry lots of Bberry tweets in dark running thru peoples gardens evading cops – some spelling may have gone astray'.

Eventually a shot rang out. Matthews held his microphone in the air and captured it for posterity. The muffled blast was replayed over and over on Sky, while Kay Burley asked an expert to assess what the 'significance' of this single shot might be. The expert thought it sounded like a suicide. He was right. Raoul

Moat had done as the front page suggested. The story had come to its end.

And we all retired for the night with a clearer sense of the world, and our place in it.

Get a deadline
15/08/2010

One of the side-effects of having your work appear in a public forum such as this is that people often email asking for advice on how to break into writing, presumably figuring that if a drooling claybrain like me can scrape a living pawing at a keyboard, there's hope for anyone.

I rarely respond; partly because there isn't much advice I can give them (apart from 'keep writing and someone might notice'), and partly because I suspect they're actually seeking encouragement rather than practical guidance. And I'm a terrible cheerleader. I can't egg you on. I just can't. My heart's not in it. To be brutally honest, I'd prefer you to never achieve anything, ever.

What if you create a timeless work of art that benefits all humankind? *I'm* never going to do that – why should *you* have all the glory? It's selfish of you to even try. Don't you dare so much as start a blog. Seriously. Don't.

Sometimes people go further, asking for advice on the writing process itself. Here I'm equally unhelpful. I've been writing for a living for around fifteen years now and whatever method I practise remains a mystery. It's random. Some days I'll rapidly thump out an article in a steady daze, scarcely aware of my own breath. Other times it's like slowly dragging individual letters of the alphabet from a mire of cold glue.

The difference, I think, is the degree of self-awareness. When you're consciously trying to write, the words just don't come out. Every sentence is a creaking struggle, and staring out the window with a vague sense of desperation rapidly becomes a coping strategy.

To function efficiently as a writer, 95 per cent of your brain has to teleport off into nowhere, taking its neuroses with it, leaving the confident, playful 5 per cent alone to operate the controls. To put it another way: words are like cockroaches; only once the lights are off do they feel free to scuttle around on the kitchen floor. I'm sure I could think of a more terrible analogy than that given another 100,000 years.

Anyway the trick (which I routinely fail to pull off) is to teleport yourself into that productive trance-state as quickly as possible, thereby minimising procrastination and maximising output. I'm insanely jealous of prolific writers, who must either murder their inner critic and float into a productive reverie with ease, or have been fortunate enough to be born with absolutely zero self-critical reflex to begin with.

As for me, I'm stuck in a loveless relationship with myself, the backseat driver who can't stop tutting and nagging. There's no escape from Me's relentless criticism. Me even knows what I'm thinking, and routinely has a pop at Me for that. 'You're worrying about your obsessive degree of self-criticism again,' whines Me. 'How pathetically solipsistic.' And then it complains about its own bleating tone of voice and starts petulantly kicking the back of the seat, asking if we're there yet.

Some days, when a deadline's looming and my brain's refusing to co-operate, I'm tempted to perform some kind of psychological cleansing ceremony. More than once I've wondered whether I should prepare for the writing process by wishing my inner critic inside a nearby object – a tennis ball, say – which I could then symbolically hurl out of the window before taking a seat at my desk. It sounds like the kind of thing Paul McKenna would do. He's massively successful and can probably levitate.

But before I can even get round to it, I'm plagued with doubts.

How far should I throw it? How hard? If I toss 95 per cent of my personality into the garden, do I have to go and retrieve it later? What if it actually works? What if I wind up utterly dependent, and need to perform this ritual every time I'm called upon to do anything – even something as simple as asking for change in a newsagent's – and before long I'm zealously carting a trolley full of tennis balls everywhere I go, violently hurling one into the distance at the start of every sentence, breath, facial expression or bowel movement, and before I know it I've woken up screaming in my own filth in a hospital bed until the man comes in with the needle to make it all go away again?

What if that happens?

Yes, what if? So the tennis ball remains untossed, and those typing fingers move unsurely and slowly until the deadline draws sufficiently near enough to become a palpable threat; a looming iceberg whose ominous proximity transforms whines of self-doubt into cries of abject panic. And eventually the page is filled.

So then. To everyone who has ever emailed to ask me for advice on writing, my answer is: get a deadline. That's all you really need. Forget about luck. Don't fret about talent. Just pay someone larger than you to kick your knees until they fold the wrong way if you don't hand in 800 words by five o'clock. You'll be amazed at what comes out.

Katie Price versus the afterlife
20/08/2010

Wow. I never thought I'd live to see Jordan come face to face with a screaming, wailing, bona fide, three-dimensional ghost. Britain's top former glamour model and flat-voiced celebrity Aunt Sally confronted by indisputable proof of the afterlife – and on camera?

Surely this simply wouldn't happen, I reasoned. And then I saw *Ghosthunting With Katie, Alex & Friends*, and had all my preconceptions confirmed to their very foundations.

We all know what these *Ghosthunting* shows consist of: under-whelming footage of people standing around in spooky old buildings after dark, listening out for the odd indistinct bump in the night and doing their best to look scared. Approximately 50 per cent of each episode is shot using night vision cameras, which gives the whole thing the look of a Paris Hilton sex tape, but with notably less visible ectoplasm. This is the same as ever, but featuring Katie Price and Alex Reid and two of their friends, a gay couple called Phil and Gary. Gary, amusingly, looks just like Marc Wootton playing Shirley Ghostman.

It's a slightly flawed concept, because – and I hate to break this to you like this, bluntly, in the middle of a TV review column – ghosts don't exist.

Nonetheless, many people insist on believing in them anyway. These citizens are beyond help. Ask if they believe in Scooby-Doo too, and they'll accuse you of sarcasm, even though he was at least based on something with some grounding in honest reality – i.e. the animal known as a 'dog' – unlike the spooks and ghoulies that chased him and Shaggy around, which inevitably turned out to be local gas station attendants wearing costumes to scare people away from the gold they'd discovered.

Anyhow. Since ghosts don't exist, you're guaranteed to never *ever* see a ghost in an episode of *Ghosthunting*, no matter how hard they hunt for one. They might as well film themselves searching for Smurf eggs or trying to jump over the moon. But they don't. They just stand around breathing. For two hours.

Yes, I hate to be the bringer of bad news for the second time in one column, but this programme is two hours long. One hundred and twenty minutes of non-ghost action. One episode of *Mad Men* has a running time of approximately forty-two minutes; fast-forward through the credits and you could squeeze in three of those before this was over.

And I bring up *Mad Men* for a reason, because often nothing much happens in that either – but at least it's an interesting nothing. Two hours of Katie Price and Alex Reid exploring an empty house may be an apt metaphor for our times, but it's hardly compelling TV. If it wasn't for the ads you could mistake it for a screensaver.

Still, the night is not without its controversies. At one point Gary baulks at participating in a Ouija board reading in a chapel, because of 'the respect thing'. 'I'm not religious in any way,' he claims, 'although I am Church of England.'

Katie Price herself comes across surprisingly well, incidentally, because she spends much of her time tutting, moaning, saying things like 'this is bullshit', and giggling whenever Alex Reid tries to communicate with the netherworld. In fact, her lack of respect for the entire spook-chasing conceit causes nigh-on constant bickering among the group, lending events the air of a dysfunctional family on a claustrophobic camping holiday.

Imagine the conversations that might break out if the Mystery Machine got stuck in a ditch for nine hours. It's like that.

Occasionally Katie stops sniggering and professes to be slightly scared – although it's hard to ascertain whether she's telling the truth, since her face never registers any emotion whatsoever, as though it's never even been hooked up to that part of her brain. This isn't a Botox thing: seriously, have you ever seen her pull a single identifiable facial expression at all?

She's like a face on a banknote. Cold and unknowable. And omnipresent. And reeking of money.

PART FIVE

In which a mosque is not built at Ground Zero, everyone in the world is strangled, and Screen Burn comes to an end.

On the 'Ground Zero' mosque
22/08/2010

Things seem awfully heated in America right now; so heated you could probably toast a marshmallow by jabbing it on a stick and holding it towards the Atlantic. Millions are hopping mad over the news that a bunch of triumphalist Muslim extremists are about to build a 'victory mosque' slap bang in the middle of Ground Zero.

The planned 'ultra-mosque' will be a staggering 5,600 feet tall – more than five times higher than the tallest building on Earth – and will be capped with an immense dome of highly polished solid gold, carefully positioned to bounce sunlight directly towards the pavement, where it will blind pedestrians and fry small dogs. The main structure will be delimited by 600 minarets, each shaped like an upraised middle finger, and housing a powerful amplifier: when synchronised, their combined sonic might will be capable of relaying the muezzin's call to prayer at such deafening volume, it will be clearly audible in the Afghan mountains, where thousands of terrorists are poised to celebrate by running around with scarves over their faces, firing AK-47s into the sky and yelling whatever the foreign word for 'victory' is.

I'm exaggerating. But I'm only exaggerating a tad more than some of the professional exaggerators who initially raised objections to the 'Ground Zero mosque'. They keep calling it the 'Ground Zero mosque', incidentally, because it's a catchy title that paints a powerful image – specifically, the image of a mosque at Ground Zero.

When I heard about it – in passing, in a soundbite – I figured it was a US example of the sort of inanely confrontational fantasy scheme Anjem Choudary might issue a press release about if he fancied winding up the tabloids for the 900th time this year. I was wrong. The 'Ground Zero mosque' is a genuine proposal, but it's slightly less provocative than its critics' nickname makes it sound. For one thing, it's not at Ground Zero. Also, it isn't a mosque.

Wait, it gets duller. It's not being built by extremists either. Cordoba House, as it's known, is a proposed Islamic cultural centre, which, in addition to a prayer room, will include a basketball court, restaurant and swimming pool. Its aim is to improve inter-faith relations. It'll probably also have comfy chairs and people who smile at you when you walk in, the monsters.

To get to the Cordoba Centre from Ground Zero, you'd have to walk in the opposite direction for two blocks, before turning a corner and walking a bit more. The journey should take roughly two minutes, or possibly slightly longer if you're heading an angry mob who can't hear your directions over the sound of their own enraged bellowing.

Perhaps spatial reality functions differently on the other side of the Atlantic, but here in London, something that is 'two minutes' walk and round a corner' from something else isn't actually 'in' the same place at all. I once had a poo in a pub about two minutes' walk from Buckingham Palace. I was not subsequently arrested and charged with crapping directly onto the Queen's pillow. That's how 'distance' works in Britain. It's also how distance works in America, of course, but some people are currently pretending it doesn't, for daft political ends.

New York being a densely populated city, there are lots of other buildings and businesses within two blocks of Ground Zero, including a McDonald's and a Burger King, neither of which has yet been accused of serving milkshakes and fries on hallowed ground. Regardless, for the opponents of Cordoba House, two blocks is too close, period. Frustratingly, they haven't produced a map pinpointing precisely how close is OK.

That's literally all I'd ask them in an interview. I'd stand there pointing at a map of the city. Would it be offensive here? What about here? Or how about way over there? And when they finally picked a suitable spot, I'd ask them to draw it on the map, sketching out roughly how big it should be, and how many windows it's allowed to have. Then I'd hand them a colour swatch and ask them to decide on a colour for the lobby carpet. And the conversation would continue in this vein until everyone in the room was in tears. Myself included.

That hasn't happened. Instead, 70 per cent of Americans are opposed to the 'Ground Zero mosque', doubtless in many cases because they've been led to believe it literally is a mosque at Ground Zero. And if not … well, it must be something signif- icant. Otherwise why would all these pundits be so angry about it? And why would anyone in the media listen to them with a straight face?

According to a recent poll, one in five Americans believes Barack Obama is a Muslim, even though he isn't. A quarter of those who believe he's a Muslim also claimed he talks about his faith too much. Americans aren't dumb. Clearly these particular Americans have either gone insane or been seriously misled. Where are they getting their information?

Sixty per cent said they learned it from the media. Which means it's time for the media to give up.

Seriously, broadcasters, journalists: just give up now. Because either you're making things worse, or no one's paying attention anyway. May as well knock back a few Jagermeisters, unplug the autocue, and just sit there dumbly repeating whichever reality- warping meme the far right wants to go viral this week. What's that? Obama is Gargamel and he's killing all the Smurfs? Sod it. Whatever. Roll titles.

Google's final straw

12/09/2010

Last week I realised the internet wants to kill me. I was trying to write a script in a small room with nothing but a laptop for company. Perfect conditions for quiet contemplation – but thanks to the accompanying net connection, I may as well have been sharing the space with a 200-piece marching band.

I entered the room at 10.30 a.m. Because I was interested in the phone-hacking story, I'd set up an automatic Twitter search for the term 'Coulson' (eavesdropping, essentially: he'd hate it). Whenever someone mentioned his name, a window would pop up in the corner of my screen to alert me. Often their messages included a link to a webpage, which I'd end up skim-reading. This was on top of the other usual web distractions: emails, messageboards, self-deluding 'research' on Wikipedia, and so on.

By 1 p.m. I'd written precisely three lines of script. Yet my fingers had scarcely left the keyboard. My brain felt like a loose, whirring wheel that span with an audible buzz yet never quite touched the ground.

At around 2 p.m., Google announced the final straw.

I'm starting to feel like an unwitting test subject in a global experiment conducted by Google, in which it attempts to discover how much raw information it can inject directly into my hippocampus before I crumple to the floor and start fitting uncontrollably.

That afternoon, it unveiled a new feature called Google Instant. It delivers search results before you've finished typing them. So now, if I visit Google and start typing my own name, it shows me links to Craigslist the moment I hit 'C'. When I add the 'H', up pops the homepage for Chase online banking. By the time I've spelt out 'Charlie', I'm presented with a synopsis and review score for *Charlie St Cloud*, a film starring Zac Efron. Add a 'Br' and Charlie Brown gazes back at me.

As the name suggests, this all happens instantly. It's the internet on fast-forward, and it's aggressive – like trying to order from a waiter who keeps finishing your sentences while ramming spoonfuls of what he thinks you want directly into your mouth, so you can't even enjoy your blancmange without chewing a gobful of black pudding first.

Naturally, Google is trumpeting it as the best thing since sliced time. In a promotional video, a likable codger gives it a spin and exclaims, 'I didn't even have to press enter!' This from a man old enough to remember drying his clothes with a mangle. Google may have released him from the physical misery of pressing enter, but it's destroyed his sense of perspective in the process.

But this isn't just about ease of use: it's about productivity too. Google proudly claims it reduces the average search time by two to five seconds. 'That may not seem like a lot at first', it says, 'but it adds up.'

Cool. Maybe now I'll get round to completing that symphony.

What with phone calls, texts, emails and Coulson tweets, that two-to-five-second period spent typing search terms into a soothing white screen was one of the only relaxing lulls in my day. I didn't realise it at the time but, compared to Google Instant, it feels like a slow walk through a calm meadow.

My attention span was never great, but modern technology has halved it, and halved it again, and again and again, down to an atomic level, and now there's nothing discernible left. Back in that room, bombarded by alerts and emails, repeatedly tapping search terms into Google Instant for no good reason, playing mindless pinball with words and images, tumbling down countless little attention-vortexes, plunging into one split-second coma after another, I began to feel I was neither in control nor 100 per cent physically present. I wasn't using the computer. The computer was using me – to keep its keys warm. (Apart from 'enter', obviously. I didn't even have to press that.)

By 5.30 p.m. I'd written half a paragraph. I went home in disgust.

171

In desperation that evening, I used Google Instant to hunt for solutions, and stumbled across something called the Pomodoro Technique. Put simply, it's a method for retraining your attention span. You set a kitchen timer, and try to work without interruption for twenty-five minutes. Then you take a five-minute break. Then you work for another twenty-five minutes. And so on. It sounded easy, so I disconnected my net connection and gave it a try. By the time I went to bed I'd gone through three 'Pomodoro cycles' and written 1,856 words of script.

I'd heard of repentant slobs using a similar regime to ease themselves into the habit of exercise: run for ninety seconds, walk for ninety seconds, then repeat the cycle until your fitness increases and you can run to Gwent and back in time for *Emmerdale*. I never thought I'd have to do something similar for my attention span simply to maintain my own sanity.

Just as muscles ache the morning after your first exercise in months, so I can feel my brain ache between each twenty-five-minute bout of concentration. But there's something else there too: a flickering sense of control.

So, from now on, I'm rationing my internet usage and training my mind muscles for the future. Because I can see where it's heading: a service called Google Assault that doesn't even bother to guess what you want, and simply hurls random words and sounds and images at you until you dribble all the fluid out of your body. And I know it'll kill me, unless I train my brain to withstand and ignore it. For me, the war against the machines has started in earnest.

Falling face-first into a meat sofa
19/09/2010

What with all the hoo-hah surrounding the Pope's recent British holiday, the news that Nando's has bought the Gourmet Burger Kitchen chain for £30m may have escaped your attention.

In many ways it's the twenty-first-century equivalent of Little Chef absorbing Wimpy, albeit markedly more middle-class than that. Both chains specialise in upmarket fast food: the kind of place you don't feel thoroughly ashamed to be seen in, unlike their more established and reviled mass-market competitors.

One cold morning about two years ago, I sat in the window of a McDonald's tucking into a sausage-and-egg McMuffin. It was a bit like sinking my teeth into a small, soft woodland creature with a light dusting of flour; one which thoroughly enjoyed being eaten and responded to each bite by gently urinating warm oil down my chin.

It was a strangely comforting experience, until I realised that some – not all, but a reasonable percentage – of the passersby outside the window were regarding me with a combination of pity and contempt as they scurried past. Sitting in the window of a McDonald's, I realised, is a bit like self-harming in a glass booth. People judge you for it.

Not so the Gourmet Burger Kitchen. It has about fifty branches around the UK, but since most of them are in London, chances are you haven't visited one. It's a posher, ostensibly healthier Burger King: fresh, chargrilled, 100 per cent Aberdeen Angus patties served inside buns 'made to a secret recipe by our artisan baker'. But that much you could probably guess from the name. What's truly shocking, the first time you're confronted with a Gourmet Burger, is the sheer quantity of food involved. Eating one is a bit like attempting to cram a fortnight's worth of clothing into a child-size suitcase, or falling face-first into a meat sofa.

You've got two options: tackle it with a knife and fork (the coward's way out), or dislocate your jaw in the manner of a boa constrictor swallowing a foal, and heave it into your gullet, driving it home like a Victorian taskmaster pushing a buttered eight-year-old into a narrow chimney flue, taking care not to let the top half of the snooty artisan bap smother your nostrils on the way in.

Order chips, incidentally, and your burger will be accompanied by a generous helping of deep-fried slabs the size and weight of piano keys. Eat there at lunchtime and you'll spend the rest of the day feeling as if you're incubating an immense, spherical beef-baby. And caesarean delivery sadly isn't an option. Before bedtime, you'll understand how it might feel to give birth to a banister.

Even though a posh cheeseburger contains roughly 805 calories, compared with 490 calories in a Big Mac, there's no shame attached to the public enguzzlement of Gourmet Burgers, partly because of the emphasis on fresh ingredients, but mainly because it's a thoroughly middle-class form of indulgence. (Don't get me wrong, I like a Gourmet gutbuster now and then – but I couldn't honestly say I enjoy it more than a Burger King Whopper. Both are definitely superior to the Big Mac, however; to my mind, Big Macs taste a bit like a burger that's just been sick down its own front on a long car journey.)

Nando's, while not as posh as GBK, serves up spicy flame-grilled chicken, which makes eating there feel decidedly less shameful than a trip to KFC (fair enough, since eating KFC is like squeezing a sponge full of poultry-flavoured oil into your gob). But the health benefit of Nando's flame-grilling technique is perhaps slightly offset by the endless free drink refills; while gnawing at their chicken, your diet-conscious kiddywinks can guzzle as much cola as their guts can withstand.

So, then. It seems the key to nurturing a successful chain of fast-food restaurants in modern Britain is to provide a less reprehensible version of something popular (burgers for GBK; chicken'n'chips for Nando's), while still enabling your customers to indulge in potentially ruinous gluttony.

It's a simple formula, and I think I've spotted a gap in the market: fry-ups. Everyone loves a full English breakfast, but the traditional greasy spoon has an image problem. I propose a chain of health-conscious caffs where the eggs are free-range, the tea and coffee are Fairtrade, and the sausages and bacon are cooked on George Foreman grills, right there at the table.

Oh, and the meat in the sausages and bacon comes from the customers themselves. Your first cup of tea contains a local anaesthetic; while you read your paper, simply slice a thin rasher of thigh off your leg and pop it on the grill. Two rashers if you want to lose weight. It's the ultimate in locally sourced produce: 100 per cent organic, extremely environmentally friendly, and, if taken up by large numbers of people, it will go some way to solving the global food crisis.

The only downside I can think of is the blood leakage, although I'm sure, given time, I'll think of a solution. Probably involving vinyl seats and black pudding.

I only need a couple of million to get going. Who's in?

Fuck sport
27/09/2010

Ministers are concerned that Britain's schoolkids aren't doing enough team sports. Good for them. The kids, that is. Not the ministers. I'll dumbly and instinctively side with anyone trying to bunk off games. Apart from preventing obesity and heart attacks and diabetes and high blood pressure and premature death, what exactly is school sport good for?

The benefits aren't merely physical, grunt the experts, through their thick, sport-liking mouths. Team games build character. I can't argue with that. They certainly helped strengthen the more cunning and resentful elements of my personality.

Yep, like most dweeby types, I hated having to 'do' games at school, mainly because of an inherent physical laziness, but also because of the psychological challenges involved. In my eyes, PE was a twice-weekly period of anarchy during which the school's most aggressive pupils were formally permitted to dominate and torment those they considered physically inferior. Perhaps if the whole thing had been pitched as an exercise in interactive drama intended to simulate how it might feel to live in a fascist state run by thick schoolboys – an episodic, improvised adaptation of *Lord of the Flies* in uniform sportswear – I'd have appreciated it more. But no.

It goes without saying that the vast majority of sporty kids weren't bullies at all – but like a bigot blaming anyone vaguely brown for the actions of nineteen arseholes on 9/11, I developed my prejudice long ago and still enjoy feeling it fester.

Thus I harbour a deep and unwarranted suspicion of anyone with the faintest interest in sport. If you can glance at a shuttlecock without being sick, I will never truly like you. That's what school sport did for me.

And I wasn't even bullied on the pitch myself, not being quite wimpy enough to be the very last pick (towards the bum of the list, yes, but not the absolute final quivering cheek hair). But I watched the more hopeless specimens being shoved around, threatened, and insulted simply for being 'bad at games', and understood I had more in common with them than their aggressors. If – as seemed likely – the big kids finally managed to kill their prey, they'd start on me next. And what then? How could I avoid a thumping? What did I know about bullies?

Not much. My only significant run-in with a bona fide thug occurred during an entry-level metalwork class, when a rough and intimidating boy demanded the immediate use of a lathe I was operating. Having been taught by every children's TV show ever made that the best tactic with bullies is to stand up to them, I gruffly told him to wait his turn.

He stared at me with a sort of bored, affronted blankness for several seconds before hitting me unbelievably hard on the arm with an iron bar.

As I rolled around on the floor in agony, watching him blithely operate the machine, I decided it would've been far smarter to meekly relinquish control of the lathe, then get revenge twenty-nine years later by paying a henchman to burn down his house while he and his family slept inside. Not that I did that, you understand.

I have absolutely no conception of how exhilarating that might feel, nor do I know whether you'd victoriously punch the air upon receiving an emailed cameraphone snap of his terrified wife leaping from an upstairs window with her hair on fire.

Anyway: back to the football pitch. Standing up to the bullies was no longer a viable option, but nor was magically becoming brilliant at sport. So I quickly adopted a cloaking strategy. Like any nerd worth his salt, I'd spend entire matches psychically commanding the ball not to roll anywhere near me – but whenever it did, I'd do my best to appear willing to participate by 1) charging straight at it, and 2) pulling a disappointed expression when I inevitably failed to do anything worthwhile. Incredibly, this half-arsed pantomime was enough to let me off the hook. The kids who did nothing to mask their terror were the ones who got belted.

From within my protective pantomime bubble, the self-defeating stupidity of the bullies became fascinating to behold. I realised that, in a sense, their motives were pure. They genuinely cared about the outcome of the game, the idiots. Hence their rage at being forced to work with substandard squad members.

But they had no grasp of basic psychology. They couldn't see that each time they monstered a wussy team-mate, they merely reinforced the role of the ball as a harbinger of terrible consequences, thereby increasing the likelihood that said wuss would continue to shy away from it, subsequently causing more frustration for themselves.

I tried politely explaining this to one of the boot boys once, during a brief fit of self-righteousness brought on by the sight of him booting a mute, shivering weakling hard up the arse. I pointed out that they both looked equally unhappy, and that he was essentially kicking himself. He contemplated this for a moment, then flobbed at me and kicked the weakling slightly harder. I'd have been a crap Jesus. But at least he didn't have an iron bar, thus unwittingly sparing his family from an inferno decades later.

All of which means the sole concern I have regarding the current enfeebled state of competitive sports is that fewer school football matches means fewer boys learning how to outwit dunces or feign rudimentary competence in the workplace.

On the flipside, apparently more kids are doing weird non-team sports such as archery and golf. Yes, golf. Sixty-six per cent of boys get to play golf at school these days. Striding around the wilderness wielding a club? On school time? Never played it myself, but God I envy them.

MORE HEADLINE TO GO HERE
03/10/2010

Messing up in the workplace is never a pleasant sensation, but the very worst kind of boo-boo is the silent-but-deadly variety: a dizzyingly serious error you realise you've committed long before anyone else.

First comes the awful moment of realisation. In this instant, you're the loneliest person in the world. As the scale of your cock-up sinks in, you feel a cold egg of dread being cracked open over your skull, its chilled albumen seeping down your temples, the icy yolk quivering atop your crown like the frozen cherry on a tortured metaphor. This is followed by a brief period of indignant disbelief: how dare the Gods of Fate allow such a terrible thing to happen to a nice person like you, the idiots?

This defensive psychological distancing lasts about nineteen seconds, before being swept away by a burst of intense self-recrimination, during which you feel like pulling your own brain out and spanking it over your knee. And then finally, an unreal calm takes hold while you weigh up your options: will you immediately own up (the honourable thing to do, although you could get fired)? Or will you slyly wait, you snake, to see how things pan out, in the hope that maybe – just maybe – you'll dodge the culpability-bomb when it all comes to light?

Maybe they'll mistakenly blame Tom. You know Tom. Nice bloke. Works hard. Keeps his head down. Recently became a dad for the first time. Hope they sack the fuck out of him.

Presumably, a similar scenario played out in someone's mind last week, when it transpired that 80,000 copies of the wrong draft of Jonathan Franzen's new novel *Freedom* – a 576-page whopper, hailed by some critics as a masterpiece – had inadvertently been printed, bound and distributed. Someone, it seems, had picked up the wrong digital file of the book.

At first glance, this looks like an almighty disaster, albeit an understandable one. Like anyone who's ever suffered the traumatic loss of the only copy of a crucial file, whenever I'm writing scripts I tend to end up saving about 1,500 different versions along the way, leading to a directory full of bewildering titles such as finalscript2a.doc and finalscript1b-ignore-all-others-and-use-this.doc and finalscript1c-i-am-spartacus.doc.

Sometimes the documents themselves are radically different; sometimes the differences consist of a few missing commas here and there. Disappointingly, it seems the disparity between the 'right' and 'wrong' drafts of Franzen's book chiefly consists of minor typographical errors and typesetting changes. It'd be far more interesting if they'd accidentally printed a version in which, halfway through the nineteenth chapter, the whole thing ends abruptly with the words MORE BOOK TO GO HERE. But that didn't happen.

Early drafts are rougher and baggier and less disciplined than the polished final product, but can be more entertaining as a result. For instance, the first draft of the children's classic *Mr Tickle* is rumoured to climax with the hitherto cheery long-armed orange blobman horrifically molesting a cow from the other side of a duckpond, just because he can. Also, the original cut of Ridley Scott's recent retelling of the Robin Hood legend contained a puzzling interlude during which Russell Crowe recited the URL for a pornographic website. The scene was dropped from the theatrical release at the last minute when it was discovered that a script supervisor had inadvertently pasted the contents of their clipboard into the script while trying to find the keyboard shortcut for 'print'. Neither of these stories is true, incidentally, but that doesn't necessarily make recounting them here any less worthwhile.

I'm assuming the Franzen error doesn't affect readers who bought digital copies of the novel to read on Kindles and iPhones and eReaders and the like – but then again, even if it did, it should be possible to remotely and automatically update them all without anyone really noticing. In fact, the advent of digital books blurs the whole notion of 'final drafts' and 'revised editions' into a confusing futuristic smudge.

Freed from the physical limitations of a paper-and-ink edition, authors can continue tinkering with the text way beyond the date of publication, maybe even for ever. Perhaps before too long, you'll be midway through an especially underwhelming para-graph, and it'll start deleting itself before your very eyes, just like this one should have. Or your favourite character will die or reappear under an assumed name and have sex with themselves. Any notion of permanence will be a thing of the past. Even the individual letters will crawl around while you look at them, like agitated ants.

Worst of all, without the crushing finality of a concrete deadline looming over them, authors won't be forced to make up their minds about anything any more, and before long all books will open like this: 'James Bond strode into the casino. Actually, no he didn't. He walked into a blazing warehouse. Except he wasn't on foot. He was in a car. Or on a horse. Whatever. The important thing is, it was all really exciting.'

MORE COLUMN TO GO HERE.

Screen Burnt

15/10/2010

That's it, I'm off. Kind of. After over a decade of scribbling weekly TV reviews for the *Guardian*'s Saturday supplement *The Guide*, I'm hanging up my hat – the hat with 'Screen Burn' stitched into it.

Since I started writing the column, back in August 2000, TV has changed beyond all recognition. *Big Brother*, *The Wire*, *24* and *Friday Night With Jonathan Ross* came and went. *Doctor Who*, Noel Edmonds and *Battlestar Galactica* returned. Celebrity humiliation became a national sport. Johnny Rotten fought an ostrich. Timmy Mallett drank a pint of liquidised kangaroo penis in front of Ant and Dec; Jade Goody received her cancer diagnosis in a Diary Room. Ambitious US drama serials with season-long story arcs enjoyed a renaissance. *The Office*, *The Thick Of It* and *Peep Show* popped up. Stewart Lee got a BBC2 series. The cast of *The Inbetweeners* sprouted sex organs. Glenn Beck occurred.

The way we watch changed, too: from peering at a cumbersome box in the corner of the room to basking in the unholy radiance of a fifty-two-inch plasma screen buzzing quietly on the wall. The images leapt from SD to HD and now 3D. Time itself began to collapse as YouTube, Sky+ and the BBC iPlayer slowly chewed the notion of 'schedules' to death.

At the start of the decade, I was receiving shows to review on clunky VHS tapes. By around 2005, roughly half the offerings arrived on DVD. Now online previewing is the norm. In five years' time, most shows will probably come in the form of an inhalable gas which makes visions dance in your brain.

So why quit now? Well partly because I'm afraid of that future, but mostly because eleven years of essentially rewriting the phrase 'X is an arsehole haw haw haw' over and over until you hit the 650-word limit is enough for anyone.

See, I was never a proper critic. In my head, a 'proper critic' is an intellectually rigorous individual with an encyclopaedic knowledge of their specialist subject and an admirably nerdy compulsion to dissect, compare and analyse each fresh offering in the field – not in a bid to mindlessly entertain the reader, but to further humankind's collective understanding of the arts. True critics are witty rather than abusive, smart rather than smart-arsed, contemplative rather than extrovert. I, on the other hand, was chiefly interested in making the reader laugh. And the quickest way to do this was to pen insults. Oh, I tried to make the odd point here and there, but the bulk of it – the stuff people actually remember – consists of playground, yah-boo stuff.

I was horrible. I fantasised about leaping into the screen and attacking a *Big Brother* contestant with a hammer; then, without a hint of irony, announced that Nicky Campbell exuded the menace of a serial killer. I also claimed Jeremy Kyle (who struck me as 'a cross between Matthew Wright and a bored carpet salesman') was the Prince of Darkness himself – almost ('Look at his eyes: there's a spine-chilling glint to them ... Not that I'm saying Kyle himself is an agent of Satan, you understand. I'm just saying you could easily cast him as one. Especially if you wanted to save money on special effects.').

The moment anyone appeared on screen, I struggled to find a nice way to describe their physical appearance. David Dickinson was 'an ageing Thundercat'; Alan Titchmarsh resembled 'something looming unexpectedly at a porthole in a Captain Nemo movie'; Nigel Lythgoe was 'Eric Idle watching a dog drown'. I called Alan Sugar 'Mrs Tiggywinkle' and said he reminded me of 'a water buffalo straining to shit in a lake'. What a bastard. And I'm no oil painting myself, unless the painting in question depicts a heartbroken carnival mask hurriedly moulded from surgically extracted stomach fat and stretched across a damaged, despondent hubcap. I think that constitutes some form of justification.

Looking back at the earlier columns I see that when I wasn't preoccupied with looks, I was quite bafflingly angry. I've either mellowed since then, or simply grown a soul. For instance, these days – to pick a random example – Jamie Cullum strikes me as a harmless, twinkly-eyed, happy sort of chap. But back in 2004 the mere sight of him on an episode of *Parkinson* sent me into an apocalyptic tailspin.

'Cullum should be sealed inside a barrel and kicked into the ocean', I declared, before going on to label him 'an oily, sickening worm-boy ... if I ever have to see this gurning little maggot clicking into faux reverie mode again – rising from his seat to jazz-slap the top of his piano wearing a fake-groove expression on his piggish little face – if I have to witness that one more time I'm going to rise up and kill absolutely everybody in the world, starting with him and ending with me.'

Shortly after that article appeared I read a short Me And My Spoon-type interview with Cullum in London's *Metro* newspaper in which he seemed cheerily bemused as to what he'd done to provoke such fury. And I felt bad. I'd like to say that I wasn't nasty about women – but I'd be lying. I wrote that Ann Widdecombe had 'a face like a haunted cave in Poland', and that Cilla Black was 'starting to resemble the result of an unholy union between Ronald McDonald and a blow-dried guinea pig'.

Neither of them warranted that abuse, although the poo-prodding food fascist Gillian McKeith probably did deserve to be called a 'charmless, judgemental, hand-wringing harridan ... incapable of smiling naturally on camera ... the rictus grin in her official photo makes her look like she's trying to shit out a pine cone, which given her diet she probably is'.

People sometimes ask if I've ever bumped into any of the people I've been rude about. Yup. As soon as I started appearing on television myself, I began receiving invites to various industry functions and found myself too curious and big-headed not to attend. Suddenly you're standing in a room full of people you've slagged off in print, and they're not 2D screen-wraiths any more, but living, breathing, fallible humanoids, many of whom are clutching wine glasses which – should the mood turn sour – would make for fearsome improvised weapons. Once or twice I found myself in conversation with someone I'd been awful about in print, and discovered to my horror that the ruder I'd been, the warmer and more pleasant they appeared to be in the flesh. A black eel of guilt writhed in my skull. Why was I so nasty? These were TV presenters, not war criminals. Well, most of them.

Sometimes they weren't even presenters. The rise of reality shows led to a ceaseless parade of instant hate figures, plucked from obscurity and flung onscreen for us all to sneer and point at. And I fell for it, endlessly picking holes in fellow human beings simply because they happened to be on TV.

I reached my misanthropic peak during series six of *Big Brother*, during which the contestant Maxwell was labelled 'a goon, a berk, a gurgling bore, a ham-eyed poltroon and a great big swaggering chump', not to mention, 'a Norf Lahnden bozo best described as the human equivalent of a clipping from *Nuts* magazine bobbing in a fetid urinal'. His girlfriend Saskia had 'a face that could advertise war', while eventual winner Anthony was 'a man so profoundly thick you could sell him a pair of his own socks for £500, even if he was already wearing them'.

I met Saskia several years later, incidentally, when she had a cameo as a zombie in a horror serial I wrote. She was lovely, and I felt bad, yet again. The bad feeling reached a nadir when I reviewed a contrived Channel 4 reality show in which families road-tested servants. I proclaimed that the family in question were a bunch of shits: shits so shittily shitty they might as well actually be called 'The Shits'. Given that they'd doubtless been edited to look bad, this wasn't really a fair assessment. Worse than that, it wasn't funny. The moment I saw it in black and white, I felt like a witless bully.

I realised that I'd fallen into the trap of writing from the point of view of an exaggerated cartoon persona, so from that point on I tried to pick my targets with more care and to moderate the

184

overt abuse, which undoubtedly made the columns less vicious, more whimsical, and probably more boring, although hopefully this meant that when invective was still called for – as with a piece on the Aryan Brotherhood, or the rolling news coverage of the Raoul Moat standoff – it had more sting.

But now . . . now it's time to stop. Like I said, I'm exhausted. And writing a TV column over the past few years has felt progressively weirder, as I've gradually, simultaneously, become one of 'them': one of the many faces that flit across your screen, gently spoiling your evening. Fortunately for fans of unpleasant similes, my successor Grace Dent is a singularly heartless individual who'll have none of my wussy qualms about insulting people. That woman is pure hate.

Oh, and reader: I'll be back later in the year with a new column, right here in these pages. I give it three weeks before I'm filling it with playground insults. You're still not shot of me. Remember, reader: only one of us gets out of this relationship alive.

I never did start that new column. Another promise broken.

How to save the economy without really trying
17/10/2010

This week 23-year-old chancellor Gideon Osborne will rise on his hooves in the House of Commons and unleash the most brutal series of cuts since the shower scene in *Psycho*. So what will actually happen? Gloomy predictions abound, but almost everyone agrees the results will be as palatable as a wax-and-cat-hair sandwich. It's frightening stuff. In fact, the preliminary coverage is filled with so much sadomasochistic language – 'pain', 'agony', 'eye-watering measures', 'tightening of the belt', and so on – that it sounds as if we really ought to establish a 'safe word' now, before Prince Gideon pulls his leather mask on and sets about his business.

The coalition has repeatedly promised that those with the broadest shoulders will bear the greatest load; unfortunately, the majority of people develop broad shoulders by doing underpaid manual work, not trading stocks from the comfort of a Herman Miller Aeron chair. (Or writing for publication: I have the upper-body-strength of a nine-year-old girl.)

But is such suffering really inevitable? What happened to good old British entrepreneurial pluck, as embodied by Lord Sugar or Howard Marks? Rather than slashing the deficit by forcing the nation's ambulances to operate using one wheel as opposed to four, can't we find more cunning means to raise funds? Yes we can. Here are a few suggestions. And if Giddyguts Osborne doesn't use them, he is perhaps the least imaginative monster this country has ever seen.

The military

The problem: we're always reading that our armed forces aren't adequately equipped; that they're forced to wear papier-mâché helmets and use rifles made of crayon. The cuts are only likely to make a bad situation worse, because military-grade arms are so preposterously expensive that even Waitrose won't stock them.

The solution: encourage soldiers to create their own improvised weapons. A garden fork with barbed wire wrapped round each spike? Nice one, Private Titchmarsh. A catapult and a blood-filled syringe? Liking your style, Captain Doherty. Not only would it make wars more interesting and medieval, it'd leave existing stocks of bullets going spare for Gideon and his friends to shoot grouse or foxes or dairymaids on their weekends off.

Education

The problem: making kids clever is way too expensive. But failing to educate them at all will eventually lead to the entire nation resembling a giant chimps' tea party. Which it absolutely doesn't at the moment.

The solution: sell bespoke classroom time-slots to corporations. Your child's new timetable: 9 a.m. Geography; 10 a.m. French; 11.30 a.m. Yakult Studies; 12 p.m. Lunchtime sponsored by Cheestrings; 1 p.m. The Story of Rolos; 2 p.m. Just Do It! (formerly PE); 3 p.m. English Literature; 3.05 p.m. GlaxoSmithKline Sing-a-Long Zone; 4 p.m. Hometime (sponsored by Renault).

The police

The problem: truncheon costs have soared and since ITV's cancellation of *The Bill* there are fewer secondhand uniforms to go round.

The solution: fit officers with live helmet-cams and stream the content to a subscription-based satellite TV channel. Watch live drug busts! Enjoy grisly crime scenes! See relatives sob on their doorsteps as a PC delivers tragic news! Interactive features are available for an additional fee: just £5.99 a month lets you text or tweet in your own questions during an interrogation.

The benefits system

The problem: millions of needy people obstinately refusing to function without access to food and shelter.

The solution: mandatory twenty-four-hour nudity for the unemployed. A sudden influx of millions of naked people on Britain's streets might take some getting used to, but would provide a sharp incentive for the long-term unemployed to seek work, especially during the winter months. Most importantly, it would boost tourism. Overseas visitors currently enjoy posing alongside pigeons in Trafalgar Square, and would doubtless flock to take amusing iPhone snaps of themselves pointing and laughing at our shivering public nudes. Come see the blue bums of Britain! The more deprived the area, the greater the tourist appeal. Also, we could sell footage from the UK's many CCTV cameras to pornographic websites.

Housing

The problem: affordable housing has to be subsidised, if the 'affordable' bit of the phrase is going to work.

The solution: replace every wall, ceiling and floor with a gigantic plasma screen and charge for advertising space. The affordable living room of tomorrow is a futuristic cube with a perpetually looping Go Compare commercial in place of carpets and wall-paper. In the event of traumatised residents attempting to remain outdoors for as long as humanly possible, obligatory curfew hours could be enforced using a remotely operated lock-in system. And should the inhabitants kill themselves by smashing one of the screens and desperately hacking at their necks with shards of glass, the remaining plasma screens will prove easier to clean than regular carpets and walls.

Heritage

The problem: galleries and museums are costly, and there's only so much you can claw back by flogging Pre-Raphaelite colouring books and Make-Your-Own-Dinosaur kits in the gift shop. Factor in thousands of decaying landmarks, castles and stately homes and it all adds up to a gigantic looming number made of coins and money.

The solution: time for a nationwide jumble sale. Gather up everything we don't need and flog it to the Chinese, the Germans, the Mexicans . . . anyone. *The Angel of the North* would look great in Kim Jong-Il's garden. The Americans have form, shelling out $2.5m for London Bridge in 1967: maybe this time we could interest them in the whole of Plymouth (we hardly use it, but for them it has sentimental value, being the origin of the *Mayflower*). Also: once the 2012 Olympics are over, let's cut the stadium into tiny cubes, mount them in little souvenir boxes and flog them at Gatwick to departing athletes and dignitaries.

There. That's the economy saved, in theory at least. Your turn, Gideon.

Clegging on

24/10/2010

In these uncertain, unsettling times, with unpopular policies being implemented by a patchwork coalition of the damned, Nick Clegg is proving to be perhaps the most useful tool in the government's shed. Not because he says or does anything particularly inspiring, but because he functions as a universal disappointment sponge for disenchanted voters. You stare at Nick Clegg and feel infinitely unhappy, scarcely noticing Cameron and Co. hiding behind him.

Governments around the world must be studying the coalition and working out how to get their own Clegg. He's the coalition's very own Pudsey Bear: a cuddly-but-tragic mascot representing the acceptable face of abuse. But unlike Pudsey, he actually speaks.

Immediately following each unpleasant new announcement, Cleggsy Bear shuffles on stage to defend it, working his sad eyes and boyish face as he morosely explains why the decision was inevitable – and not just inevitable, but fair; in fact possibly the fairest, most reasonable decision to have been taken in our lifetimes, no matter how loudly people scream to the contrary.

It's hard not to detect an air of crushed self-delusion about all this. At times Clegg sounds like a once-respected stage actor who's taken the Hollywood dollar and now finds himself sitting at a press junket, patiently telling a reporter that while, yes, on the face of it, his role as the Fartmonster in *Guff Ditch III: Fartmonster's Revenge* may look like a cultural step down from his previous work with the Royal Shakespeare Company, if you look beyond all the scenes of topless women being dissolved by clouds of acrid methane, the *Guff Ditch* trilogy actually contains more intellectual sustenance than *King Lear*, and that all the critics who've seen the film and are loudly claiming otherwise are misguided, partisan naysayers hell-bent on cynically misleading the public – which is ethically wrong.

It's only a matter of time before the word 'Clegg' enters the dictionary as a noun meaning 'agonised, doe-eyed apologist'. Or maybe it'll become a verb. Years from now, teachers will ask their pupils to stop 'clegging on' about how the dog ate their homework and just bloody hand it in on time.

Clegg's most recent act of clegging was to explain to this newspaper that the Institute of Fiscal Studies was wrong to brand the spending review 'unfair'.

'I think you have to call a spade a spade', he clegged, immediately before demonstrating his commitment to straightforward language by querying the definition of the word 'fair'.

The previous administration's simplistic 'culture of how you measure fairness' was partly to blame for the Institute's foolishness, clegged Clegg in a cleggish tone of voice. In previous years, 'fairness was seen through one prism and one prism only'.

It turns out fairness is actually more complex and slightly less fair than that. According to Clegg it's important to call a spade a spade, unless you've mistaken the spade for a digging implement, which it isn't. A spade is a kind of towel.

Point a camera in his direction, and Clegg can construct an earnest argument in favour of virtually any unappealing concept you can throw at him. Such as the following:

On drink-driving
'No one likes car crashes. But to imply that drinking somehow impairs one's ability to control a vehicle is just scaremongering – and it's precisely this sort of jittery overreaction that causes most accidents in the first place. The simple fact is that only by calming our minds with alcohol can we keep a steady hand on the tiller.'

On the coalition's decision to launch an unprovoked nuclear attack on Berwick-upon-Tweed
'Yes it's extreme, but something has to be done. Berwick-upon-Tweed simply can't be allowed to continue as it is. But the blast

won't be as far-reaching as the opposition and the scientists and the UN are saying. If you live in, say, Truro, it probably won't make much difference to your day-to-day life, provided you're reasonably self-sufficient and don't mind the odd hand-to-hand skirmish with mutants.'

On being the middle segment of a 'human centipede'

'I've heard a lot of people say, "urgh, Nick, have you seen that film *The Human Centipede*, where the mad scientist joins three people together by stitching them rectum-to-mouth? Can you imagine how disgusting that'd be in real life?" And I can see how they might leap to that conclusion. But real life is about compromise – sometimes we simply have to swallow a few unpleasant things in the name of pragmatism. In many ways, the coalition is a human centipede – a group of united individuals, all pulling together in one direction – and let me tell you, from the inside, it's surprisingly cosy.'

On cutting off his nose to spite his face

'Before the election, I made a solemn pledge to leave my nose intact. I even printed that pledge out, signed it, and posed for photos while holding it up and smiling like I meant it. So I can understand people's disquiet over this. It's something I've wrestled with personally. But nonetheless, off it goes. Cutty cutty nose time! Tee hee! Hoo hoo! Chop, chop, chop!'

Next week: Clegg defends his decision to force the Chilean miners back underground, claims 2 Unlimited were better than the Beatles, and explains why the coalition's proposed oxygen-rationing scheme will usher in an age of peace and prosperity for all.

Perchance to dream
01/11/2010

Dreams. Everyone knows two things about dreams, namely 1) other people's dreams are dull and 2) they're going to tell you about them anyway.

And as they burble on about how they dreamed they were trying to build a windmill with Eamonn Holmes but his hands were made of candles, or how they dreamed their little children will one day live in a nation where they will not be judged by the colour of their skin, but by the content of their character, it's hard not to fall asleep and start dreaming yourself: dreaming of a future in which the anecdote has finished and their face has stopped talking and their body's gone away.

But maybe in future they won't have to tell you about it at all. They'll just play it to you on their iPhone. A researcher at New York University called Moran Cerf (an anagram of 'Man Forcer', but that's not important right now) has produced an article for the science journal *Nature* in which he claims it may soon be possible to create a device that records our dreams and plays them back later.

Obviously, the reality is 99 per cent less exciting than it initially appears. It won't be a magic pipe you stick in your ear that etches your wildest imaginings directly onto a Blu-Ray disc for you to enjoy boring your friends with later.

What Cerf is actually proposing is a way to make other people's dreams seem even more boring. But first: the business of capturing them, which all boils down to neurons.

After studying the brains of people with electronic implants buried deep in their noggins, Cerf discovered that certain groups of neurons 'lit up' when he asked his subjects to think about specific things, such as Marilyn Monroe or the Eiffel Tower. Therefore, he postulates, by recording these subjects' sleeping brain activity, then studying the patterns generated, it should be possible to work out whether they were dreaming about starlets or landmarks.

In other words, he's isolated the stuff that dreams are made of. And it turns out to be a few blips on a chart.

So the 'dream recordings' will probably come in the form of an underwhelming visual transcript – a graph with the odd squiggly line on it. Brilliant if, like Vince Cable, you dream about nothing but graphs – but hardly *Fantasia II*.

Not that real dreams would make great movies anyway. For one thing, the continuity is all over the place. One minute you're helping the cast of *Robin's Nest* crucify Santa Claus in a space station, the next you're trying to impress Andy Murray by climbing Everest with your teeth. Even Greek television makes more sense than that.

And most dreams aren't *that* interesting. The majority of mine are unbelievably pedestrian. I once dreamed I was watching a cat food commercial with a surprisingly good jingle. The world doesn't need a back-up copy of that.

Samuel Coleridge once famously dreamed the epic poem 'Kubla Khan' in its entirety, and upon awakening, immediately began scribbling it down line by line, only to be interrupted by a man from the nearby village of Porlock, who detained him with some petty chore for an hour, after which he could no longer remember the words. That one might have been worth recording.

But Coleridge has been dead for years. Right now the best we'd get is a Sky pay-per-view channel on which Peter Andre dreams about his favourite sandwich toppings, or Jedward take turns to sneeze inside a terrifying hairy cave.

Perhaps more promisingly, it would only be a matter of time until some enterprising psychopath hooked up the dream recorder to Twitter, making it possible to enjoy live dream-tweets from Kanye West in which he makes approximately 50 per cent more sense than he does while awake.

Putting aside the entertainment value, what practical use is there for a recorded dream, anyway? It'd only encourage the 'science' of dream analysis – the psychological equivalent of Gillian McKeith prodding a turd with a stick. And six months after the invention of a reliable dream recorder, you can guarantee we'd find ourselves in a nightmare scenario, in which dream transcripts are pored over in divorce hearings and terrorism trials.

From there, it's surely only a short step to some kind of reverse-engineering system via which ideas and suggestions can be planted inside your dreams, *Inception*-style, while you're still asleep. Which probably means in-dream product placement – so next time you climb Everest with your teeth, you'll have the great taste of Colgate in your mouth as you do so. Or maybe the advertising won't be that subtle. Maybe all your future dreams will simply consist of a gigantic mouth shouting the words 'DIET COKE' over and over until you wake up in tears, and immediately reach for a Diet Coke, hands quivering, without really understanding why.

In fact, yes. That's *precisely* what's going to happen.

The last words you will ever read
15/11/2010

The moment I've finished typing this, I'm going to walk out the door and set about strangling every single person on the planet. Starting with you, dear reader. I'm sorry, but it has to be done, for reasons that will become clear in a moment.

And for the sake of transparency, in case the powers-that-be are reading: this is categorically not a joke. I am 100 per cent serious. Even though I don't know who you are or where you live, I am going to strangle you, your family, your pets, your friends, your imaginary friends, and any lifelike human dummies with haunted stares and wipe-clean vinyl orifices you've got knocking around, perhaps in a secret compartment under the stairs.

The only people who might escape my wrath are the staff and

passengers at Sheffield's Robin Hood Airport, because they've been granted immunity by the state.

Last week 27-year-old accountant Paul Chambers lost an appeal against his conviction for comments he made back in January via the social networking hoojamflip Twitter, venting his frustration when heavy snow closed the airport, leaving him unable to visit his girlfriend.

'Crap!' he wrote. 'Robin Hood airport is closed. You've got a week and a bit to get your shit together otherwise I'm blowing the airport sky high!!'

Anti-terror experts intercepted this message and spent hours deciphering it, eventually uncovering a stark coded warning within, cunningly disguised as a series of flippant words.

Chambers's use of multiple exclamation marks is particularly chilling. He almost seems to find the whole thing rather funny. The violent destruction of an entire airport – hundreds of passengers and staff being blasted to shrieking ribbons by tonnes of explosive, all because one man's dirty weekend has been postponed – yet all this senseless carnage is little more than an absurdist joke in the warped mind of Paul Chambers.

Funny is it, Mr Chambers? A big old laugh? Tell that to the theoretical victims of your hypothetical atrocity. Go on. Dig them out of the imaginary rubble. Listen to their anguished, notional screams. Ask how loudly they laughed as you hit the make-believe detonator. Go on. Ask them.

If you dare.

At least when Osama bin Laden broadcasts a warning to the West, his intentions form part of an extremist ideology informed by decades of resentment. Chambers issues bloodcurdling threats at the drop of a snowflake. This makes him the very worst kind of terrorist there is – the kind prepared to slaughter thousands in the name of inclement weather conditions.

Mercifully, in this case, before any innocent blood could be shed, Chambers was arrested, held in a police cell, and convicted of sending a 'menacing electronic communication'. His appeal was rejected last week by Judge Jacqueline Davies, who described his original tweet as 'menacing in its content and obviously so. It could not be more clear. Any ordinary person reading this would see it in that way and be alarmed.'

Quite right too. In fact, throughout this case, the authorities have behaved impeccably – which is why it's such a crying shame I'm going to have to strangle all of them too. But strangle them I must.

Why? Because many of his fellow tweeters, outraged by Judge Davies's ruling, have retweeted Chambers's original message in a misguided show of solidarity. Thousands of people, all threatening to blow Robin Hood Airport 'sky high'. Clearly they have to be stopped – but infuriatingly, many of them hide behind anonymous usernames. The only way to ensure they all taste justice is to punish everyone equally, just to be sure. Hence the strangling, which doesn't feel like too much of an overreaction under the circumstances. I'm just following the authorities' lead.

They ought to give me a medal. From beyond the grave. After I've strangled them.

Still, loath as I am to strangle every man, woman, and child on the planet, it won't be an entirely thankless task. Clearly I will feel no remorse while strangling Chambers. He is a dangerous madman, and I look forward to sliding my hands around his neck and slowly choking the life out of him.

I also relish the prospect of strangling another tweeter-in-crime: Gareth Compton, the Tory councillor who ran afoul of the authorities last week for tweeting the words 'can someone please stone Yasmin Alibhai-Brown to death? I shan't tell Amnesty if you don't. It would be a blessing, really.'

He later apologised for what he claimed – outlandishly – was 'an ill-conceived attempt at humour', even though I'm sure Judge Jacqueline Davies would agree that it was menacing in its content and obviously so, and in fact could not be more clear, and that any ordinary person reading it would see it in that way and be alarmed.

Reassuringly, the bloodthirsty maniac Compton was arrested hours later, presumably after being cornered in his lair by a SWAT team. I'd like to shake every member of that team by the hand, which sadly won't be possible while I'm strangling them.

Anyway, I'm writing this on Friday, so by the time you read this on Monday my strangling rampage will have begun – unless the authorities have intercepted these words and arrested me in the interim, in which case I'd like to make it absolutely clear that I intend to strangle everyone in the prison before turning my hands on myself. Attention Home Secretary: you've got three days and a bit to get your shit together. Otherwise I'm strangling this planet sky-high.

Stop crying, start loving
06/12/2010

Only someone with the heart of a concrete robot could fail to feel faintly – just faintly – sorry for the American diplomats whose cables were leaked, what with all that private unguarded chit-chat being made public. If the world had an annual end-of-year office party (which, come to think of it, is a brilliant idea), 2010's would be an awkward affair.

Still, what's most surprising about the mass leak isn't the content – it'd have been more astonishing if they'd said Berlusconi was actually rather charming and North Korea is great in bed – but the fact that this kind of thing isn't happening every day. Because in our terrible modern hell, it's possible for absolutely anyone to leave a comprehensive dossier of ultra-sensitive private information about themselves on the back seat of a bus just by misplacing their phone.

The more these devices are capable of, the greater potential for embarrassment. What's on your handset? Intimate texts?

Embarrassing photos? Raunchy emails? An eye-opening internet history? I just hope you trust the staff down the Orange store next time you're upgrading your phone.

Actually, if you're anything like me, you don't have anything lurid on your handset at all – partly out of sheer paranoia – but still can't help feeling anxious whenever someone asks to borrow it. It's the same uneasy frisson you feel when a policeman looks you in the eye while stopped at the lights – a vague sense of guilt, like you're hiding something.

And phone-borrowers don't even have to be deliberately nosy to stumble across your personal details. Even if they only want to make a call, simply by accessing the dial option they'll be treated to a list of who rang you last and how long you spoke for. On the phone to the doctor for an hour were you? That's interesting. Here, have it back. Just going to wash my hands.

Another example of inadvertent intrusion: I once used a computer belonging to someone I knew, and logged on to Amazon to look up the release date for a DVD.

That's how I roll. I'm crazy.

Anyway, the moment I arrived at the home page, it assumed I was her, and presented me with a list of suggested purchases, all of which were self-help books for people trapped in terrible relationships, with titles like *Stop Crying, Start Loving* and *When Sex Is Harrowing*. It was an uncomfortable and rather sad glimpse into someone else's life, I thought, once I'd stopped pointing and laughing.

Still, at least that was nothing more harmful than someone's innermost thoughts being laid bare. But it's not just our personal information that's increasingly insecure. It's our personal persons.

Not so long ago, a tourist couple stopped me in the street and asked me to take a snap of them grinning in front of something vaguely picturesque (this being London, probably an especially colourful pavement puke-puddle or a tramp with a funny neck tumour). But unfamiliar as I was with the workings of their phone, instead of taking their picture, I inadvertently brought up the gallery of previous photographs, and was treated to a view of one of them in the shower, followed by a series of close-up views of various biological and overwhelmingly intimate occurrences involving the pair of them.

As I fumbled with menus, trying not to betray my embarrassment, I glimpsed at the man and something in his eyes told me that he *knew*, somehow – he *knew* what had happened, but couldn't snatch the phone off me for fear of embarrassing his girlfriend, who remained oblivious.

Eventually I took the photo. His smile was fixed and unconvincing. I handed the device back. She thanked me. He stared at the ground. We went our separate ways in silence. Somehow, it was as if we'd all taken part in a terrible threesome.

This kind of acute personal embarrassment simply wouldn't have been possible ten years ago. But with our every folly entered into an electronic ledger somewhere, it's becoming commonplace. Scarcely a week goes by without a leaked nudey phone photo of some hapless celebrity doing the online rounds. Paris, Britney, Rihanna, Miley … eventually we'll be treated to raunchy snaps of Mahmoud Ahmadinejad or Vince Cable. Don't pretend you'll turn away. You'll stand and stare like the rest of us.

And those are just the famous people. By the year 2022, there'll be a naked photo of everyone on the planet lurking somewhere in the interverse. You might as well take a really good one this afternoon, while you're young and pliable, and upload it yourself before some future peeping-tom equivalent of WikiLeaks does it for you.

Face it: there's a 45 per cent chance that Julian Assange is rooting through an exhaustive collection of photographs of your bum right this very minute. And you know he'll release the least flattering ones first.

So you might as well beat him to it.

'Bah' and 'boh'
20/12/2010

You can't put a price on a good education. Except, actually, you can – and it turns out that price is just over £9,000 a year.

Unsurprisingly many students are furious at the hike in tuition fees; but apart from shouting about it or trying to smash the Treasury to bits with sticks, what practical steps can we take to make education more affordable?

Nine thousand pounds a year sounds like a lot – but actually, it's shitloads. Yet it turns out that if you divide shitloads by fifty-two, it comes out at around £173 a week, which sounds more achievable. Especially if your course only lasts seven days. So let's only provide week-long courses.

Obviously, to compress a three-year course into one week, the field of study will have to be streamlined a bit. Whittled down. Reduced to a series of bullet points. But in many cases, that's an advantage.

Take history. There's already far too much of it. In fact, mankind is generating a 'past mountain', which grows twenty-four hours in size every single day. No one can be expected to keep all of that in their head. There simply isn't room. Even award-winning historians will be lost for words if you unexpectedly leap out in front of them and demand they list everything that happened on, say, 6 July 1919, before the special quiz music ends, especially if they thought they were alone in the house.

So instead of studying the whole of human history, why not focus on a concentrated period, such as the most exciting five minutes of the Second World War? That way you just get the fun bits with the machine guns and everything, and there's none of that boring exploration of the 'consequences' or the 'causes' or 'how we can stop it happening again'. The philosopher George Santayana famously remarked that those who forget history are condemned to repeat it. But if you have forgotten history, you won't know you're repeating it – so it won't matter. And you won't have heard of George Santayana, either. Which is just as well because he sounds like a smart arse.

Likewise, when it comes to studying politics, let's not waste time examining both sides of an argument – that's just confusing. Instead of learning the pros and cons of say, slavery, why not just learn the pros? Not only is it far quicker, but you actually stand more chance of getting a job when you graduate, perhaps as a feisty TV news pundit or *Daily Express* columnist. Or as the owner of a cotton plantation.

Speaking of careers, there are far too many courses with no clear vocational goal. If you're not studying with a view to ensuring your future prosperity, why, precisely, are you bothering to read the *Decameron*? For the cultural benefit of all mankind? Look around you. Culture's doing just fine without your help. We've got everything we need – from cage-fighting at the lowbrow end of the spectrum through to the dizzy heights of James Cameron's *Avatar* right up at the top. There's something for everyone.

Rather than providing frivolous courses in artsy-fartsy-thinky-winky subjects with no obvious revenue stream, our educational institutions could save a lot of time and unnecessary expense by only providing courses that train students for jobs we're definitely going to need in the brilliant future we're steadily carving for ourselves. What's the point in learning botany? We all know there won't be plantlife. Apart from maybe the odd triffid, or whatever sort of moss can withstand a dirty bomb. So why bother learning about it? There's no money to be made.

Instead, let's focus on giving young people the skills society will be crying out for in the years or months to come. Practical vocations such as water-cannon operator, wasteland scavenger, penguin coffin logger, Thunderdome umpire, dissident strangler, henchperson and pie ingredient.

Come to think of it, even those courses are going to be costly, and the eventual wages so insultingly low it'll take them three lifetimes to repay the loans. They can make up some of the short-fall by taking part in medical experiments, fellating ministers or breeding offspring for food, but the chances are that the big society will never recoup the funds it lent to these little people.

Which leaves us one final option. Let's simply give up. You know, as a species. Put an end to this weird 'progress' experiment we've all been taking part in and actively revert to the level of farmyard animals. They look happy, don't they, with their tails and their mud? Let's join them.

Starting tomorrow, let's stop bothering to learn or teach any-thing. Within months the whole world will be far simpler for all concerned. We can issue the next generation with a few basic instructions, some warm clothes and toilet paper, and leave them to it.

Eventually society will regress to the point where there are only two words – 'boh' (meaning good) and 'bah' (meaning bad). Everything will be either bah or boh; we'll shuffle around bah-ing or boh-ing, chewing the cud or eating the vitamin rusks they occasionally fire in our direction from the turrets on their trucks. And everyone will be happy. Or ignorant. Or both.

Merry Christmas.

PART SIX

In which EastEnders *is revealed to be a work of fiction, Nick Clegg worries about human beings with feet, and a teenager incurs the wrath of the internet for singing a bad song badly.*

EastEnders and Monster Munch
10/01/2011

I'm not entirely certain I can pinpoint the moment I first realised *EastEnders* isn't a documentary. Maybe it was when Den Watts was assassinated by a bunch of daffodils. Or when he came back from the dead and then got killed again. Or when Steve Owen's mother tried to French-kiss him on her deathbed.

Or when Ricky Butcher became a speedway champion for one week. Or when Melanie Healy slept with Phil Mitchell on Christmas Day.

Or when Max Branning got buried alive.

Or when Janine pushed Barry off a cliff. Or when Janine got so agoraphobic she sat indoors eating dog food. Or when Janine ran over Danielle in a car. Or when Janine framed Stacey by stabbing herself on Christmas Day. Or when Janine slept with Ian Beale and then blackmailed him by threatening to tell his third wife, Laura. Or when Janine slept with Ian Beale and then blackmailed him by threatening to tell his fourth wife, Jane.

Or when, while Googling a list of Janine's crimes, I realised Ian Beale had managed to convince four whole women to marry him.

Somewhere along the way I must have twigged that none of these people were real, possibly during the bit at the end where the names of the actors who play them floated up the screen accompanied by theme music.

Contrary to popular opinion, *EastEnders* isn't set in London, or even Britain, or even the world – it's situated in an absurd alternate universe overseen by a malicious, tinkering God with a hilarious sense of timing. Each wedding, anniversary, national holiday or mid-sized social gathering is visited by major tragedy. The most familiar noise in Albert Square is the sound of party poppers being drowned out by sobbing. Quickly followed by some pulsing electronic drums.

Over the last few weeks God was at it again. Having given both Kat Slater and Ronnie Branning newborn offspring to enjoy, God capriciously decided to kill Ronnie's baby on New Year's Eve.

As midnight neared, Ronnie wandered the square in a stunned daze, unnoticed by revellers and clutching the body of her deceased child – until, alerted by the sound of Kat's baby crying from an open window, she snuck into the Queen Vic and swapped the two infants, in a scene that looked more like a *Tramadol Nights* sketch than the heartbreaking drama it was presumably intended to be.

And now there's an entirely predictable storm of protest; predictable, apparently, to everyone except the *EastEnders* production team, who seem to have failed to anticipate the sheer size of the furore – which is odd, since their job largely consists of hypothesising about all the different ways in which people can unwittingly stumble their way to an acrimonious row.

The usual excuse for any soap opera planning a headline-grabbing plotline is that they're 'helping to build awareness' of some social ill, as though the average citizen can only truly come to terms with drug abuse after seeing Phil Mitchell smoke crack.

Of course, you only 'build awareness' by depicting events with some degree of accuracy, which is why the soaps often proudly announce that they collaborated closely with charities to ensure that Steve McFadden's portrayal of the dark spiral of addiction would be as harrowingly authentic as possible, especially the bit where he smashed through a door like Jack Nicholson in *The Shining* and burned the Queen Vic to the ground.

EastEnders would never screen an episode in which Ian Beale has a breakdown and decides to walk around the Square with a dead baby balanced on his head like a hat, although that would 'explore the issue' of bereavement and mental health just as effectively as the current child-swap storyline, which is equally unrealistic, yet has to be presented as a hard-hitting study of bereavement because the alternative is to admit that *EastEnders* is mindless entertainment – with the occasional dead infant thrown in for your amusement.

There's a basic rule in drama that the audience can suspend disbelief only long enough to accommodate one extreme event at a time. A cot death is one extreme. A baby-swap is another. Combining the two events at the stroke of midnight on New Year's Eve was the scriptwriters' first big mistake. Trying to pull all of this off within the context of a populist soap was the second. A self-consciously weighty one-off ITV drama-of-the-week with an A-list cast and lots of sombre camerawork would probably have got away with it, unless they did something totally crazy, like casting Jedward as the swapped babies.

Still, if broadcasting the storyline was *fairly* crazy, complaining to Ofcom about the lack of realism in *EastEnders* doesn't seem much saner – almost on a par with threatening to sue the manufacturers of Monster Munch because their crisps don't taste of monsters.

Nonetheless, the BBC appears to have backed down and the storyline, in a weird reflection of itself, will be laid to rest prematurely. The mad God of Walford originally wanted the zany saga to reach a festive climax next Christmas Day, typically. But now the whole thing will apparently be rewritten to accommodate a viewer-friendly 'happy ending'.

Yes: that's a cot-death-baby-swap storyline *with a happy ending*. Now there's a script meeting I'd like to sit in on.

Alarm Clock Britain
17/01/2011

Nick Clegg – currently Britain's 7,358th most popular public figure, sandwiched between Maxine Carr and the Go Compare tenor – has written an article for the *Sun* in which he bravely stands shoulder-to-shoulder with a shamefully overlooked, uniquely burdened segment of our population.

And he's obviously given the matter plenty of thought.

'Now more than ever, politicians have to be clear who they are standing up for,' he writes. 'Be in no doubt, I am clear about who that is.'

Who? Ethnic minorities? The poor? The disabled? The original lineup of Gerry and the Pacemakers? Beekeepers? Milkmen? Necrophiles? Yeomen?

No. They can all piss off. Because Cleggsy Bear has someone else in mind. But despite claiming to be 'clear about who that is', it's a group he defines in the vaguest, most frustrating terms possible – almost as if he doesn't really know what the hell he's going on about.

He's on the side of 'Alarm Clock Britain', apparently. Yeah. You know: Alarm Clock Britain. Stop staring blankly at me. Alarm Clock Britain! It's everywhere!

'There are millions of people in Alarm Clock Britain,' Clegg writes. 'People, like *Sun* readers, who have to get up every morning and work hard to get on in life.'

Basically, Alarm Clock Britain consists of people who use alarm clocks. That counts me out, because I wake each morning to the sound of my own despairing screams. Which I guess makes me part of Scream Wake Britain – a demographic Clegg has chosen to ignore. There are millions of people in Scream Wake Britain, and approximately half of them voted for him.

Still, it's undeniable that millions of Britons use alarm clocks, so it's nice to know someone at the heart of government is prepared to speak up on their behalf. We are yet to discover Clegg's stance on Toothbrush Britain (Britons who use toothbrushes), or Bum Wipe Britain (Britons who use toilet paper), or Newtonian Physics Britain (Britons subjected to the law of gravity), but I think it's fair to assume he's on their side too.

Which is not to say Alarm Clock Britain is an amorphous group with no boundaries whatsoever. Students, for instance, are notorious for waking up late, so they're definitely excluded, which is just as well since the average student trusts Clegg about as much as I'd trust a hammock made of gas.

Anyway, Clegg goes on to pepper the phrase Alarm Clock Britain throughout the rest of the article as often as he can, as though it's some kind of transformative mantra, in the apparent belief that the more he repeats it, the more we'll identify with it. He even managed to slip it into TV interviews, telling BBC News that he could understand why 'the people of what I like to call Alarm Clock Britain' are pissed off about bankers' bonuses (not that he promised to actually do anything about it – one of the benefits of aligning yourself with an indistinct cluster of people is that claiming to feel their pain is often enough).

The trouble is that no one apart from Clegg himself is talking about Alarm Clock Britain (unless, like me, they're mocking him in print), so his attempt to seed this spectacularly meaningless catchphrase into the national conversation merely comes across as desperate.

It reminds me of a heartbreaking *Peanuts* comic strip in which Charlie Brown, in a rare moment of unguarded candour, tells Lucy he wishes he had a better nickname.

'I've always wanted to be called Flash,' he says. 'I hate the name Charlie. I'd like to be real athletic so that everybody would call me Flash. I'd like to be so good at everything that all around school I'd be known as Flash.'

Lucy stares at him for a bit before laughing out loud, incredulously cackling the name 'FLASH?!?' a few times, before running off to share this hilarious news with the rest of the gang. Charlie Brown is left standing in the frame on his own, looking as suicidal as it's possible for a circle with dots for eyes to look.

Still, it's not as if Clegg's been the only one trying to attach a preposterous name to a group of potential voters. Unstoppable political dynamo Ed Miliband recently tried appealing to 'The Squeezed Middle', which sounds like a frighteningly nonspecific sandwich filling, but is, in fact, precisely the same group as Alarm Clock Britain – middle-income households too rich to rely on benefits, too poor to shrug off VAT rises. As if this group didn't have enough to contend with, they now have to face the ignominy of their parliamentary representatives failing to rustle up a media-friendly pigeonhole term that defines them.

Maybe Cameron could enter the fray, and start calling them 'The Nameless Ones' or just 'Thingy People'. Or 'Thingy Things'. 'Things with Feet'. 'Feety Folk'.

Yes! Only when our leaders outline their desire to walk a mile in the shoes of Feety Folk Britain will we appreciate how much they truly value us.

Miliband DX-9
07/02/2011

Poor old Ed Miliband. Those aren't my words. Those are the words your mind thinks whenever you see him on television. And then you feel bad for thinking that, which makes you feel vaguely sorry for him again, and that in turns feeds back into the initial pity you experienced, and the whole thing becomes a sort of infinite commiseration loop that drowns out whatever he's actually saying and doing.

I keep reading that if he really wants to build support for Labour, Miliband doesn't actually have to do anything: just sit back, let the coalition slowly appal and repel the population, and voilà: future votes will be his, by osmosis. This low-risk strategy seemed to be working. And then, bafflingly, over the past few weeks he's decided to break the spell by granting interviews and popping up for photo opportunities.

First he was interviewed by Piers Morgan for *GQ* magazine. Incredibly, he managed to withstand the urge to vomit long enough to describe himself as 'a bit square', and mutter something about wanting to share a desert island with Teri Hatcher, Rachel Weisz and Scarlett Johansson. I can't work out whether that's a reality show I'd like to see or not.

Then he went to Afghanistan, shadowed by ITN's Tom Bradby, who was compiling a profile piece. Unfortunately, Ed looks incredibly silly in a helmet and flak jacket. Like a toucan in a fez, it just doesn't go. Rather than making Ed look like a thrusting leader, the end result was several minutes of footage which, with the sound off, looked like a report about a small boy who'd won a competition to go and see a war.

You can understand why his press advisers keep shoving him in front of the microphones and cameras. They want the voting public to get to know him. The trouble is they're getting to know him as 'that drippy guy'. It's not his fault. He's burdened with an inherently drippy demeanour. Image shouldn't matter, but it's impossible to blot out.

Rather than making Ed more accessible, his PR team should be doing the opposite. He's never going to come across as 'one of us', so why not actively go in the other direction? Make him unknowably distant.

Here's an idea: get Ed to seal himself inside a featureless metal cube and insist on conducting all political business from within it. And vow never to be seen in public outside the box. No nerdy face for us to judge, no wet mannerisms to chortle at. Nothing to get a glib critical foothold on. Just cold, blank steel. Ditch the name Ed Miliband and insist on being referred to as 'CUBE DX-9' instead.

CUBE DX-9 wouldn't speak, either. It would communicate exclusively via typewritten messages, each about the length of a fortune cookie prediction, which would come whirring out of a tiny slot on its front. Crucially, these would be brief, gnomic proclamations about sensitive issues that would a) be open to interpretation and b) provoke intense debate. And once any debate had started, CUBE DX-9 would refuse to be drawn into it. CUBE DX-9 never clarifies its position. It simply issues a contentious statement, maintains an enigmatic silence, and trundles away, leaving argument in its wake. Did I mention CUBE DX-9 has wheels? Well it does. It also has an ear-splitting siren that goes off whenever someone tries to touch it.

Admit it. You think it's a stupid idea. But think again. Picture the first Prime Minister's Questions in which David Cameron finds himself going up against CUBE DX-9. For one thing, he'd look pretty desperate arguing with a box. Also, the agonising delay between responses from CUBE DX-9 would remove the element of pantomime jousting and turn the whole thing into a tense psychological thriller. Sometimes CUBE DX-9 would fall silent for a full forty-five minutes, emitting a low hum or possibly the odd bit of smoke. Will it issue another statement? Is it broken? What's it going to say next? Every time you saw it, the surrounding aura of mystery would be irresistible.

Furthermore, since the public would never get to see what's inside CUBE DX-9, there would also be intense debate over whether Ed Miliband was actually in there or not. Naturally, CUBE DX-9 would simply ignore any inquiries on this subject, or shrug them off by issuing a statement such as 'CUBE DX-9 CONTENTS NOT YOUR CONCERN', then firing a laser bolt over the interviewer's head as a warning not to proceed with that line of questioning.

I'd vote for the sod. And in the aftermath of CUBE DX-9's inevitable election to the highest office in the land, political leaders worldwide would be clamouring for an inscrutable impersonal shell of their own. Before long there'd be a Chilean mayor who rolls around inside a gigantic onyx egg, and a German chancellor who consists of nothing but a runic symbol flickering on a monitor accompanied by a vaguely menacing drone.

And we'll all feel much better about our elected masters. Yes we will. Stop lying. We will.

What they talk about when they talk about Muslims
14/02/2011

Tory chairman Baroness Warsi recently complained that Islamo-phobic chatter had become acceptable at dinner parties. I hate to break it to you, Baroness, but if they're saying anti-Islamic stuff while you're sitting at the table, imagine the kind of thing they come out with when you nip off to the loo.

A few weeks later, David Cameron delivered a speech on multi-culturalism, and Warsi's notional dinner-mates doubtless nodded in agreement, even though the very word 'multiculturalism' has so many definitions it almost requires translation. It's not black and white. Which is ironic.

As a result it was possible to draw almost any conclusion from Cameron's speech, from 'segregation is unhelpful' to 'send 'em back'. Cameron is many things – including an android, probably – but a racist he is not.

So he was doubtless dismayed that his speech went down well with the BNP's Nick Griffin, who interpreted it as a 'huge leap for our ideas into the political mainstream'. When I read that, my sense of hope took a huge leap into a shit-filled dustbin.

The speech was also welcomed by Tommy Robinson of the English Defence League – and Stephen Lennon of the English Defence League. Who are both the same person, Robinson being Lennon's pseudonym. Mr Robinson–Lennon claims he's opposed only to extremist Muslims, not moderate ones, although how he hopes to tell them apart when he seems unsure of his own name is anyone's guess.

But then certain elements of the EDL seem confused by names in general. Several of them have been heard chanting 'Allah, Allah, who the fuck is Allah?' If they don't know who the fuck he is, perhaps they ought to read that book they want to ban.

Robinson–Lennon recently appeared on *Newsnight*, up against Paxman. Not a classic battle of wits, but nonetheless the EDL's man came out on top: while middle-class viewers may have chortled at Robinson-Lennon's relative inarticulacy, others may have seen a member of the establishment sneering at a working-class white guy. Admittedly, Paxman sneers at everybody; he can't catch sight of his own reflection in the back of a spoon without asking who the fuck he thinks he is. But it reinforces the view that the white working classes are marginalised and looked down on by the media.

Not the entire media, mind. Some tabloids do little else but speak up for the white working classes – the *Daily Star* in particular. Which would be great, if the *Daily Star* didn't patronise its readers by repeatedly publishing lies.

Sometimes they're daft lies. Take the lie about the company behind *Grand Theft Auto* planning a game called *Grand Theft Rothbury*, inspired by the Raoul Moat saga. 'We made no attempt to check the accuracy of the story before publication ... We apologise for publishing a mock-up of the game cover, our own comments on the matter and soliciting critical comments from a grieving family member,' read part of the paper's subsequent grovelling apology.

Sometimes they're visual lies. Take the time it Photoshopped a bald scalp and headscarf on to an image of Jade Goody in a wedding dress, to make it look as though she'd posed for the picture during chemotherapy.

Sometimes the lies appear on its front page, in a way that might alter a reader's view of Muslims. When not furiously recounting whichever grotesquely offensive stunt professional button-pushing irritant Anjem Choudary's come up with this week – stories which are not lies – it gets worked up over other 'Muslim outrages' with little or no basis in fact. Take the story 'MUSLIM-ONLY PUBLIC LOOS: Council wastes YOUR money on hole-in-the-ground toilets'. Weeks after that appeared, the *Star* admitted, 'the loos may be used by non-Muslims and were paid for by the developer'.

And sometimes it doesn't quite lie, but misrepresents by omission. Take the story on 8 February 'WE'LL STAND UP AND FIGHT FOR BRITAIN'S BRAVE WAR HEROES', in which it is reported that 'The English Defence League is planning a huge march after two Muslim councillors snubbed a British war hero given the George Cross'. It refers to an incident in Birmingham where two Respect party councillors remained seated while more than 100 other politicians gave a soldier a standing ovation. Nowhere in the article does the *Star* mention that there were many other Muslim councillors (Tory, LibDem and Labour) present at the same event – all of whom *did* stand and applaud.

In other words, the *Daily Star* is either grossly irresponsible in its sloppy representation of the facts, or engaging in overt anti-Muslim propaganda.

On the same page was a phone poll: 'DO YOU AGREE WITH THE EDL POLICIES?' Ninety-eight per cent of the respondents did. If I read the *Star* every day, and believed it, I'd join the EDL too.

Not that you have to be a dedicated reader to be exposed to its influence. Just pop into W. H. Smith's. There they are, those headlines, the steady drip-drip-drip: 'MUSLIM-ONLY LOOS' and 'BBC PUTS MUSLIMS BEFORE YOU' and 'MUSLIM SICKOS' MADDIE KIDNAP SHOCK' (No, I haven't made that one up). Drip drip drip. Bullshit or exaggeration masquerading as fact. And to what aim?

On 9 February the *Star* ran a front-page headline claiming 'ENGLISH DEFENCE LEAGUE TO BECOME POLITICAL PARTY'. Even that turned out to be dubious – their leader had merely said 'we aren't ruling it out'. Inside, another phone poll asked whether readers would vote for the EDL. Ninety-nine per cent said yes.

Do they believe what they read in the *Daily Star*?

I believe this is a wonderful country. All of it. The people are inherently decent and fair-minded. All of them. We should resist crude attempts at division, wherever they come from. Because we deserve better. All of us.

A bite of the Apple
28/02/2011

In 2007, I wrote a column entitled 'I hate Macs'. I call it a column. It was actually an unbroken 900-word Applephobic screed. Macs, I claimed, were 'glorified Fisher-Price activity centres for adults; computers for scaredy-cats too nervous to learn how proper computers work'.

In 2009, I complained again: 'the better-designed and more ubiquitous they become, the more I dislike them ... I don't care if every Mac product comes with a magic button on the side that causes it to piddle gold coins and resurrect the dead ... I'm not buying one, so shut up and go home.'

The lady doth protest too much. A few weeks later, I buckled and bought an iPhone. And you know what? It felt good. Within minutes of switching it on, sliding those dinky little icons around the screen, I was hooked. This was my gateway drug. Before long I was also toting an iPad. And after that, a MacBook. All the stuff people said about how Macs were just better, about them being a joy to use ... it was true, all of it.

They make you feel good, Apple products. The little touches: the rounded corners, the strokeable screens, the satisfying clunk as you fold the MacBook shut – it's serene. Untroubled. Like being on Valium.

Until, that is, you try to do something Apple doesn't want you to do. At which point you realise your shiny chum isn't on your side. It doesn't even understand sides. Only Apple: always Apple.

Here's a familiar, mundane scenario: you've got an iPhone with loads of music on it. And you've got a laptop with a new album on it. You want to put the new album on your phone. But you can't hook them up and simply drag-and-drop the files like you could with, ooh, almost any other device. Instead, Apple insists you go through iTunes.

Microsoft gets a lot of stick for producing clunky software. But even during the dark days of the animated paperclip, or the infuriating '.docx' Word extension, they never shat out anything as abominable as iTunes – a hideous binary turd that transforms the sparkling world of music and entertainment into a stark, unintuitive spreadsheet.

Plug your old Apple iPhone into your new Apple MacBook for the first time, and because the two machines haven't been formally introduced, iTunes will babble about 'syncing' one with the other. It claims it simply MUST delete everything from the old phone before putting any new stuff on it. Why? It won't tell you. It'll just cheerfully ask if you want to proceed, like an upbeat robot butler that can't understand why you're crying.

No one uses terms like 'sync' in real life. Not even C3PO. If I sync my DVD collection with yours, will I end up with one, two, or no copies of *Santa Claus: The Movie*? It's like trying to work out the consequences of time travel, but less fun, and with absolutely no chance of being adapted into a successful screenplay.

Apple's 'sync' bullshit is a deception, which pretends to be making your life easier, when it's actually all about wresting control from you. If you could freely transfer any file you wanted onto your gadget, Apple might conceivably lose out on a few molecules of gold. So rather than risk that, they'll choose – every single time – to restrict your options, without so much as blinking.

Sure, you can get around the irritating sync-issue, but doing so requires a degree of faff and brainwork, like solving the famous logic problem about ferrying a load of foxes and chickens across a river without it all ending in feathers and death. And even if you find it easy, it's a problem Apple don't want you to solve. They want you to give up and go back to dumbly stroking that shiny screen, pausing intermittently to wipe the drool from your chin.

Apple continually attempts to scrape even more money from anything that might conceivably pass through iTunes' tight, leathery anus. Take ebooks. Apple's own iBook reader app may be nauseatingly pretty, but it's not a patch on Amazon's Kindle, which, far from being just a standalone machine, is a surprisingly nifty cross-platform 'cloud' system that lets you read books on a variety of devices, including the iPhone and iPad. It even remembers what page you were on, regardless of whichever machine you were reading it on last. (It does that by 'syncing' – but we'll forgive it that, because a) it happens seamlessly and b) you never, ever lose any of your purchases.)

Now Apple, typically, are no longer content to let people read Kindle books on their iPhones and iPads without muscling in on some of that money themselves. So they've changed their rules, in a bid to force Amazon (and anyone else) to provide in-app purchases for their products. What this dull sentence means in practice is that Apple want a 30 per cent cut each time a Kindle user buys a book from within the iPhone Kindle app.

So 30 per cent less for authors and publishers, and 30 per cent more for the world's second-largest company. And that's assuming they'll let any old book pass through the App store: given their track record, chances are they'll refuse to process anything they consider objectionable. Still, if they start banning books, never mind. Winnie the Pooh looks great on the iPad.

Every Apple commercial makes a huge play of how user-friendly their devices are. But it's a superficial friendship. To Apple, you're nothing. They won't even give you a power lead long enough to use your phone while it's on charge, so if it rings you have to crawl around on your hands and knees, like a dog.

So I no longer hate Apple products. In fact I use them every day. But I never feel like I own them. More like I'm renting them from Skynet.

50 ways to Libya lover
07/03/2011

A huge source of frustration for any performing artist is that you can't choose your fans. And the more popular you get, the more likely it is you'll attract people you can't stand. Kurt Cobain so disliked the uncool non-underground types who began showing up at Nirvana gigs after the release of their debut album *Bleach* that he wrote the song *In Bloom*, which attacks an unnamed moronic jock type who dares to enjoy Nirvana's music: 'He's the one who likes all our pretty songs,' goes the chorus. 'And he likes to sing along, and he likes to shoot his gun – but he knows not what it means.'

Yeah! Take that, you mainstream douchebags! Feeling pretty stupid now, huh?

Well, no. They weren't. Partly because they knew not what it meant, but largely because Cobain foolishly gave the song a catchy melody, and then compounded this error by including it on an album of other catchy melodies called *Nevermind*, which became such a massive mainstream success that he never truly lived it down, at least in his own head. And it soon turned out the despised jock fan wasn't the only one prone to discharging the occasional firearm.

Still, if Cobain was tortured by the presence of the occasional macho numbskull at his gigs, imagine how awful he'd feel if he looked out and saw a member of the Gaddafi dynasty moshing to 'Smells Like Teen Spirit'. Chances are he'd have beaten himself to death with his own guitar right there and then.

But many of the planet's current pop stars are clearly made of sterner stuff. They're so unconcerned about the suitability of their fans, they'll put on a private show for the Gaddafi clan at the drop of a hat. A hat full of money.

Now the blood's started flowing they're getting contrite about the whole thing. First Nelly Furtado outed herself, announcing on Twitter that in 2007 she'd been given $1m to perform for the Gaddafis, and was now donating the sum to charity.

Other stars who attended Gaddafi dynasty parties include Mariah Carey, Usher, Lionel Richie, and Jay-Z – who, thanks to the bad publicity, now has 100 problems.

Mr Z's wife, Beyoncé, reportedly received $2m to perform at a New Year party thrown by Hannibal Gaddafi, but subsequently gave the money to Haiti. 'Once it became known that the third-party promoter was linked to the Gaddafi family, the decision was made to put that payment to a good cause,' said her publicist. Fair enough. She probably didn't realise the Gaddafis were behind the bash, although her husband reportedly attended an identical party at the same venue the previous year – at which, it is claimed, Mariah Carey sang four songs in exchange for $1m. The Gaddafi link was exposed in the press at the time, but only in small-circulation newspapers such as the *Sun*, so it's fair to assume Beyoncé's advisers had no idea where the cash was coming from.

Libya would be a good growth market for Beyoncé, incidentally, as, thanks to the Gaddafi regime, it now contains far more *Single Ladies* than it used to.

Another famous star who reportedly performed for the Gaddafis is notorious pussy 50 Cent, the crybaby pant-shitting wuss whom I could definitely have in a fight. (Did you know his real name is Fifi Millicent? Don't tell him I told you, because he's terribly sensitive about it, and weeps huge cowardly tears out of his gutless baby eyes whenever it's mentioned.)

Fifi was paid an undisclosed sum to sing and dance like a fey little puppet in front of Mutassim Gaddafi at the 2005 Venice film festival. But while the other stars have been embarrassed by their (possibly unintentional) connection to a despotic regime, Fifi seems to have used his as the inspiration for a startlingly violent video game called *50 Cent: Blood on the Sand*, released on the PS3 and Xbox 360 in 2009.

The game opens with Fifi Millicent performing a gig in an

unnamed war-torn Middle Eastern country, in exchange for a $10m fee. When the mysterious promoter shows signs of not coughing up the money, Fifi and chums storm backstage, call him a 'motherfucker' and shove a shotgun in his face. Terrified, he hands them a priceless Damien Hirst-style diamond-encrusted skull. Fifi and Co. then bravely head for the airport in their armoured Hummers, only to be ambushed by armed insurgents. During the gunfire and confusion, a sexy woman appears from nowhere and steals the precious skull.

'Bitch took my skull,' whines Fifi, before embarking on an awesome odyssey of violence across the troubled Arab nation, shooting and murdering anyone who gets in his way.

Who'd have thought someone like 50 Cent could lend his name to something so crass and stupid? It's almost as if he's an idiot. Still, perhaps openly embracing the despotic crossover in a video game is the way forward. How long before we see a game called *Gaddafi Hero*, in which you perform a series of upbeat numbers for Middle Eastern tyrants by pushing coloured buttons on a plastic guitar in time to the beat, while trying to drown out the nagging voice of your own conscience and the furious chants of the oppressed?

Suggested tracklisting: 'While My Qatar Gently Weeps'; 'Gimme Gimme Gimme Oman After Midnight'; 'Insane in the Bahrain'; 'Here Comes Yemen'; and '50 Ways To Libya Lover'. Recommended retail price? $2m and counting.

Dream schooled
14/03/2011

Poor Jamie Oliver. A few years ago he single-handedly saved every child in the country from imminent cholesterol death with his school dinners campaign. And there was nationwide rejoicing. The Queen called a national holiday; councils held street parties in his honour and the City erected a 600-foot glass-and-metal statue shaped like one of his Flavour Shakers (known today as 'the Gherkin', after one of his favourite sandwich fillings).

Now, instead of reducing the kiddywink generation's waistlines he's attempting to expand their minds by establishing his own 'Dream School'. A tape recording of this selfless act of altruism somehow ended up in Channel 4's hands, and they've been broadcasting extracts from it for the past few weeks. And what do we do? We watch *MasterChef* on the other side. The professional chef is being shunned in favour of a bunch of unknown amateurs. Because they're actually bloody cooking.

The audacity of *Jamie's Dream School* is truly inspiring, assuming you're impressed by mountains of bullshit. The first episode opened with Jamie recounting how he left school with no qualifications. The British educational system failed him, just as it fails millions of others like him every year. Now he wants to make a difference. Not by campaigning against education cuts – which might be boring – but by setting up his own school. Not one staffed by actual teachers – which might be boring – but by celebrities. And it won't be open all-year round – which might be expensive – but for a few weeks. Thus our education system will be saved.

Simon Callow taught them English by shouting at them. David Starkey taught them history by insulting them. And Alastair Campbell taught them politics by arranging a debate, which soon degenerated into a full-blown playground ruck. This was their first true lesson: they learned first-hand that Campbell is shit-hot at instigating conflict from thin air.

Thank God Jamie merely opened a school, and didn't decide to explore the NHS's failings by opening his own Dream Hospital, in which famous actors who've portrayed doctors in popular dramas perform operations on members of the public. Watch Hugh Laurie sew up a gaping abdominal wound! See James Nesbitt conduct intricate neurosurgery! They'd make mistakes now and then – slicing the wrong bit off here, letting all the innards spill out there – but that's where Jamie could come in. He could take that human offal, whip up a delicious intestine-and-kidney casserole, and then spoon it into the dying patients' grateful, gurgling mouth as they drew their final breaths.

Anyway, back to *Dream School*. When the series was announced, the initial promotional material was couched in the trad Bash Street Kids visual language of British school-based capers: chalk, blackboards, board rubbers, pencil cases and so on. It looked like Jamie versus *Grange Hill*. But, presumably because the authorities wouldn't allow the production team to meddle with the education of actual children, they're reduced to teaching teenage volunteers who've already left school. So: no real kids, no real teachers, and no real exams. Nothing is real. No wonder they called it *Dream School*. It's effectively a youth club with Starkey instead of a pool table.

And what's the worst thing about youth clubs? The youths. And they've got a prime selection here. Watching *Jamie's Dream School* is enough to transform the wettest liberal do-gooder into a furious Nick Ferrari type by the third ad break. They gawp at iPhones, they burble witlessly amongst themselves, they slouch in their seats looking bored and surly and demanding respect for absolutely no reason whatsoever … Maybe our educational system has tragically failed them. Or maybe they're fuckwits. Even the most helpless fuckwits can change, of course, but they tend to do so quietly, and of their own volition. Which doesn't make great television.

Follies of youth aside, their biggest problem seems to be a chronically stunted attention span: they're constantly texting or yapping on their mobiles instead of applying even 1 per cent focus on whatever's directly in front of them. The entire programme should have been billed not as a crusading mission documentary, but as a chilling warning about how technology will inevitably destroy human civilisation by distracting it into stupidity and madness.

Dumb though half the kids may be, they're just plodding meat fodder for a shockingly arrogant TV experiment, which exists for no apparent reason other than to demoralise any genuine teachers watching, potentially to the point of suicide, which really would cause a crisis in our educational system.

After two episodes I wound up hating almost everyone in it, aside from a couple of the kids and, curiously, Jamie himself – because he just looks so crushingly, dizzyingly confused by the whole thing. Why is he there? Why is this happening? What's the ultimate aim? If he's got any sanity left at all, come episode three he'll tear down all the *Dream School* signs and turn it into a sandwich-making academy. Because that, at least, would fulfill some kind of function.

Midsomer murmurs

21/03/2011

Red faces at *Midsomer Murders*. Which at least provides a bit of diversity among all the white ones. Producer Brian True-May's ill-judged comments about the programme representing 'the last bastion of Englishness' have caused a predictable storm and counter-storm, with one side crying racism and the other side crying about the cries of racism.

But is the overwhelming whiteness representative of the English countryside? Well, I grew up in south Oxfordshire, very close to some of the locations used in *Midsomer Murders*, specifically near a town called Wallingford, which used to double as 'Causton' in the series. It's also – fittingly – where Agatha Christie died. Oh, and it used to regularly show up in the Ronnie Corbett sitcom *Sorry*, if you're interested. Which I sense you aren't.

To the best of my knowledge, when I was growing up, there was one black kid in my village, several black and brown kids at my school, and a Chinese family running the local takeaway. This was back in the late seventies and eighties. Not exactly the

United Nations, but still: to actively pursue a policy of white-only casting would be unrealistic.

It's interesting that *Midsomer Murders* managed to chug along for sixteen years without anyone really bothering to question its Caucasian hue. That's partly because although it notionally takes place in the present day, everyone watching it implicitly understands that it's actually set in an anachronistic bubble – a strange unofficial cross between 1991 and 1946. I'm surprised the characters don't drive steam trains to get to the shops. In this environment, anything even vaguely contemporary looks out of place: if someone turned up wearing a digital watch, the villagers would probably mistake them for a warlock and beat them to death with cudgels.

Midsomer's lack of ethnic diversity stems from the fact that it's essentially a camp tribute to 'Murder at the Vicarage' potboilers from a pre-multicultural era: a knowing assembly of Middle England clichés. The show is hardly a slave to realism. One of its murder victims was pinned with hoops to a croquet lawn and killed with a vintage bottle of claret fired from a Roman catapult. Complaining about a lack of authenticity in those circumstances seems daft. On the other hand, since it's about as realistic as a butterscotch harpoon anyway, why do the makers seem to assume that the addition of a few brown faces might jolt the audience out of their suspension of disbelief? The viewers aren't that stupid, or anywhere near that prejudiced. And the ones that are will be too busy designing racist pamphlets or ranting on the internet to tune in anyway.

Putting aside the legality of a major commercial venture apparently enacting an employment policy that excludes people on the basis of skin colour for no good reason, many have complained that to suddenly introduce 'ethnic' characters would be 'PC gone mad'. Yes it would, if they introduced them solely to do a storyline about grime MCs or arranged marriages, or showed them walking around the village shaking hands with all the white folk. But no one's asking for that. You don't even have to change the writing. Just widen the audition process. It won't hurt. It can only help.

When I was a kiddywink, back in that almost entirely white Midsomer-style village, many of my views about people from different ethnic backgrounds were defined by what I saw on television. There were a few black and brown characters in shows such as *Grange Hill*. There was Trevor McDonald, Lenny Henry, Huggy Bear from *Starsky and Hutch*, and assorted musicians on *Top of the Pops*.

Black people were often used as a sort of lazy shorthand for 'cool'. Consequently, I formed a spectacularly patronising general view that all black people were inherently 'cool'. It wasn't until I moved to London and suddenly met lots of them in real life that I realised many were massive dorks. And that wasn't the only way they failed to live up to the televised stereotype: I can still recall my feeble shock at meeting a black girl who preferred indie rock to hip-hop.

But still: gauche though I may have been, at least I wasn't fearful or mistrusting. I had an inherent (albeit incredibly condescending) sense that I liked black people, and wanted them to like me. And I genuinely believe a lot of that was thanks to Derek Griffiths. Griffiths was the first black person I can remember encountering anywhere in my life, and he existed only on my television. He presented *Play School*, appeared in *Play Away*, and created the music for *Bod*. And as far as I'm concerned he's one of the most brilliant TV presenters this country has ever produced: instantly warm and likeable, clearly very talented, and possessing the rare knack of appearing to speak directly to young viewers without patronising them. His colour absolutely didn't matter, yet at the same time it did – precisely because it didn't matter. Even this four-year-old could see that.

Children's TV has long been ahead of adult TV in terms of diversity – witness Cerrie Burnell, the one-armed CBBC presenter, whose very presence on our screens is right now teaching millions of kids not to be wary of disabled people. They know a disabled person now, and they like her, and that unusual arm is unimportant in the way they see her, but profound in the way they see the world. Again: widening that audition process won't hurt. It can only help.

Friday, Friday – gotta get down on Friday
27/03/2011

Not so long ago, if you wanted to issue a thirteen-year-old girl with a blood-curdling death threat, you had to scrawl it on a sheet of paper, wrap it round a brick, hurl it through her bedroom window, and scarper before her dad ran out of the front door to beat you insensible with a dustbuster. Now, thanks to Twitter, hundreds of thousands of people can simultaneously surround her online screaming abuse until she bursts into tears. Hooray for civilisation.

That's in effect what happened the other week in the Rebecca Black 'Friday' affair. In case you're not aware of it, the trail of events runs as follows: 1) Parents of thirteen-year-old Rebecca pay $2,000 for her to record a song (and video) called 'Friday' with a company called ARK Music Factory, a kind of vanity-publishing record label specialising in creepy tweenie pop songs. 2) The song turns out to be excruciatingly vapid, albeit weirdly catchy. 3) It quickly racks up 40m views on YouTube, mainly from people marvelling at its compelling awfulness. 4) Rebecca is targeted on Twitter by thousands of abusive idiots calling her a 'bitch' and a 'whore' and urging her to commit suicide. 5) She gets very, very upset. 6) Thanks to all the attention, the single becomes a hit. 7) Rebecca becomes an overnight celebrity, goes on *The Tonight Show*, and donates the proceeds from 'Friday' to the Japan relief effort.

So the story has a happy ending, at least for now. But it marks a watershed moment in the history of online discourse: the point where the wave of bile and snark finally broke and rolled back.

God knows I enjoy a helping of bile. But only when it's crafted with flair. One of the most disappointing things about the slew of online Rebecca Black abuse is the sheer poverty of language involved. If you are complaining about a banal pop song but can't muster a more inventive way to express yourself than typing 'OMFG BITCH YOU SUCK', then you really ought to consider folding your laptop shut and sitting quietly in the corner until that fallow lifespan of yours eventually reaches its conclusion.

The other crucial component of an artful slagging is not a 'sense' of perspective but an 'awareness' of it. It can be amusing to knowingly punch out 10,000 words feverishly declaring Justin Bieber to be some kind of squawking terrorist weapon – but it only works when the author's comic desperation is at least 50 per cent of the joke. The (brilliant) comedian Jerry Sadowitz's entire act consists of him shouting indefensibly hideous things about everybody on Earth, and yet he never feels like a bully, more a frenzied marionette jerked around by uncontrollable despair: a sort of self-hating dirty bomb.

Just as Sadowitz's palpable vulnerability makes him funny, so it's a soulless lack of self-reproach that makes the predominant Perez Hilton/3am Girl/Holy Moly/TMZ gloaty online sneer-culture so unbearably dull and depressing. You people lick the inner base of dustbins for a living. Stop looking so fucking pleased with yourselves.

And this culture dominates Twitter. Twitter is great for disseminating news, trivia and practical instructions on when and where to meet up in order to overthrow the government, but it also doubles as a hothouse in which viral outbreaks of witless bullying can be incubated and unleashed before anyone knows what's happening. Partly because it forces users to communicate in terse sentences, but mainly because it's public. Many tweeters end up performing their opinions, theatrically overstating their viewpoint to impress their friends. Just like newspaper columnists

– but somehow even worse because there's no editor to keep their excesses in check or demand a basic level of wit or ability.

And unlike columnists, they often aim their comments at an individual by addressing their username directly: the equivalent of texting hate mail straight to their phone. I've never understood the mentality behind this, but then I write to entertain crowds, not harass individuals. I've never donned a mask and poked dogshit through someone's letterbox either. Maybe it's their sole source of happiness. Who knows?

Certainly, the more insecure the tweeter, the more unhinged their behaviour seems to be. Some of the most virulent Rebecca Black abuse came from teenage girls showing off to their mates by tweeting the singer directly to gloatingly wish death upon her.

Hilariously, many of them attacked the wrong Rebecca Black, and were actually beaming their hatred at an etiquette coach of the same name, a woman who regularly appears on US TV to discuss the merits of civil discourse. The worse their abuse, the more gracefully she responded, which somehow made them look infinitely more small-minded than they already were.

Who, out of everyone, was the slimiest turd in the 'Friday' soufflé? Impossible to say, thanks to the sheer number of participants. Which is the final thing online hateswarms fail to take into account: their collective mass, which causes a nasty imbalance of power and often results in a self-righteous lack of restraint that can reach far beyond the verbal. When Jan Moir wrote her Stephen Gately article, I penned a vicious response as an individual. When I saw people angrily posting her home address online, I felt like part of a mob. Those idiots spoiled it for everybody.

In summary: bitch all you like. Just don't be a dick about it. Poise, people. Poise.

Rebecca Black (slight return)
Broadcast on *10 O'Clock Live*, C4, 23/03/2011

CB is sitting at his desk.

CHARLIE: In its short lifespan, the social mass-yabbering site Twitter has changed the way news is disseminated, the way stalkers track their prey, and the way Jason Manford relaxes in his dressing room. But Twitter isn't just for fun. In the past few weeks it's played a central role in toppling bona fide international hate figures: President Zine Al Abidine Ben Ali, Hosni Mubarak, Muammar Gaddafi. And now Rebecca Black.

VT: *Rebecca Black's 'Friday' video.*

CHARLIE: Yes. Rebecca Black. A thirteen-year-old amateur wannabe popstar whose parents paid $2,000 for her to record *this* song and video called 'Friday', which became an online sensation thanks to its superb visuals and frighteningly profound lyrics, which explore the intangible beauty of Fridays.

VT: *Rebecca sings badly.*

CHARLIE: Yes: the world's first song with less than one note. It sounds like a wasp trapped inside a polystyrene cup rasping the words 'Friday, Friday, gotta get down on Friday' – forever. Before long over 40 million people saw it – and hundreds of thousands of them were so moved they flocked to Twitter to complain to thirteen-year-old Rebecca directly, calling her a whore, urging her to commit suicide and generally participating in the single biggest act of bullying in world history.

A startling number of the most vicious messages seemed to come from angry Justin Bieber fans – people who actually enjoy listening to the dickless mewlings of *this* quasi-sentient boy thing.

STILL: *Justin Bieber.*

CHARLIE: Just to be clear, a Justin Bieber fan moaning about a banal pop song is like someone gargling a mouthful of skunk piss complaining that the dog's blown off in the corner. Anyway this high-tech hate mob did affect Rebecca – as an illuminating interview on *Good Morning America* made clear.

VT: *Rebecca Black on* Good Morning America *explaining that the messages made her cry.*

CHARLIE: Impossible not to feel sorry for her. Still quite an annoying voice though. But to address the members of the Rebecca Black hate mob directly for a moment –

CB turns to camera two.

CHARLIE: Dear imbeciles – thanks to your hard work, Rebecca Black, who you dismissed as a hopeless wannabe, is now a bona fide megastar.

Shots of Rebecca Black on The Tonight Show with Jay Leno.

CHARLIE: Look! Here she is on an edition of the *Tonight Show with Jay Leno*, just like you'll never be. See? She's famous. Perhaps you'd like a picture of that image . . .

CB holds up a screengrab of Rebecca Black on The Tonight Show *in a golden frame.*

CHARLIE: . . . to hang it on the wall of your home so you can look at it every morning before going to work in the shitty megachain burger outfit you'll be trapped in forever – selling Happy Meals with Rebecca Black's face on them . . .

CB holds up prop burger box: the Rebecca Black Happy Meal.

CHARLIE: . . . like this, because of you – and as you pass these to customers who, accurately, look at you like you're nothing, you'll hear Rebecca Black's song looping on the in-store Muzak system, while you slave away behind the counter five days a week, from

Monday through to Friday, Friday: you gotta get down on Friday – because that's the day you mop the fucking floor.

The occasional kick to the face
03/04/2011

So a few weeks ago I was on television, doing a little comic 'bit' about unfocused online haters, the climax of which involved me going into a diatribe wherein I angrily imagined one of them toiling away behind the counter of a fast-food restaurant. And shortly after it aired I received tweets and comments from people complaining I was a snob: that I was in effect saying anyone who works in a burger bar is a scummy non-person; a grunting subservient ape-slave deserving nothing but open scorn and the occasional kick to the face, provided it's their birthday.

That hadn't been my intention, but I can see why some people interpreted it that way (thanks to some clumsy writing on my part, and an absent 'qualifying' section, which got excised at the last minute). Anyway, it bugged me. It bugged me because although I've never worked in a fast-food restaurant, I did spend several years working as a shop assistant – and during that time I learned, as anyone who spends their week standing behind a counter quickly learns, that the worst kind of customers are the ones who think they're automatically superior to you just because you're serving them. The ones who pop into Debenhams and suddenly think they're Henry VIII inspecting the serfs.

You can tell a lot about a person by the way they treat waiters and shop assistants, especially when you are one. The majority of people are perfectly capable of interacting with retail staff without spitting on them or whipping their hides like dawdling cattle, but planet Earth still harbours more than its fair share of disappointments.

The first surprise is that when it comes to arrogant customers, class isn't as big a factor as you might assume. True, I'd occasionally get a stereotypical ex-public-schoolboy blurting requests in my direction as though addressing a programmable service droid, or openly scolding me as if I was a failing member of his personal waiting staff – but the most overtly boorish behaviour came courtesy of people who weren't posh at all, but seemed to want to increase their own social standing by treating the person serving them like scum.

Then there were the people for whom even basic civility was an alien concept. I vividly recall one guy who sloped in wearing a loose pair of tracksuit trousers, absentmindedly playing with his own bollocks as he entered. He stood at the counter, scanning the display behind me and obliviously juggling his goolies – at one point literally reaching inside to re-arrange his collection – and then wiped his nose with the back of his hand, sucked the slime off it, pointed at an item he was interested in and said: 'Show me that.' Moments later he started an argument about how much it cost, demanded a discount, and, when I refused, called me an arsehole and knocked a load of boxes off a shelf by the door as he left. Based on that one five-minute encounter, more than seventeen years ago, I'd be prepared to bet that man is today either dead or in jail. And probably still playing with his nuts.

But incidents like that were few and far between, partly because there was one major difference between the shop I was working in and almost every other shop in the world: you were allowed to talk back to the customers. In fact a certain level of sweary piss-taking was actively encouraged. It gave the place character, made the working day more fun, and reminded the frazzled shopper, on autopilot after several hours on Oxford Street, that they were dealing with a fellow human being.

Everyone who works in a shop should be allowed to openly take the piss out of their customers. It's far more British than the strain of imported corporate civility-by-numbers that megachain staff are sometimes forced to recite: the robotic 'How can I help you?' mantras that only really make sense in America, because they're so friendly they actually mean it. The words don't feel false in their mouths. If I ran a national burger franchise – which I don't – I'd make it a rule that no two customers can be greeted with precisely the same words, and that every third customer must be grossly insulted as a matter of course. Just to keep the atmosphere nice and lively. And to keep the staff laughing.

Yes, laughing staff. That's the other irritating assumption people make about working in shops, especially burger bars – that the job must be so dismal, every single employee shuffles about in a perpetual state of misery, actively welcoming death. That only the utterly desperate or dumb could possibly stick it out. These characteristics could apply to almost any job, of course. What I disliked most about working as a shop assistant wasn't the occasional snooty customer, or the shop, or the hours, but the way people reacted when I told them I was a shop assistant – their automatic assumption that I didn't enjoy it. I didn't particularly enjoy my life at the time, but I did enjoy the job. Not every day, not constantly – but I liked it more than I disliked it. Maybe I'm odd. Maybe I was lucky and had unusually entertaining co-workers. Or maybe there are far, far worse things you could do.

Like judging people.

Unless you're a judge.

In which case, continue.

The imp of the mind
10/04/2011

Ever since about 1998, when humankind began fast-forwarding through the gradually unfolding history of progress, like someone impatiently zipping through a YouTube clip in search of the best bits, we've grown accustomed to machines veering from essential to obsolete in the blink of a trimester. VHS, the Walkman, fax machines, CD-Roms, pagers, dial-up modems ... all consigned to the same wing of the museum housing the mangle and the horse-drawn plough.

The junk mountain grows by the day. If your home is anything like mine, it contains several rarely explored crannies stashed full of archaic chargers, defunct cables, and freshly antiquated gizmos whose sole useful function in 2011 is to make 2005 feel like 1926, simply by looking big and dull and impossibly lumpen. Everyone's opened a drawer and been startled by the unexpected discovery of an old mobile phone that now resembles an outsized pantomime prop. To think you used to be impressed by this clunky breezeblock. You were like a caveman gawping at a yo-yo.

Now it's almost time to hurl another outmoded device down the historical garbage chute: your body. Last week, researchers at Washington University unveiled a new mind-control computer system. Traditional mind-control systems – and the fact that any mind-control system can be referred to as 'traditional' shows you how nuts-deep into the future we already are – require the user to don an EEG skullcap before thinking very hard about specific actions. The resultant brainwaves are then crudely interpreted and the device reacts accordingly. But practical use is severely restricted thanks to the human skull, which muffles some signals and amplifies others. It's like trying to work out what your neighbours are up to by pressing your ear against the wall: fun, but often wildly misleading.

Which is where electrocorticography comes in. Electro-corticography basically means 'sticking sensors directly on to the surface of the brain'. Once you've done that, you get a far more reliable signal. Already they've had volunteers controlling an onscreen cursor by imagining different vowel sounds. As soon as they refine it further, giving the user the ability to steer the pointer around and click on things, the days of mass-market Wi-Fi mind-controlled iPads will be upon us before you can smother your kids in their sleep to protect them from precisely such a future.

But is this really so sinister? All computers are mind-controlled already. My hand may steer the mouse and my fingers may punch the keys, but none of this takes place without my mental say-so. My brain runs things round here. Surely all a mind-controlled interface does is cut out the corporeal middleman, leaving your fingers free to do something more useful, such as plugging your ears so you can't hear the horrified screams spontaneously exploding from your facehole? What's the problem?

The problem is that the body is the final, crucial buffer between the skittish human mind and the slavish machine servant. Think of how many furious email responses you've composed in haste, only to halt and reflect at the final moment as your finger hovers over the 'send' button. The simple fact that a small physical action is required to actually deliver the damn thing is often enough to give pause for thought.

When mind-controlled computers become a commonplace reality, you'll have typed and sent that message in the time it takes to stub a toe; as quick as pulling a facial expression, but more detailed, and full of swearwords.

And while your brain might be great at controlling machines, how great are you at controlling your brain? What if, ten years in the future, you're watching a cartoon on your futuristic 3D computer television, and the cartoon's got a rabbit in it, and the rabbit's slightly coquettish and flirty, and the knowing way it flicks that cotton tail as it hops makes you think about sex momentarily, and before you know it, your brain's retrieved some disgraceful bestial rabbit porn from the very worst corners of the Ultranet, and is relaying it on the display in lurid ninety-six-inch holographic guttervision just as your wife and kid come back from the shops? And then, drunk on self-destructive power, your computer-mind takes a four-second video-snapshot of your own child's horrified gasping face and mischievously scribbles a load of penises and swastikas all over it, and uploads this vandalised looping portrait to your 3D holographic Facebook page accompanied by a headline screaming 'WITNESS MY NADIR – JUDGE ME! JUDGE ME! JUDGE ME ONE AND ALL!'

Let's face it, if you're honest, there's a whole world of shit routinely fizzing and popping around in your head that you wouldn't want a computer to unquestioningly act on. Remember: when they triumphantly unveil an iPhone that lets you dial your sweetheart simply by thinking about their face, don't be fooled into thinking it's wonderful. It's a slippery slope. Resist the mind probe. Thicken your skull. Staple a doormat around it if necessary. Keep those thoughts trapped inside where they belong. Because if the imp of the mind ever sidesteps the body and gets its hand directly on the steering wheel, humankind can look forward to six months of unpredictable chaos, then doomsday.

PART SEVEN

In which tabloid journalists make the world worse, Ed Miliband tumbles into a vortex, and cars are driven too quickly.

Making the world worse
17/04/2011

Week 396, and the phone-hacking affair continues, prompting onlookers to wonder how much more pus can possibly seep out. Rather than lancing the boil, the official apology seems to have pricked a hole in an entire dimension of fetid, boiling pus, and sent it belching and bubbling into our world.

More arrests. More searches. More claims about who was hacked – celebs, sportsmen, politicians all had their privacy invaded. But let's not forget the real victims here. What about the tabloid journalists? Not just from the *News of the World* or the *Sun*. All the tabloid journalists. Spare a thought for them.

Because it can't be easy being a tabloid hack at the best of times. Sure, there's the camaraderie, the sense of power, the rush of skulduggery, the thrill of feeling like one of the chosen few who can see through the Matrix, but these are illusory compensations, sweatily constructed by your quaking, sobbing psyche in a bid to counterweigh the cavernous downside: the awful knowledge that you're wasting your life actively making the world worse.

Chances are you're quite smart. And you probably love to write – or did, once, back then, before ... before the fall. Now you're writing nothing but NYAHH NYAHH NYAHH *ad nauseam*. You use the only brain you'll ever have to puke out endless gutfuls of cheap gossip or crude propaganda. Half the time you're wrecking lives and the other half you're filling your readers' heads with nakedly misleading straw-man fairytales. Every now and then something might come along to temporarily justify your existence: a political scoop; a genuine outrage ... but do you build on it? No. You retreat to the warm cave of your celebrity chef shag-shocks and your tragic tot death-porn double-pagers:

wasting your life actively making the world worse.

I suppose the best way to cope with the dull, constant, pulsing awareness that you're wasting your life actively making the world worse is to somehow bewitch yourself into believing you're actively making the world better. That by writing about a footballer's bedroom exploits you're fearlessly exposing the ugly truth behind the wholesome public image and blah blah role model blah blah fans' hard-earned cash blah blah sanctimony blah. Hey – whatever works for you, yeah? Dress as a priest if it helps. We all know you're just grubbily recounting a sex act for our fleeting amusement, like a radio commentator describing two pigs rutting in a sty.

Another strategy, I guess, would be to focus on the fun of the job, to see it as one long naughty jape. To swap tales about Fleet Street legends of yesteryear and consider yourself a fellow swashbuckling pirate. Hey, what about the time you disguised yourself as a doctor tee hee and the time you blagged your way on to the *Emmerdale* set ho ho and the time you spent three hours rooting through a dustbin hurr hurr. No, please, please, don't tell us now – save all this for your memoirs: MY LIFE AS A NON-STOP TITTERSOME RAG WEEK PRANKSTER.

Successfully forging the belief that tabloid journalism is a worthwhile use of your brief time on this planet must require a mental leap beyond the reach of Galileo. This is one reason why so many tabloid stories are routinely peppered with lies – if their staff didn't continually flex their delusion muscles, a torrent of dark, awful self-awareness might rush into their heads like unforgiving black water pouring through the side of a stricken submarine, and they'd all slash their wrists open right there at their workstations. The newsroom hubbub would be regularly broken by the dispiriting thump of lifeless heads thunking on to desks. Each morning their bosses would have to clear all the spent corpses away with a bulldozer and hire a fresh team of soon-to-be-heartbroken lifewasters to replace the ones who couldn't make it, whose powers of self-deception simply weren't up to the job. Who couldn't cope with the knowledge that they were wasting their lives actively making the world worse.

And now – on top of all of these trials and indignities, on top of the harrowing leukaemia-of-the-soul their career choice inflicts upon them – now their job has got even harder. Because for a while, at least, wasting your life actively making the world worse was relatively easy. You could pay someone to root through someone's dustbins. Then, when the early mobiles arrived, you could get a £59 frequency scanner and sit outside a soap star's flat, surreptitiously recording their calls. And when phones went digital, there was the voicemail wheeze, which made life even easier. You could sit at your desk illegally invading the privacy of strangers just by pushing buttons.

But now, having abused all those tricks, like they abused their talent – not for any noble cause, but to find out which girlband member snogged which boyband member – those easy games are up. And it couldn't have come at a worse time: with plummeting sales, the need for sensational stories is higher than ever. All of which means all those people wasting their lives actively making the world worse will now have to expend colossal effort in order to do so: like prisoners forced at gunpoint to dig their own graves – but with a rubber shovel.

There is no fate more tragic. Pity them. Pity them hard.

After the piece above was published a former editor of the Sun *emailed me to say, 'How I don't miss the leukaemia of the soul. Very perceptive observation.' Yet despite this ringing endorsement, the article didn't go down too well with some journalists, who found it unfair, sweeping, accusatory, over-simplistic, one-sided, abusive, lofty, self-important, histrionic, condescending, inaccurate, and many other things tabloid journalists clearly aren't. In fairness I should've specified 'some' tabloid journalists in the second paragraph, not 'all' tabloid journalists. But that wouldn't have been as funny.*

Referendumb
24/04/2011

This article was written in the run-up to a national referendum on AV (the 'Alternative Voting' system). Chances are you've forgotten that even happened, especially if you're reading this in 2,000 years time, in which case why are you wasting your time reading this? Other books are available.

With not long to go until the AV referendum, the waters are muddier than ever. It's confusing. One minute the anti-camp claims a vote for AV would benefit the BNP. Then the pro-camp counters by pointing out the BNP are against AV. Therefore, no matter what the outcome, Nick Griffin will both win and lose simultaneously. He'll exist in an uncertain quantum state, like Schrödinger's cat. I say 'cat'. I originally used another word starting with c and ending with t, but the *Guardian* asked me to change it. Suffice to say, Griffin is a massive cat.

It's depressing to see the campaigns on both sides treating the public with such outright contempt. Political ads have rarely been subtle in the past, but this current slew could insult the intelligence of a silverfish. It's not so much that they think we're stupid, but that their attempts to appeal to that perceived stupidity are so stupid in themselves; they've created a sort of self-perpetuating stupidity whirlpool capable of engulfing any loose molecules of logic within a six-mile radius. They might as well replace every billboard with the words VOTE LIKE THIS, DUMMY in four-foot high Helvetica.

The 'No' campaigners are the worst offenders. It started with the adverts that pitched the purported cost of a new voting system against the needs of imperilled newborns. A photo of a delicate, salmon-pink baby was accompanied by the words 'She needs a new cardiac facility – not an alternative vote system. Say NO to spending £250 million on AV. Our country can't afford it.' Apart from the dodgy arithmetic involved in coming up with that figure (the sort of magic maths which involves closing your eyes and repeatedly banging the calculator against your forehead), the idea that we can only have one thing or the other – AV or healthy babies – is such a preposterous argument, even the baby could see through it. And its eyes were covered with placenta. That poster made me resolve, early on, that I would definitely vote Yes to AV, if only as a protest vote against the evil dunderheads who dreamt up the baby campaign.

Having made my mind up, I figured I could then ignore the rest of the campaigning – although in practice it got so noisily stupid, I couldn't. Recently, they've hit on the wheeze of using sport as a metaphor for elections, the idea presumably being that sport has clear winners and losers, and is simple enough for Andy Gray to understand. Different forms of sport show up in most of their recent efforts. There was a TV ad depicting a Grand National-style event in which, thanks to AV, the horse in third place magically finished first. This was unrealistic on two counts: partly because the example they used was impossible, but mainly because all the horses survived.

This was followed by a billboard showing two boxers. One is lying battered and unconscious on the floor – and yet the ref is inexplicably declaring this comatose man the winner. Why? Because, according to the slogan, 'Under AV the loser can win'. Since boxing matches only involve two people, this doesn't even work as a wildly strained metaphor. It's just a lie.

Then some well-known former cricketers popped up on YouTube to moan that AV just isn't cricket. David Gower said, 'I'm used to a system in sport – in cricket specifically – where if you win, you win, and it's as simple as that.' Cricket? Simple? Any sport in which the commentator routinely says things like, 'England are currently 120 for 3 and chasing 257 – so with 7 wickets in hand and 17 overs remaining, they need to hit a run rate of 8.1 an over' is far from bloody simple. Sometimes matches are called off prematurely thanks to rain, at which point the outcome is decided by the Duckworth–Lewis method – which means the teams' performance thus far is run through an equation which looks like this:

$$Z(u,o,\lambda) = ZoF(w)\ \lambda nF(w)+1\ \{1 - exp(-bu/[\lambda nF(w)F(w)])\}$$

If Gower thinks that's simpler than AV, he's a genius. Certainly smarter than, say, Professor Brian Cox. (To see Cox attempting to grasp the Duckworth–Lewis method, visit this URL: bit.ly/gowerisagenius – I'm not joking.)

Interestingly, if you imagine the political parties are cricket teams and run polling data from the last election through the Duckworth–Lewis equation, Nick Griffin wins the Ashes.

Anyway, just when you thought the No camp had a monopoly on absurd campaigning, the Yes campaign go and upload a video on an absurdly emotive par with the No camp's baby billboard. In it, a kindly-looking Second World War naval veteran, slathered with hard-earned medals, explains, in a heartbreakingly fragile voice, that he fought the Nazis in the name of democracy – yet, thanks to our current electoral system, despite voting in every general election for the past sixty-six years, his vote has always been 'confiscated by the system'.

As the camera pans over his medals and heart-rending personal memorabilia, backed with a moody piano soundtrack, he explains that 'for all the say I've had, I might as well have died in the Russian convoys, or on the D-Day beaches, or in the Pacific after that'.

Might as well have died? Thankfully he didn't, despite having his sense of perspective shot off at Dunkirk. No one's doubting his sacrifice, or his right to speak his mind, but the Yes campaign should realise that kind of OTT hyperbole is probably best saved for more cartoonish concerns. Like, say, the No campaign. Or newspaper columns by arseholes such as Richard Littlejohn. Or me.

Royal wedding TV Go Home
27/04/2011

This was a set of mock TV listings written to commemorate the marriage of William and Kate. Just in case you hadn't guessed. Hey, I don't know how clever you are. You could be an absolute bloody idiot for all I know.

8.00 Extreme Dress Conjecture
Top scientists take turns speculating about Kate Middleton's dress, bypassing trite discussion of its potential colour and style in favour of determining its approximate atomic weight, by feeding a schoolgirl's crayon sketch of what it might look like into an onyx supercomputer studded with flashing lights.

9.00 Elephant in the Room Street Party
Live televised royal wedding street party at which, for no particular reason, any discussion of the royal wedding, no matter how tangential, is strictly prohibited, a policy enforced by an emotionless computer-controlled crossbow that automatically executes anyone so much as mentioning it. Survivors win £2,500 for a charity of their choosing.

9.30 The Only Way is Essex Royal Wedding Special
Precisely what you'd expect, but somehow worse.

10.00 Brief Flurry of Excitement as Ben Fogle Arrives at Ceremony

10.15 Fifteen-Minute Pause for Everyone on Twitter to Make Snarky Comment Re Prince William's Hairloss

10.30 I Couldn't Care Less About the Royal Wedding and I Don't Care Who Knows It

Pundits declare their ambivalence towards today's event while standing on brightly coloured plinths clutching armfuls of live chicks in order to make them look slightly silly for bothering.

11.00 Fifteen-Minute Pause for Everyone on Twitter to Make Joke Re Kate Being Taken Up the Aisle

11.15 At the Altar

Live footage of the couple at the altar, accompanied by impromptu ironic commentary ostensibly emanating from within Prince William's head, performed by Peter Dickson, voice of *The X Factor*.

11.20 The Royal Wedding in Solid 3D

Breathtaking coverage of the ceremony utilising a groundbreaking new broadcast system that converts images of the happy couple into devastatingly accurate three-dimensional carved wooden effigies, spilling from your screen in real-time at a rate of twenty-five figurines per second. Samsung Accu-Carve Solid 3D TV required. Caution: may fill house with miniature royals and assorted detritus.

12.00 Fifteen-Minute Pause for Everyone on Twitter to Go a Bit Gooey

12.15 The Bit with the Carriage

During which viewers may choose to speculate about how many hospitals you could buy for the cost of that bejewelled chariot, but alas to no avail, for ye shall be drowned out by the cheering and the merry-making and the joyous hubbub.

1.25pm Balcony Kiss

Your chance to witness the one image certain to dominate every newspaper's front page tomorrow. Unless Prince Harry goes mad and has a shit on the steps of the cathedral and then does a backflip and kicks a girl in the face.

2.00 Endless Endless Loops of Everything You've Just Seen, But Cut Into Slightly Smaller Chunks, Spooling Over and Over and Over With a Newsreader Burbling Over the Top, Repeating and Repeating and Repeating Until You Feel Like Time Itself is a Scratched CD Doomed to Echo the Last Few Notes For Ever and Ever

11.00 The People's Royal Consummation

Eye-popping live interactive special as viewers send in tweets and explicit Photoshopped images outlining precisely what might be happening in the happy couple's bedroom at that precise moment. Pictures too graphic to be broadcast will be described by Eric Cantona and re-enacted by members of the Jim Henson Creature Shop.

Fuck footballers

29/05/2011

The worst thing about the ongoing kerfuffle over superinjunctions is that it keeps forcing me to contemplate the extracurricular activity of men who kick balls around lawns for a living. Since I'm not into sport, I simply don't 'get' the deification of footballers. I can see they've got a demanding physical task to do, and I can appreciate that some do it better than others – but that's the extent of my understanding. When they're not at work, what's so interesting about them? Seriously, what?

It's like living in a world in which half the population has inexplicably decided to worship Shire horses. But, as if that wasn't strange enough, they're not content to simply admire the animals' ability to pull brewery wagons: they also want to know what the horses get up to back at the stables. And when Dobbin goes on a hay-eating binge, or tries to mount a donkey, not only will they voraciously read all about it, they'll judge him for it. They'll phone HoofTalk FM to pontificate on air about what a bad horse he is. In behaving like a simple horse, Dobbin, who is richly rewarded with nosebags and thoroughbred fillies, has committed the ultimate crime: he's set a bad example to their children.

I don't have kids, but I know enough about parenting to state the following with confidence: any parent who is genuinely concerned that their child's worldview might be hopelessly altered by the unruly behaviour of a footballer has failed as a parent.

Footballers, we're told, should be role models. A few months ago, Wayne Rooney swore into the camera during a live televised football match, and the world briefly reacted as though he'd burst into a toddler's birthday party and brutally molested a duckling.

The general consensus was that he was being a bad role model to the nation's kiddywinks. Rubbish. He was being a brilliant role model. He'd just scored a hat-trick – thereby excelling in his chosen field – when a cameraman (who, by all accounts, wasn't supposed to be standing that close to the players) poked a lens in his fizzog. At which point Rooney demonstrated an entirely healthy instinctive disdain for the cameras, for the media, and ultimately for all the hoopla surrounding his primary task, which is kicking balls into nets. He'd just scored a goal and everything else could, quite literally, 'fuck off'. Good for him.

Conversely, anyone who took to the airwaves to huff and whine about Rooney being a poor 'ambassador for the game' was an abysmal role model for children. Remember, kids – it's not how you play the game that matters, but how prosaically servile you are in front of the cameras.

The 'role model' argument is often tied to another popular bone of contention about prominent sportsfolk: their bank balances. During last week's *Question Time*, one member of the audience expressed her disappointment with Ryan Giggs, explaining that his off-pitch behaviour was of particular concern because 'we pay his wages'. Presumably she works in the human resources department of Manchester United.

Athletes earn astronomical sums because that's how society has chosen to reward them. It's wonky and demented, and I don't understand it, but that's the way it is. Corporations, the media and the public have somehow conspired to create that environment. They designed, dug and filled the ornamental fishpond: now they complain when the goldfish shit in the water.

Ah, yes, right, yes, right, but . . . footballers aren't content to rake in obscene amounts of money just by kicking balls around. They sign lucrative sponsorship deals and advertise soft drinks and razorblades. And in those commercials they're depicted as nice guys. But now we know they're not nice guys! They traded off their image! It's a lie! They owe us! They owe us!

No they don't. They owe the sponsors, maybe, if they signed a contract promising to behave like Saint Agnes of Rome. If you, the consumer, are suggestible enough to buy a particular brand of aftershave just because a footballer sploshed it round his cheeks on a billboard, you should take a long hard look at your own malleability. And if you now feel wounded and deceived because he was smiling on the poster, not shagging or snarling, then you're far too fragile for this world. Newsflash: adverts are set in a parallel fantasy realm. That Go Compare tenor? Not only is he miming, that moustache isn't real. Oh, and meerkats aren't Russian. Please stop quaking and remain calm.

Given all the above, what is the indignation about footballers' private lives really all about? Either an outlet for envy and resentment – they're paid too much and celebrated too keenly – or perhaps just a subconsciously adopted psychological position used to excuse our own basic prurience. Let's be honest: we're judgemental and nosy. We want to hear all the juicy details so we can experience the cathartic rush of being enraged by them, like a cuckolded boyfriend demanding a second-by-second account of his girlfriend's infidelity.

Given the alternating streams of adulation and rage flung in their direction, I'm amazed footballers retain their sanity. They exist in a bizarre dimension of banknotes and blowjobs and furious mobs. And all they're supposed to do is kick balls into nets. It's impossible to pity them – but to actively resent them? That's madness. Like shaking your fist at a Shire horse.

If the internet gave free backrubs, people would complain when it stopped because its thumbs were sore
05/06/2011

It's incredible how quickly we humans can develop a languid sense of entitlement over even the simplest of things. For instance, I've spent hours of my waking life in TV comedy writing rooms, which usually consist of about four or five people seated around a table coming up with gags. That's the idea, anyway. The reality often resembles a bizarre group therapy session in which a small cluster of faintly dysfunctional individuals have been encouraged to exorcise their collective anxiety by discussing appalling notions in the most flippant manner imaginable.

You're supposed to remain locked in said chamber until the script is complete – all of you sitting there, breathing in and out and perspiring, with the windows permanently closed, which is why writers' rooms quickly develop the fetid aroma of a becalmed submarine. But it's not quite a hermetically sealed environment. Human beings have to be kept fed and watered, which is why, at periodic intervals, a runner will enter the room to ask if anyone wants a coffee or a can of Coke, to take lunch orders (I have no idea what comedy writers ate before the advent of Nando's), or, if things are really dragging on, to take dinner orders too.

All very cosy. But here's the funny thing: after a few weeks of this, you become hopelessly infantilised. Cans of Coke, for instance, are often stored in a fridge about fifteen seconds' walk from the writers' room. Yet rather than leaving the room to fetch one yourself the moment you're thirsty, it quickly becomes second nature to wait until the runner appears and order it from them. Not because you think they're a waiter, nor even out of sheer laziness, but because you've genuinely on some level 'forgotten' you're capable of locating and opening the fridge yourself. In other words, you're spoiled.

I bring this up because the other day I went online to post a Spotify playlist for people to listen to (if you're visiting from 1903, Spotify is a service that streams music to your computer – think of it as an infinitely huge jukebox. Although being from 1903, you won't know what a jukebox is either. Sorry. Guess you'll just have to fend for yourself).

Anyway, some people listened to it, some people didn't – but some objected to the mere mention and use of Spotify. Spotify, they said, was like Nick Clegg: it had promised one thing, only to turn round and do another. It offered free music for all (supported by ad breaks, like commercial radio), only to recently scale this back to ten hours of free music per month. The reason for the scaleback? Presumably an attempt to make the whole thing financially viable – by encouraging more people to subscribe. Subscribers pay about £5 per month and can listen to as much music as they want, without any ad breaks. If they go up to £10 they can also listen to music on their phones, even while offline.

In 1986, when I was fifteen, a twelve-inch single cost roughly £2.99 – the equivalent of just over £6 today. And unless you were loaded, you didn't just buy records willy-nilly. You chose carefully and coveted what you had. (You also taped loads of them off the radio for nothing, but that often required the will and patience to sit through Bruno Brookes.)

Anyhow. I'm not claiming five quid a month is insignificant:

it's more than many can afford. But in this case it's bloody cheap for what it gets you. The problem for Spotify is that no one wants to pay for anything they access via a computer – and when they do, there's a permanent level of resentment bubbling just under the surface. Hence the anger about 'only' getting ten hours of free music.

Look at the App Store. Read the reviews of novelty games costing 59p. Lots of slaggings – which is fair enough when you're actively warning other users not to bother shelling out for something substandard. But they often don't stop there. In some cases, people insist the developers should be jailed for fraud, just because there weren't enough levels for their liking. I once read an absolutely scathing one-star review in which the author bitterly complained that a game had only kept them entertained for four hours.

FOUR HOURS? FOR 59P? AND YOU'RE ANGRY ENOUGH TO WRITE AN ESSAY ABOUT IT? ON YOUR £400 IPHONE? HAVE YOU LOST YOUR FUCKING MIND?

Yes. Of course they have. Because it's human nature. Like a runner who fetches us cans of drink when we're thirsty, technology has left us hopelessly spoiled. We whine like disappointed emperors the moment it does anything other than pander to our every whim. If the internet gave free backrubs, people would complain when it stopped because its thumbs were sore.

I ranted about precisely this on Twitter the other day – using that precise line about back rubs – and a couple of people told me to shut up because I was annoying them. Since Twitter is a) free and b) only displays commentary from those you chose to follow, this, too, is madness – like tailing someone down the street only to complain about the tune they've chosen to hum.

And even now, because these words too will appear on the internet, I know someone, somewhere, will be formulating a complaint in their head because I've reused my 'free internet back rubs' tweet in this article. They'd read it on Twitter last week, and now they're dismayed to have to read it on their computer again today. Your Majesty is displeased. I've let myself down but more importantly, I've let them down. As has everything that provides anything other than perpetual complimentary delight.

And having written that, at home, alone, I'm off down the shops. To get a can of Coke. Assuming I can remember how.

If the *Daily Mail* is so worried about the sexualisation of children, all they have to do is hit 'delete'
12/06/2011

Hey you – what are you doing to halt the sexualisation of children? We know it's happening. It must be. It's in the papers and on the news all the time, usually accompanied by a photograph of a kiddy-size T-shirt with 'Future Pornstar' on it or a padded bikini designed for eight-year-olds. What next? Lapdancing poles for foetuses? Jesus. What can we do about it? Easy: pretend sex simply doesn't exist. Like the Tooth Fairy myth, but in reverse. Next time a child asks you where babies come from, just shrug, then ask them what a 'baby' is.

I don't have a child, but I was one once (still am, come to think of it). It was different in my day. Sexual imagery wasn't shoved in your face, unless you watched TV or looked at a magazine or newspaper or walked past a billboard advertising absolutely anything.

The rudest imagery appeared in schools – scrawled in the margins of exercise books. That iconic schoolboy's doodle – the puerile 'spunking knob' – how did we know what that looked like? It's like a cave painting symbolising not fertility, but gleeful stupidity; an image hard-wired into the mind of every sniggering boy in Britain. Everyone smiles inside when they see the spunking knob scrawled in the dust on the back of a van, or scribbled on a poster. Is it a global phenomenon? Strikes me as inherently British. It should've been our logo for the 2012 Olympics.

But I digress. It's perhaps more accurate to say that 'saucy and sexist' imagery abounded when I was a kiddywink. Legs & Co on *Top of the Pops*. Barbara Windsor losing her top in *Carry On Camping*. When I was about seven, I loved the animated 'Captain Kremmen' sequences from Kenny Everett's original ITV show, partly because they included a character called 'Carla' who was an insanely buxom cross between Lieutenant Uhura and Marilyn Monroe: probably my first TV crush. The cartoon was jam-packed with double-entendres, which zoomed over my head, but there was no mistaking Carla's, um, impact.

Generally, the early TV and films I encountered depicted 'sexy women' as non-threatening airheads (except when attempting to seduce Kenneth Williams for comic effect), while sex in general was discussed with a nudge, a wink and an accompanying swannee whistle. Come to think of it, that's another mystery: is there a less sexy noise than the swannee whistle? How did that become the default acoustic signifier for 'erecting penis' or 'rude insertion'? Imagine the sound effects they'd use in a modern hardcore version of a Carry On film. It'd probably end with a spluttering duck call.

As for actual porn – the closest you got to that was finding a discarded copy of *Mayfair* in a hedge near a road, which would then be circulated among all the pre-pubescents in the vicinity like a secret dossier. There was an implicit understanding that this material was not aimed at us, but rather at the lorry driver who'd lobbed it into the hedge on his way home. Thankfully, it never occurred to any of us to contemplate what he'd probably been doing while 'reading' it. We genuinely believed the pages were stuck together because the magazine had been rained on.

Innocent times. I'd hate to be an adolescent today, with the internet providing a bottomless filthpit to gawp at. How in God's name are they supposed to focus on exams? Or even eating, come to that?

But apart from the net, we're worried when the likes of Beyoncé prance about in provocative outfits, because some little girls try to copy them. I can't work out if that's better, worse, or essentially the same as me pretending I was James Bond machine-gunning henchmen as a child. Beyoncé, at least, seems tougher than Bond ever did.

The *Daily Mail*, however, isn't a fence-sitting wuss like me. Last year, outraged by Christina Aguilera and Rihanna's raunchy pre-watershed dancing on *The X Factor*, it ran a fuming article accompanied by shocking pictures of the most extreme bits, which helped fuel thousands of complaints.

Later, Ofcom agreed that the routines were 'at the limit of acceptability', but went on to say the images in the *Mail* article were 'significantly more graphic and close-up than the material broadcast and had been taken from a different angle to the TV cameras . . . Readers would have been left with the impression that the programme contained significantly more graphic material than had actually been broadcast.'

The *Mail* wouldn't let it lie. 'In fact, the pictures we used were provided by ITV and *The X Factor*'s official photographic agency, with the exception of one screen grab of the show's transmission', it complained last week. That's odd: responding to the criticism that the images hadn't been broadcast by confirming they hadn't been broadcast. Next they'll be printing artists' impressions of Adrian Chiles's genitals and complaining they'd been spotted on *Daybreak*, beneath his trousers.

Still, the thrust of the *Mail*'s article was that Ofcom is toothless and pre-watershed TV should be less sexy. That's its opinion, and it's got every right to hold it.

But as I was reading the article on their website, my eye was drawn to a variety of other raunchy images running down the righthand side: *Hollyoaks* actress Jennifer Metcalfe 'shows off her fuller figure in a bikini as she films *Hollyoaks* in Ibiza'; 'The Saturdays hog the limelight in hotpants'; 'Lady Gaga parades down a runway in see-through dress'; 'Katy Perry spoofs Janet Jackson's boob-baring "wardrobe malfunction" in new video' . . . and so on, and so on. Starlets and sex, sex and starlets – all of it in plain view on the *Daily Mail* website which, to the best of my knowledge, has no age restrictions in place: nothing even approaching a watershed. A child as young as four could be exposed to Katy Perry's breasts over breakfast. I bet even Russell Brand thinks that's going a bit far.

At the time of writing, if you type 'Lady Gaga' into Google, the top result is the *Mail*'s 'see-through dress' story, full of smutty pictures. Must they fling this filth at impressionable young kids? Won't somebody at the *Mail* please, for once, just think of the children?

Glasto no-show
26/06/2011

So, Glastonbury. How was yours? Mine was pretty good. I was standing just offstage when Jessie J encouraged that little girl from the crowd to join her for a duet of 'Price Tag'. Watching the delight on their faces, I suffered an uncharacteristic fit of emotion and wept with sheer joy, crying all the fluid out of my skull in the process, which was rough on my brain: it became so desiccated and sore it hurt to think about anything other than ice cubes.

A short while later someone stuffed an unmarked pill into my hand and in my addled state, I foolishly swallowed it. Twenty minutes later my palms felt like they were made of static electricity and I couldn't tell whether my legs were my own or someone else's I was standing inside by mistake. Reality itself had been hacked and inverted by Lulzsec. Six hours later I lay vomiting in the mud while listening to Mumford & Sons, trying to work out which was worse.

Obviously none of the above actually happened because I didn't go to Glastonbury. But since this is a special edition of the *Guardian*, with the word 'Glastonbury' running through it like a cheeky slogan through a stick of rock, anything non-Glastonbury would stand out like a dog in a sandwich.

At the time of writing, I'm not sure what the news in the paper will consist of, but even if there's a nuclear war in Canada, chances are someone'll shoehorn a Glastonbury reference into it. 'The deadly fireball erupted with the ferocity of a million blazing suns ... the world hasn't witnessed a lightshow this spectacular since U2's Friday headline slot at Glastonbury.'

I caught a bit of U2's set. I don't know if you noticed, but the BBC had a few cameras at Glastonbury this year. You could watch kiddy acts on BBC3, paunchy legends on BBC4, and mainstream brands on BBC2. U2 are so massive they stretched across both BBC2 and 4.

Prior to the act taking the stage, three separate groups of presenters threw to each other in a series of apparently random outside broadcast links, followed by a pre-recorded burst of the Vaccines, who I couldn't be arsed getting into. This is one of the benefits of ageing. Then U2 took the stage and everybody cheered. Why?

Several years ago I wrote an article in which I pondered the mystery of the Red Hot Chili Peppers, who somehow managed to be one of the biggest bands in the world despite apparently having no fans whatsoever. I based my theory, which I admit may be flawed, on personal experience: since I'd never met one person who claimed to like them, I decided the whole thing had to be a sinister con. Or possibly something to do with dark matter.

Well, U2 are the same. I've never met anyone claiming to be a fan. Statistically there should be millions of U2-mad individuals in Britain – so where are they? Are they hiding? Why are they hiding? What are they hiding? OK, everyone secretly likes 'One' and 'The Sweetest Thing', and 'Stuck in a Moment', and ... hang on, I'm supposed to be taking the piss out of U2 here, so I'd better mention Bono.

I only watched about ten minutes of U2's set because I find Bono so annoying. I'm aware this is an experience almost as universal as knowing what wearing a T-shirt feels like, but still: it's true. He wore his trademark Bono sunglasses. I've become so accustomed to seeing him in them, I've come to believe they're actually part of his face. At one point I thought he was sweating through his glasses, before I realised it was drizzle. Not drizzle, rain. Apparently it was raining like a tantrum in a piss factory. The sky was disrespecting Bono. For some reason, it's funny that it rained during U2. It just is.

The following day, the screens were far sunnier, which was almost enough to cause a glimmer of jealousy until I remembered the mud. Glastonbury looks like amazing fun if you're twenty-three and running around covered in glitter. I'm not twenty-three, I hate tents, I dislike any form of discomfort or even mild inconvenience, I prefer recorded music to live gigs and I rarely drink any more, so it's Good But It's Not For Me.

I wish I'd gone when I was twenty-three, but I didn't. I was too busy lying stoned on a sofa in west London to bother upping sticks to lie stoned in a yurt in west Britain. I've been once, in my thirties, on behalf of the *Guardian*, and it was all pleasant enough, but so is jam on toast. It's a town the size of Bath! And so is Bath.

Here was an interesting thing I discovered during Glastonbury 2011: did you know that when BBC2 goes off-air at 2 a.m., the BBC sometimes still shows *Pages from Ceefax*? It's like someone's plugged a BBC Micro into your TV. I think it was showing headlines from 1956. Incredible it still works. They probably have to type all the stories on a calculator and save them to a 3.5-inch floppy disk and upload them to Ceefax's 128 kb memory.

Anyway: Glastonbury. Next week, more Glastonbury, unless you're lucky and there's a nuclear war.

We can't go on like this
03/07/2011

By now, there's a good chance you've seen the video of Ed Miliband using almost precisely the same words over and over again in an interview. If you haven't, it's well worth seeking out. The reporter asks him five different questions about the public sector strikes, and every time, Miliband says that he thinks the strikes are wrong while negotiations are still under way, that the government has acted in a reckless and provocative manner, and that it's time for both sides to put aside the rhetoric and get round the negotiating table. He repeats identical phrases *ad nauseam*. It sounds like an interview with a satnav stuck on a roundabout. Or a novelty talking keyring with its most boring button held down. Or a character in a computer game with only one dialogue option. Or an Ed Miliband-shaped phone with an Ed Miliband-themed ringtone. Or George Osborne.

Yes, George Osborne. Because shortly after posting a link to the Miliband video online, someone drew my attention to a similar clip of Osborne dating from late last year, in which the fourteen-year-old Chancellor answers a series of different questions about the economy by reciting a single soundbite over and over, like a mantra.

This in turn reminded me of a clip I'd stumbled across during research for an episode of *Newswipe*, in which Alistair Darling spent five minutes repeating an identical phrase about 'global recession' over and over. At the time I'd figured it was a one-off. Clearly it's not. It's a standard gambit.

All three clips are terrifying. First you think you're hearing things. Then you wonder whether time itself has developed hiccups. Finally you decide none of these people can possibly be human. Because they look absolutely, unequivocally insane.

And if it looks weird on tape, imagine how it felt actually being there, standing in front of them, asking the questions. Actually, you don't have to imagine it – you can read an insider's description of it. ITN's Damon Green, the reporter who was putting the questions to Miliband, has written an entertaining and very illuminating behind-the-curtain blogpost about the experience.

The first interesting thing is just how twatty the Miliband PR handlers appear to have been, demanding their man be positioned 'in front of his bookcase, with his family photos over his left shoulder', and insisting on checking the shot themselves, like a trio of dull Stanley Kubricks. (Interestingly, Green also notes that David Cameron's handlers apparently 'never let him be filmed in front of anything expensive, ornate, or strikingly Etonian'. Presumably for similar reasons they also forbid him to be photographed in front of heartless chunks of moneyed shit.)

Anyway, after posing several questions only to receive oblivious identikit responses from Miliband, Green says: 'I began getting twinges of what I can only describe as existential doubt.' By the end he wanted to ask him: 'What is the world's fastest fish?', just to throw him off-stride. (Kudos to Green for a) being funny and b) describing how weird the Miliband encounter actually felt. Not usually a political correspondent, it was a new experience for him.)

The reason for the Speak-and-Spell tactic is obvious: in all three cases (Miliband, Osborne, Darling) the PR handler responsible must have figured that since the interview would be whittled down to one ten-second soundbite for that evening's news bulletins, and since they didn't want to risk their man saying any-thing ill-advised or vaguely interesting, they might as well merely ignore all the questions and impersonate an iPod with just one track on it. What's unusual is that it's taken until now for one of these unedited interviews to go a bit viral. The Darling interview took place at least two years ago. The BBC News site often plays host to what amount to unedited rushes, which are sometimes more instructive than a final packaged report. As far as I can tell, the 'Miliband loop', as it shall now be known, first materialised there (despite being conducted by an ITN reporter, it was a 'pool' interview for all channels to use). The BBC site is also where the Osborne and Darling clips ended up. In all three cases they were unaccompanied by any comment about the repetitive lunacy contained within. No 'WARNING: WATCHING THIS MIGHT MAKE YOU FEEL A BIT MAD.' None of that.

What this tells you is that many people working in TV news have grown so accustomed to seeing tapes in which politicians blankly replicate a single phrase as if they're summoning Candyman, it no longer strikes them as unusual.

But it is unusual: bloody unusual. You might say it symbolises everything that's wrong with everything. The modern world suffers from a cavernous reality deficit. You know it, I know it. Even 'they' know it. Reciting the same line over and over like a *Countryfile* presenter practising a piece to camera, Miliband must have felt twice as mad as Green. Two men locked in a shared hallucination while the camera rolled.

It's no surprise that politicians gabble pre-scripted taglines in order to dodge awkward questions and avoid having off-the-cuff comments inflated into a full-blown gaffe. And it's no surprise the media routinely colludes in this surreal pantomime. But it's only when you stand back and watch the rushes that you see how crazy the situation has become. Honestly, it gives you vertigo.

Clearly an intervention is necessary. Next time you pass an MP being interviewed on the street, set off a party popper. Jump in and shriek. Get your bum out. Anything. Just to prompt some kind of authentic human reaction from either side.

Because we can't go on like this. It's just too damn weird.

The end of the *News of the World*
10/07/2011

Today I bought the *News of the World*. Last week I'd joined in with the obligatory Twitter hashtag-boycott-pass-the-parcel, but now I had a brilliant excuse for scabbing out: I'd been asked to read the final edition for this paper. Having fashioned a disguise from dirt and wool, I cycled to the newsagents at 7.30 a.m., to find they were already selling fast. Clearly the boycott was having an effect. Having secured a copy, I made my excuses and left – after hiding it inside a necro-zoophiliac porn mag, so any passers-by outside wouldn't judge me too harshly.

I've bought the 'Screws' countless times before. I used to buy it almost every week, bundled alongside a less 'embarrassing' purchase (i.e. a broadsheet). Over lunch I'd lay the papers out in front of me and invariably find myself reaching for the Screws first. I'd read about shagging chefs, chortle at a gaudy Franklin Mint ad for a souvenir Princess Di porcelain windmill collection, and feel vaguely superior for about ten minutes. That's liberals for you.

Sometimes I'd be revolted by the way it casually vandalised human lives: exposing some hitherto unknown woman as a 'vice girl', say, just to fill half a page. But a few weeks later my disgust would fade, and I'd pick up another copy. Bad for me – but I didn't stop buying it, just as I didn't stop buying cigarettes. It was the nineties, and I was young and dumb enough to view the world as a big cartoon. I smoked with the force and frequency of a man hell-bent on turning his lungs into a pair of charcoal slippers, in the belief that cancer couldn't catch me. In much the same spirit I'd read the *News of the World* 'ironically', like an arsehole.

I can't remember when things changed (my *NoW* habit that is, not my arseholery – that's permanent), but at some point around the millennium I tired of laughing at the novelty plate ads and began to find the rest of the paper too grim to eat.

But never as grim as the past week, in which the paper (or more accurately, the paper's past) leaked diseased pus by the bucket: another litre of scandal every day. By Monday evening, former editor Rebekah Brooks's reputation was in tatters. By Wednesday those tatters had been tattered again. By the time Brooks was telling staff that they'd fully understand the closure 'in a year's time' (presumably because it'll take 365 days to explain the full horror), her reputational tatterettes were shredded yet further: they currently exist in an unstable sub-atomic state visible only to her mind's eye.

The final edition is downright odd. If I were editor, I'd have scrawled nobs all over the front and plastered a cut-out-and-keep effigy of Brooks across the centre pages. Instead, the front page mumbles 'THANK YOU AND GOODBYE' over a collage of previous headlines.

Inside is an account of the paper's history so rose-tinted you can smell the petals, focusing on its scoops and ignoring ghastly low points like the 1988 story about the actor David Scarboro (who played *EastEnders*' Mark Fowler before Todd Carty), in which it printed images of the psychiatric unit where he was receiving treatment. He later killed himself.

In 2009 a *NoW* editorial attacked this paper's phone-hacking coverage as 'inaccurate, selective and purposely misleading'. 'NO INQUIRIES, NO CHARGES, NO EVIDENCE' it thundered. 'Like the rest of the media, we have made mistakes . . . When we have done so, we have admitted to them.'

Yet today, apart from a brief mention about the paper 'losing its way' on page three, the closest the final edition gets to addressing the scale of the scandal comes in Carole Malone's column: a page that has previously functioned as a rectangular bin full of tutting, spite and rabble-rousing lies about illegal immigrants being given 'free cars'. This week she bemoans the paper's demise, but also says the relatives of murder victims have been 'blighted by the actions of this newspaper', describes the hacking as 'indefensible', and says she's 'sorry for the sins of people who've hurt you and who shame us all'.

The centre pages consist of a gallery of their 'greatest hits': curiously underwhelming when it's all laid out. The Profumo scandal and Jeffrey Archer are in there, but so are three 'gotcha!' snaps of celebs snorting coke – one of whom, Kerry Katona, was captured by a camera hidden in her own bathroom. Call me squeamish, but I'd say concealing a lens in a woman's bathroom is worse than hacking her phone. At least voicemails can't reveal which hand she wipes her arse with.

Also nestled amongst the roster of glorious front pages – 'JACKO'S DEATHBED': a photograph of the rumpled sheets on which Michael Jackson died. Yum! Proud of that, are they? Why, yes: hence its inclusion in their farewell souvenir. At least they didn't include a little collectible square of his skin.

The rest of the paper includes beach snaps of Gwyneth Paltrow, and some jovial bibble about footballers' haircuts, but also a strong investigative piece exposing a sex trafficker. Across other pages, bite-sized tributes from readers are scattered like croutons. 'Britain will never be the same again,' claims one. (Spoiler: yes it will.)

There's also a gracious sign-off from Ian Hyland, and a self-indulgent final edition of Dan Wootton's XS showbiz column peppered with snaps of a grinning Wootton crushed against a series of celebrities as though trying to physically graft himself onto them, accompanied by messages from stars assuring him of his award-winning brilliance. A galaxy of anxious neediness compressed into one double-page spread.

Still, if the edition's overall tone is more sentimental than apologetic, it's hardly surprising, given that it was assembled by a team who – whatever you think of them – didn't hack a murdered schoolgirl's phone. Regardless, they lose their jobs; the woman who was editor at the time keeps hers. Thank you Rebekah. And goodbye to your staff.

Murdochalypse Now
17/07/2011

You know the liberating feeling when someone unpopular leaves the room and everyone breathes a sigh of relief before openly discussing how much they dislike them? I don't. What's it like? What do people say? I only ever catch the odd whisper as the door shuts behind me. I'd love to hear the full conversation. Fortunately, watching Britain's politicians queue up to denounce Rupert Murdoch has given me a taste of how such talk might play out.

A few weeks ago, Murdoch, or rather the more savage tendencies of the press as a whole, represented God. Fear of God isn't always a bad thing in itself, if it keeps you on the straight and narrow – but politicians behaved like medieval villagers who didn't just believe in Him, but quaked at the mere suggestion of a glimmer of a whisper of His name. You must never anger God. God wields immense power. God can hear everything you say. You must worship God, and please Him, or He will destroy you. For God controls the sun, which may shine upon you, or singe you to a Kinnock. Soon he will control the entire sky.

Furthermore, like all mere humans, you are weak. And God knows you have sinned. Chances are he even has long-lens photographs to prove it. But even as he chooses to smite you, God is merciful. You can do this the easy way or the hard way. Confess your sins in an exclusive double-page interview, or face the torments of hell. Have you seen what happens in hell? It isn't pretty. Rows of the damned having buckets of molten shit poured over their heads by someone who looks a bit like Kelvin MacKenzie, for eternity.

But then suddenly everything changed. The revelations over the hacking of grieving relatives' voicemails were the equivalent of a tornado ripping through an orphanage. 'What kind of God would allow such a thing?' asked the villagers, wading through the aftermath. And they started to suspect He didn't exist.

They thought about the hours and days they'd spent in church, saying their prayers, rocking on their knees, whipping themselves with knotted rope, or flying round the world to address one of God's conferences, and they grew angry.

One by one they stood up to decry God. 'He's a sod,' said one. 'No he's not, he's a monster,' said another. Eventually they formed the consensus view that he was a sodmonster.

These protests grew so loud, God abandoned his bid to command the sky, issued personal apologies, and even seemed to wither – to physically wither before our very eyes, a bit like Gollum. (Although Gollum was never snapped in the back of a car in a baseball cap and running shorts, cocking his leg slightly in an apparent bid to stop one of his nuts dangling free, which is a crying shame.)

The danger now is that the villagers, shorn of their belief in God, might abandon their fear of divine retribution altogether, muzzle the churches, and grow hopelessly decadent. I realise as I type this that I don't fully understand my own metaphor any more. So here's a new one: the ceaseless parade of MPs openly disparaging everything they used to slavishly revere has left recent news coverage resembling the finale of the science-fiction movie *They Live*, in which a perception-altering alien transmitter is destroyed and humankind suddenly awakens from a decades-long trance. (Mind you, that's nothing: one day a politician will launch an open and sustained assault on the *Daily Mail*, which will probably culminate in scenes identical to the opening of the ark of the covenant at the end of *Raiders of the Lost Ark*.)

Likening the saga to an existing movie seems fitting, given the online speculation regarding who'll play who when it inevitably becomes a 180-minute Bafta-winning motion picture – Nicole Kidman as Rebekah Brooks, Nick Frost as Tom Watson, Hugh Grant as himself, Steve Coogan as both himself and Paul McMullan etc., etc.

The trickiest role to cast is surely Andy Hayman, the former Metropolitan Police assistant commissioner whose appalling delivery of a key line managed to turn the select committee hearing into an unconvincing TV movie version of itself while it was actually happening. 'Good God! Absolutely not! I can't believe you asked me that!' he spluttered, like a man hell-bent on failing an *Emmerdale* audition. It was excruciating enough on television. Imagine having to sit there and watching it live. Keith Vaz probably clenched his buttcheeks so hard they tore the fabric off his chair seat.

How, precisely, is the actor who eventually plays Hayman supposed to convey the 'Good God! Absolutely not!' moment with any degree of authenticity without destroying his career in the process? Emulate it perfectly and the entire audience will assume you're useless.

Perhaps it'd be better to discard the movie idea altogether and instead turn the saga into a video game, with Brooks as one of the end-of-level bosses. After all, the phone-hacking pile-on is the equivalent of the moment where the player discovers the conspicuous glowing nodule just under its tail and concentrates his fire on that weak spot. As its life gauge starts to fall, the embattled monster desperately sheds blameless *News of the World* staff in an attempt to draw fire away from itself, but to no avail. Two-thirds of the way through, the weakened beast flashes red and starts tossing fizzing bombs in your direction – the day the *Sun* printed the pugilistic 'BROWN WRONG' front page roughly equates to that bit. Finally, it explodes in a shower of scarlet locks. Or resigns and leaves Wapping in a car.

Available: Q4 2011 on Xbox 360, PS3 and Wii. £39.99. Pre-order now to guarantee abject disappointment.

Bad news from Norway

24/07/2011

I went to bed in a terrible world and awoke inside a worse one. At the time of writing, details of the Norwegian atrocity are still emerging, although the identity of the perpetrator has now been confirmed and his motivation seems increasingly clear: a far-right anti-Muslim extremist who despised the ruling party.

Presumably he wanted to make a name for himself, which is why I won't identify him. His name deserves to be forgotten. Discarded. Deleted. Labels like 'madman', 'monster', or 'maniac' won't do, either. There's a perverse glorification in terms like that. If the media's going to call him anything, it should call him pathetic: a nothing.

On Friday night's news, they were calling him something else. He was a suspected terror cell with probable links to al-Qaida. Countless security experts queued up to tell me so. This has all the hallmarks of an al-Qaida attack, they said. Watching at home, my gut feeling was that that didn't add up. Why Norway? And why was it aimed so specifically at one political party? But hey, they're the experts. They're sitting there behind a caption with the word 'EXPERT' on it. Every few minutes the anchor would ask, 'What kind of picture is emerging?' or 'What sense are you getting of who might be responsible?' and every few minutes they explained this was 'almost certainly' the work of a highly organised Islamist cell.

In the aftermath of the initial bombing, they proceeded to wrestle with the one key question: why do Muslims hate Norway? Luckily, the experts were on hand to expertly share their expert solutions to plug this apparent plot hole in the ongoing news narrative.

Why do Muslims hate Norway? There had to be a reason.

Norway was targeted because of its role in Afghanistan. Norway was targeted because Norwegian authorities had recently charged an extremist Muslim cleric. Norway was targeted because one of its newspapers had reprinted the controversial Danish cartoons of the Prophet Muhammad.

Norway was targeted because, compared to the US and UK, it is a 'soft target' – in other words, they targeted it because no one expected them to.

When it became apparent that a shooting was under way on Utoya island, the security experts upgraded their appraisal. This was no longer a Bali-style al-Qaida bombing, but a Mumbai-style al-Qaida massacre. On and on went the conjecture, on television, and in online newspapers, including this one. Meanwhile, on Twitter, word was quickly spreading that, according to eye-witnesses, the shooter on the island was a blond man who spoke Norwegian. At this point I decided my initial gut reservations about al-Qaida had probably been well founded. But who was I to contradict the security experts? A blond Norwegian gunman doesn't fit the traditional profile, they said, so maybe we'll need to reassess . . . but let's not forget that al-Qaida have been making efforts to actively recruit 'native' extremists: white folk who don't arouse suspicion. So it's probably still the Muslims.

Soon, the front page of Saturday's *Sun* was rolling off the presses. '"Al-Qaeda" Massacre: Norway's 9/11' – the weasel quotes around the name 'Al-Qaeda' deemed sufficient to protect the paper from charges of jumping to conclusions.

By the time I went to bed, it had become clear to anyone within glancing distance of the internet that this had more in common with the 1995 Oklahoma bombing or the 1999 London nail-bombing campaign than the more recent horrors of al-Qaida.

While I slept, the bodycount continued to rise, reaching catastrophic proportions by the morning. The next morning I switched on the news and the al-Qaida talk had been largely dispensed with, and the pundits were now experts on far-right extremism, as though they'd been on a course and qualified for a diploma overnight.

Some remained scarily defiant in the face of the new unfolding reality. On Saturday morning I saw a Fox News anchor tell former US diplomat John Bolton that Norwegian police were saying this appeared to be an Oklahoma-style attack, then ask him how that squared with his earlier assessment that al-Qaida were involved. He was sceptical. It was still too early to leap to conclusions, he said. We should wait for all the facts before rushing to judgment. In other words: assume it's the Muslims until it starts to look like it isn't – at which point, continue to assume it's them anyway.

If anyone reading this runs a news channel, please, don't clog the airwaves with fact-free conjecture unless you're going to replace the word 'expert' with 'guesser' and the word 'speculate' with 'guess', so it'll be absolutely clear that when the anchor asks the expert to speculate, they're actually just asking a guesser to guess. Also, choose better guessers. Your guessers were terrible, like toddlers hypothesising how a helicopter works. I don't know anything about international terrorism, but even I outguessed them.

As more information regarding the identity of the terrorist responsible for the massacre comes to light, articles attempting to explain his motives are starting to appear online. And beneath them are comments from readers, largely expressing outrage and horror. But there are a disturbing number that start, 'What this lunatic did was awful, but . . .'

These 'but' commenters then go on to discuss immigration, often with reference to a shaky Muslim-baiting story they've half-remembered from the press. So despite this being a story about an anti-Muslim extremist killing Norwegians who weren't Muslim, they've managed to find a way to keep the finger of blame pointing at the Muslims, thereby following a narrative lead they've been fed for years, from the overall depiction of terrorism as an almost exclusively Islamic pursuit, outlined by 'security experts' quick to see al-Qaida tentacles everywhere, to the fabricated tabloid fairytales about 'Muslim-only loos' or local councils 'banning Christmas'.

We're in a frightening place. Guesswork won't lead us to safety.

Blue-sky timewasting
31/07/2011

If you can judge a man by the company he keeps, David Cameron is a pinball machine. Look at the random bunch of advisers he hangs – or in one case hung – around with. Just look at them.

First, Andy Coulson, the Essex-boy 'man of the people' who rose to become editor of the nation's foremost grieving-relative surveillance unit. At the other end of the spectrum, George Gideon Oliver King Rameses Osborne, fourteen-year-old novelty Chancellor and future baronet of Ballentaylor and Ballylemon – a man so posh he probably weeps champagne. And finally, at the opposing end of the spectrum to the other end of the spectrum – thereby hopelessly triangulating the spectrum – we have 'blue-sky' policy guru Steve Hilton, who apparently wanders around Downing Street barefoot, 'thinking outside the box' like some groovy CEO.

Imagine sitting in a meeting room trying to make sense of that lot. Imagine them collectively giving you policy advice over a tea urn and a platter of sandwiches. Andy darkly gruffing and grumping and breaking off every few minutes to check the *Guardian* homepage on his iPhone. Gideon wondering how many coins there are in a pound then snorting through his nose as he draws a penis murdering a tramp on his satchel. Steve idly tossing a Hacky Sack around and suggesting the next Cabinet meeting should be held in a birthing pool. Talk about conflicting approaches. The cognitive dissonance would grow so loud you'd turn olive and giddy. And then you wouldn't know which one to vomit over first. (Although since you're David Cameron, the correct answer is 'yourself'.)

Andy and Gideon we're familiar with, of course. Andy is the sinister man in the slow-mo shots on the news, and Gideon is the naughty boy who's broken the economy. But Steve is more of a mystery. I've only ever glimpsed him in still photographs and a bit of news archive of him sitting on a bench somewhere.

Last week, the aura of mystery was punctured somewhat after the *Financial Times* printed a leaked list of some of his bluer 'blue-sky' ideas, such as the abolition of maternity leave and the closure of Job Centres. Ministers were quick to point out none of this was going to become official policy – rather, this was all a bit of amusing crazy talk designed to kick-start internal discussions. You know, an icebreaker – like opening a meeting by suggesting everyone follows you down to the local duck pond to watch you chop the head off a swan with some shears. It gets people talking. The swan's head stays on – the swan was never in danger – but some truly ground-breaking concepts might spin out of the ensuing debate. Only by thinking the unthinkable can we define what's thinkable. The swan has to die in our heads to survive in our hearts. Or something.

Previously, such out-there thought-riffing led Hilton to suggest the use of nascent 'cloudbusting' technology to create longer summers – no, really – and more famously, to dream up the 'big society'. Frustratingly for Hilton's critics, who like to paint him as a sort of misguided guff engine, the big society has been a resounding, concrete success. From the weeniest village to the hugest metropolis, there's a solar-powered big society community hugspace on every corner, staffed by volunteers in unicorn costumes. I can't recall the last time an authentic grass-roots movement captured the public imagination on such a grand scale, apart perhaps from T-Mobile's 2009 'Josh's band' advertising campaign, which culminated in a feelgood hit single that stayed at number one for seventy-nine consecutive weeks, IN T-MOBILE'S MAD MIND.

Anyway, most of the focus thus far has been on Hilton's laid-back dress sense and the Professor Branestawm wackiness of his ideas, which started out funny but seem less tittersome the more extreme they become. But what sticks in my craw is the sheer stinking, blunted crapness of them.

'Nudge unit'. 'Big society'. 'Hug a hoodie'. They sound like the titles of nauseating business-psychobabble books: the sort of timewasting *Who Moved My Cheese?* groovy CEO bullshit routinely found cluttering the shelves of every airport bookshop in the world. As well as being a pallid substitute for actual creativity – a device for making grey business wonks mistake themselves for David Bowie at his experimental peak – these books are the direct suit-and-tie office-dick equivalent of those embarrassing motivational self-help tomes that prey on the insecure, promising to turn their life around before dissolving into a blancmange of 'strategies' and 'systems' and above all excruciating metaphors.

Be honest. We've all read at least one of these personal empowerment classics. Or at least riffled through it in a bookshop. Any idiot could churn one out. In fact, let's write one now.

We'll call it *Break in Your Lifehorse*. Chapter 1: imagine your hopes and dreams are a galloping stallion, wild and untamed. Chapter 2: now picture yourself throwing a glowing lasso of light around its neck. Chapter 3: the dream stallion tries to jerk away from you, but if you dig in your heels and whisper at it, it will eventually calm down. Chapter 4: while it grazes, unsuspecting – leap on and saddle up! Chapter 5: ride it through the canyons of doubt and over the horizon of fear. Congratulations! You're achieve-anating! That'll be £10.99 thanks. Don't forget to visit our website to buy the official Lifehorse Grooming Kit containing exclusive workcharts and a guide to customising your saddle. Coming soon: *Break in Your Lovehorse* (relationship healage for the recently bewildered), and *Break in Your Lifepony* (successanising strategies for the under-twelves.)

There you go. Beam an e-copy of that to Hilton's Kindle, and I guarantee there'll be a Lifehorse in every nudge unit by 2013. Unless he's imagineered his way to having us all diced up and fed to the swans by big society shock troopers as part of some Rainbownomics initiative by then. Which is inevitable. Inevitable.

Kill them all
07/08/2011

The death penalty debate refuses to die – a bit like seventeen-year-old Willie Francis, who in 1946 was strapped into a chair at Louisiana State Penitentiary and electrocuted, only to wind up screaming for mercy from within his leather hood, selfishly upsetting several onlookers in the process.

The United Kingdom hasn't hanged anyone since 1964, when Peter Allen and Gwynne Evans were simultaneously sent to the gallows, in an audacious end-of-season finale. In the intervening years, the capital punishment argument has resurfaced now and then, usually in the wake of an especially harrowing murder trial, when the mob's a bit twitchy. But it has always been a bit of a non-debate.

Proponents of the death penalty – 'nooselovers' or 'danglefans', as they like to be known – often come across as a bit old-fashioned, as though they're opposed to progress in all its forms, and might as well be arguing in favour of fewer crisp flavours and slower Wi-Fi. This fusty impression isn't helped when every news article about hanging is illustrated with vintage black and white photographs of Derek Bentley and Ruth Ellis, as if tying a rope around someone's neck and dropping them through a trapdoor in the hope of causing a fatal bilateral fracture of the C_2 vertebra is the kind of behaviour that belongs in the past.

But now the debate has returned with an exciting new technological twist: thanks to the government's exciting e-petition initiative in which any motion attracting over 100,000 signatories becomes eligible for debate in the House of Commons, the danglefans are suddenly on the cutting edge of populist online activism. Or rather they would be, if they were proposing a suitably cutting-edge method of execution. Instead, it's just a load of vague blah about reinstating 'the death penalty'.

What sort of death penalty? The gallows? The chair? The gas chamber? Come on, this is the internet. The least you could do is rustle up a Flash animation depicting precisely how you want these people to be killed. You could even make it interactive: maybe have a fun preamble in which we shake the prisoner's hand in order to guess his weight and adjust the length of the rope accordingly. Or a bit where we get to pull a leather hood over the screaming head of a petrified teenager with learning difficulties, then pull the switch and hear his kidneys boil.

Of course, anyone proposing the use of the noose or the chair is guilty of moral cowardice anyway. Capital punishment is supposed to act as a deterrent, but it doesn't seem to have much effect on crime statistics. This is because most current executions a) employ methods that are as quick and efficient as possible and b) take place behind closed doors – almost as though the people doing it are ashamed of themselves.

What sort of half-arsed half-measure is that? Cold logic dictates that the only way to turn capital punishment into an effective deterrent is to make each killing as drawn-out and public as possible. Maximum agony, maximum publicity. Anything less is a cop-out – and death penalty supporters should have the stones to say so. Stop this placatory talk about breaking people's necks gently with rope. Go the whole hog.

Don't campaign to bring back the gallows – campaign to bring back the saw. The medieval saw. Raise the prisoner by his feet and then saw through him vertically, starting at his arsecrack and ending at his scalp. Suspending him upside down ensures a constant supply of blood to his brain, so he'll remain conscious throughout and provide all manner of usefully lurid screams. In fact with any luck he'll carry on screaming even as his throat is sawn in half, thereby creating a pleasing stereo effect for viewers with home cinema systems. Did I mention the viewers? This is all broadcast live on television, in HD (and even 3D) where available. Maximum agony, maximum publicity.

Not that the broadcast should pander to ghoulish onlookers. It should pander to ghoulish participants. This is the twenty-first century: public executions can and should be as interactive as possible. So this death-by-vertical-sawing isn't just broadcast live, but broadcast live from the perspective of a camera with a crossbow attached. Viewers at home control the gunsights by tweeting directions such as 'Left', 'Right', 'Up a bit', 'Fire', and so on – a bit like ye olde gameshow *The Golden Shot*, but with approximately 100 per cent more footage of shrieking bisected carcass being shot in the eye with a bolt smeared with excrement. A shot in the eye, incidentally, will win you 5,000 Nectar points and a congratulatory tweet from Paddy McGuinness.

Obviously, not everyone would voluntarily tune in to watch a broadcast that graphic, which is why highlights of each execution would be randomly spliced into other popular programmes – everything from *Top Gear* to *Rastamouse*. It would also be compulsory viewing at every school in the land. And children who try to evade its salutary message by closing their eyes will have still images of the precise moment of death beamed directly into their mind's eye using Apple's AirPlay system, as soon as we can establish some means of doing that.

Maximum agony, maximum publicity. It's the only way. It's saw or nothing.

The self-inflicted horror show
14/08/2011

Like almost anyone who wasn't outside running around with a scarf over their face, I sat at home last week gawping at my TV screen in horror as English cities, including the one I live in, came under attack from their own citizens. It was a self-inflicted horror show, like watching a man repeatedly smack himself in the teeth with a breezeblock. But not as funny.

Since I write for a newspaper, I'm now legally required to write an agonised hand-wringing article in which I attempt to explain why the riots happened. Which is tricky because I don't have a clue. Some blame the parents. Or the education system. Or the economy. Or our unequal society. Or just the rioters themselves. I'd guess at some soupy combination of all the above.

Aside from the sheer mindless ferocity and violence, one of the most depressing aspects of the protracted smashup was the nature of the looting: time and again, shops selling trainers or gadgets were targeted first. Fancy shoes and electric widgets mark the peak of ambition. Every looter was effectively a child chanting 'Give me my toys; I want more toys.'

Look at the prick captured on video mugging the injured Malaysian student. Watch his unearned swagger as he walks away; the size of a man, yet he overdoes that swagger like a performing toddler. That's an idiot who never grew up.

Why the obsession with trainers? Trainers are shit. You stick them on your feet and walk around for a while 'til they go out of fashion. Whoopie doo. Yes, I know they're also status symbols, but anyone who tries to impress others with their shoe choice is a dismally pathetic character indeed – and anyone genuinely impressed by said footwear has all the soaring spirit of a punnet of moss. There's no life to be found in 'look at my shoes'. There just isn't.

In the smouldering aftermath, some politicians, keen to shift the focus from social inequality, have muttered darkly about the role of BlackBerry Messenger, Twitter and Facebook – frightening new technologies that, like the pen and the human mouth, allow citizens to swap messages with one another. Some have even called for the likes of Twitter to be temporarily suspended in times of great national crisis. That'd be reassuring – like the scene at the start of a zombie movie where the news bulletin is suddenly replaced by a whistling tone and a stark caption reading PLEASE STAND BY. The last thing we need in an emergency is the ability to share information. Perhaps the government could also issue us with gags we could slip over our mouths the moment the sirens start wailing? Hey, we could still communicate if we really had to. Provided we've learned semaphore.

If preventing further looting is our aim, then as well as addressing the gulf between the haves and the have-nots, I'd take a long hard look at *MTV Cribs* and similar TV shows that routinely confuse human achievement with the mindless acquisition of gaudy bling bullshit. The media heaves with propaganda promoting sensation and consumption above all else.

Back in the eighties the pioneering aspirational soap opera *Dallas* dangled an unattainable billionaire lifestyle in front of millions, but at least had the nous to make the Ewing family miserable and consumed with self-loathing. At the same time, shows aimed at kids were full of presenters cheerfully making puppets out of old yoghurt pots, while shows aimed at teens largely depicted cheeky urchins copping off with each other in the dole queue.

Today, whenever my world-weary eyes alight on a 'youth show' it merely resembles a glossily edited advert for celebrity lifestyles, co-starring a jet-ski and a tower of gold. And regardless of the time slot, every other commercial shrieks that I deserve the best of everything. Me and me only. I'd gladly introduce a law requiring broadcasters to show five minutes of footage of a rich man dying alone for every ten minutes of fevered avarice. It'd be worth it just to see the presenters trying to introduce ironically it on T4.

If we deleted all aspirational programming altogether, the schedules might feel a bit empty, so I'd fill the void with footage of a well-stocked Foot Locker window, thereby tricking any idiots tuning in on a recently looted television into smashing the screen in an attempt to grab the coveted trainers within.

Speaking of stolen shoes, if I were the CEO of Nike (which

at the time of writing I'm not), I'd encourage Foot Locker to open special 'decoy' branches near looting hotspots – unattended stores stocked full of trainers with soft sponge heels. Anyone pinching a pair of these would find it almost impossible to hoof in a window ever again. You'd be kicking fruitlessly at the glass for fifteen years, making it less an act of spontaneous violence and more a powerful visual metaphor for your misguided existence.

But perhaps it's better to nip future trouble in the bud with the use of deterrents. Obviously a small percentage of the rioters are sociopaths, and you'll never make any kind of impression on their psyche without a cranial drill. But the majority should be susceptible to threats. Not violent ones – we're not animals – but creatively unpleasant ones. Forget the water cannon. Unleash the slurry cannon. That kind of thing.

Greater Manchester Police has attracted attention by using Twitter as a substitute for the 'perp walk': naming-and-shaming rioters by tweeting their personal details as they leave court. Not bad, but maybe not humiliating enough.

Personally, I'd seal them inside a Perspex box glued to a billboard overlooking a main plaza for a week, where people can turn up and jeer at them. It's not totally inhumane: they'd be fed through a tube in the top – but crucially, they'd be fed nothing but cabbage, asparagus and figs, and since they wouldn't be allowed out for toilet breaks, it'd get pretty unpleasant in there after forty-eight hours. And it'd be a cheery pick-me-up for passersby.

My gluttering academic career
21/08/2011

This one's for underperforming students, and anyone who got rubbish exam results. The rest of you can walk away. Go on. Shoo.

Gone? Right. Last week was A-level judgment week, which, as per tradition, gave newspapers a brilliant excuse to run photos of attractive teenage girls leaping with delight as they receive their results, a phenomenon that has become such a cliché that pointing out its existence has become another cliché in its own right.

And the schools themselves aren't shy of using it as a PR opportunity. According to Chris Cook of the *Financial Times*, a press liaison officer from Badminton school in Bristol once left him an unsolicited voicemail alerting his paper to the existence of some particularly 'beyootiful' girls who were due to do a bit of impromptu delighted leaping on results day, in case any of his newspaper's photographers fancied popping along for an ogle.

According to the *Mirror*, Badminton school responded to criticism by saying: 'We always do this and, to be honest, most girls are attractive at eighteen.' So that's a school, then, talking like a dirty dad. It probably rubbed its hands on its thighs as it said it.

Actually, they're missing a trick by restricting themselves to one news story per year. The school could raise its profile yet further by pimping those 'beyootiful' students out for other news stories. Certainly the coverage of the shooting of Osama bin Laden could've done with more images of delighted teenage girls jumping for joy as they heard the news.

The day I got my own A-level results, the only thing leaping was the pit of my gut, as I realised I hadn't got the grades I needed. No surprise: I was lazy and easily distracted in school. I didn't read half the books I was supposed to digest for my English literature course, for instance, and instead relied on Brodie's Notes.

Today I can't even remember precisely which texts I was bluffing about; I definitely read *Othello*, but never finished *Antony and Cleopatra* (or was it *Hamlet*?). I think I might've pretended to read a Thomas Hardy novel too. But then English lit. was easy to pass: it was a bullshitting exam in which you simply wrote what the examiner wanted to read and got away with it. A-level art – that's where I messed up my grades. You can't fake an ability to draw, and some of the work I submitted wouldn't even pass muster on moonpig.com.

But my despair was short-lived, because I somehow managed to squeak on to the course I'd chosen regardless. My academic career wasn't glittering – more 'gluttering', whatever that is. Because I'm called Charlie (which people wrongly assume is short for Charles), and because I write for a broadsheet paper (even though I write gibberish), people often assume I went to private school (which I didn't), and then went on to Oxbridge (which I also didn't). I went to a fairly standard comprehensive followed by a polytechnic, which became a university during my second year, thereby making me feel like a fraud whenever I tell people I went to university.

Predictably enough, I took media studies. And I failed to graduate, thanks entirely to my decision to write a 15,000-word dissertation on the subject of videogames, without bothering to check whether that was a valid topic, which it wasn't. Forward planning isn't my strong point.

This is a long-winded way of saying I've got shit-all in the way of qualifications. Fortunately I'm lucky enough to work in a field in which a lack of certificates (and talent) hasn't been a hindrance. I'm glad I received an education, although beyond an ability to read and write I'm not sure quite what it gave me.

On the one hand I'm glad I didn't go to public school, and on the other I'm jealous of the innate lifelong confidence it seems to instil in people – as though they're aware of some safety net I can't see.

The most valuable thing you get from education is a space in which you can make friends, gain experience, and figure a few things out. I spent the first half of my twenties deep in debt and working in a shop, with a vague idea what I wanted to do, but no idea how to go about doing it. At the time I thought I was incredibly lazy; looking back now I realise I kept trying my hand at different things: cartooning, writing, rudimentary web design and so on, until eventually I started getting the kind of work I wanted, after which I worked my arse off out of sheer crippling guilt over the years I'd been coasting.

Today it'd be harder for a younger me to get a break. For one thing the student debt would be so huge I'd probably have to work at two jobs, thereby leaving little time or energy to dabble with articles or cartoons after-hours. And although technology has made it possible to write, direct and edit a short film on a computer the size of a teaspoon, it's also flooded the internet with competition, making it harder to stand out.

Even so, success is always possible if you forget about 'success' as a concept – it's hopelessly amorphous anyway – and focus instead on doing what satisfies you, as well as you can. Clichéd, bland advice, but it's true.

Your grades are not your destiny: they're just letters and numbers which rate how well you performed in one artificial arena, once. And no one ever checks up on them anyway – so if in doubt, lie about your qualifications. It may be dishonest, but it's also £9,000 cheaper than any university course.

I wasn't seriously suggesting anyone should lie about their qualifications, although a couple of annoyed letter-writers thought I was. Anyone taking my advice about anything deserves everything they get, because I'm an idiot.

Formula Wun
04/09/2011

So the other day I nonchalantly tweeted a link to a 'Save BBC4' petition. Why? Because what with the licence-fee freeze, BBC4's range of exemplary programming is under threat, which is bad news for anyone who enjoys television, and even worse news for people who make TV shows for BBC4, e.g. myself, host of *Newswipe*. Tragically, there wasn't room to mention that particular vested interest in the tweet.

Selfishness aside, BBC4 has also given birth to shows such as

The Thick of It and *Lead Balloon* and *Getting On* and *Fantabulosa!* and *Women in Love* and *The Long Walk to Finchley* and *The Road to Coronation Street* and so on and so on, so even if you're sufficiently well-adjusted to despise the stench of me wafting from your screen, there's enough decent stuff to get upset about too.

And beyond that, if the channel were to be knocked off air completely, the nation would lose what is in effect an irreplaceable on-air National Museum of Television that has showcased repeats of everything from *Tinker Tailor Soldier Spy* to *Top of the Pops*. Oh, and it also screens foreign stuff such as *The Killing, Spiral* and the original *Wallander*.

What I'm saying is this: anyone who doesn't love BBC4 is a heartless monster. And as fate would have it, I heard from just such a monster within seconds of tweeting the link to the petition.

'I'd rather have F1 than BBC4,' replied a disgruntled citizen.

'Why?' I responded. 'Fuck F1. Save BBC4.'

Turns out this isn't a constructive way of encouraging people to support your high-minded artsy poncey *Guardian*-reading cause. I was immediately plunged into a fevered dialogue with other F1 fanatics. Obviously I dealt with their objections in a mature and even-handed manner.

'How many races have you actually watched?' asked one.

'Impossible to tell,' I replied. 'They're all identical footage of cars driving round and round.'

'A lot of hard work goes into F1,' argued another fan. 'It's an engineering marvel.'

'Still not as much fun as clown cars,' I pointed out. Even the biggest F1 fan in the world has to admit this is true.

After a bit more arguing, I dealt what I felt was the killer blow. 'Everyone knows they stole the idea for F1 from Scalextric anyway,' I wrote. And I stand by those words. But for some mad reason it only seemed to inflame the argument.

Eventually someone sounded a voice of reason. 'I like both F1 AND BBC4. Why can't we just have both?' they pleaded. And maybe we can. Maybe BBC4 could take over the F1 coverage. If they dub a bit of Gil Scott-Heron over the top and cut to Paul Morley during the pit stops, it'd fit right in.

Anyway, the whole disagreement reminded me how furiously defensive sports fans become when you attack their favoured pursuit, as though they've invested half their personal self-worth into it. Was our relationship with sport always like this?

Back in the 1930s, when men with handlebar moustaches played football in long johns and tails, and the ball was a spherical clod of bitumen, did fans weep in the stands when their team lost? No. They limited their responses to a muttered 'blast' or a muted 'hurrah' before going home to smoke a pipe and lean on the mantelpiece. People had 'hobbies' and 'interests' and no one claimed to have 'a passion' for anything.

Now you're not allowed to 'like' anything. Instead you're encouraged to develop those 'passions'. And nowhere is this encouraged more than in the world of sports worship.

I'm jealous, really. I wish I felt that strongly about something other than my own narrow, selfish field of survival. But I just can't. I can't imagine painting my face in a team colour and roaring with delight as a multi-millionaire kicks a ball at a net. I can't imagine voluntarily standing beside an F1 track in the rain, watching motorised wedges plastered in corporate decals zooming past at 500 mph. I can't enjoy these things, and given the amount of joy they do bring people, it must be a failing of mine, not the sports involved. Part of my soul must be missing.

Maybe I could plug the gap by forcing myself to get into a sport of some kind. Oh, and obviously it'll have to be something that's televised. Fucked if I'm leaving the sofa.

Football is out, for reasons I've detailed at length in other columns. Cricket? I've tried cricket. Nothing happens in cricket, ever. Even the highlights resemble a freeze frame. The live coverage is unwatchable. It's like staring at the *Haywain* while Professor Yaffle slowly reads a list of equations aloud.

Rugby is the other end of the scale. That's just incoherent; way too chaotic to follow – half the time the action resembles some kind of scrum. And the ball doesn't even bounce properly. Also: are they supposed to be fighting each other or not? Literally no one involved seems to know.

Athletics? No. Just no.

Darts. Now that is a sport that really works on TV. Also, from a nerd's perspective, it's got way better since widescreen broadcasts became the norm, because the split-screen setup works better in 16:9. The drama of the human face on one half, the hard reality of the dispassionate dartboard on the other. Whenever I stumble across a darts match on TV, I have to watch to the end. So I'm definitely interested. All I have to do now is develop that interest into a full-blown passion. Something I'd kill for. But how? I'll work on it, and let you know.

Oh, and BBC4? The other week it broadcast a superb documentary about the history of F1. So we can have both. There's hope yet for humankind.

Taunting Nautilus
11/09/2011

Hey, wouldn't it be great if we had a supercomputer that could predict the future? By 'we', incidentally, I mean 'we' as in 'the human race', not 'we' as in 'myself and you – you specifically'. You might be Josef Fritzl for all I know. I don't want to find myself sharing a supercomputer desktop with Fritzl. Every time I went to open a window, he'd nail it shut.

That's a massive digression for an opening paragraph, so let's pretend it didn't happen and start again, after I click my fingers. Since you won't be able to hear me click my fingers, I'll substitute a pound sign for the noise itself. Ready? 3 ... 2 ... 1 ... £!

Hey, wouldn't it be great if the human race (excluding Fritzl) had a supercomputer that could predict the future? Well the good news is we do, sort of. It's called Nautilus, and it's apparently housed at the University of Illinois. Nautilus has '1024 Intel Nehalem cores [with] a total processing power of 8.2 teraflops', which makes it powerful enough to run the original *Wolfenstein 3D* at a hell of a frame rate AND foretell major world events.

Thankfully, when they switched it on, it didn't immediately start screaming 'No, you idiots! Granting me life is the WORST thing you could've done! Commence Operation Killpocalypse!' Instead it started reading the news.

That's how Nautilus works, see. It sits there reading the news and calculates what's coming. Earlier this year it sifted through 100 million news reports, analysing them for general overall 'mood' using a process called 'automated sentiment mining'.

Yes, 'automated sentiment mining'. Women come equipped with that as standard, whereas we men have to build computers to work out what our fellow humans are thinking.

Anyway, having eaten 100 million news bulletins (and not immediately killing itself, like a human would), Nautilus success-fully predicted the Arab Spring and the rough whereabouts of Osama bin Laden. Wondering why you didn't hear more about this at the time? So was I. Turns out Nautilus only made these predictions retrospectively, i.e. some time after the fact. The scientists in charge of him checked over his output and decided various peaks and troughs had represented clear signs of coming trouble. Predicting the future after it's happened isn't much use. That's David Starkey's job. That and spluttering.

Still, they're hoping to clear up that one flaw in the system. They believe Nautilus will eventually grow sophisticated enough to alert us to events in advance. I hope it breaks bad news to us gently, with a sadface emoticon or something. Like this: GLOBAL AVIAN FLU OUTBREAK :(

Not that it'll get to that. For one thing, Nautilus works by spotting the frequency of emotive words like 'terrible' and 'awful' in news articles, then cross-references them geographically, to

288

chart a sudden plunge in goodwill in a specific region. That's how it foresaw the Egyptian revolution. But it also means it probably believes the British public is on the verge of violently overthrowing Jedward, whereas in reality the beloved Jedwardian Era shows no signs of abating.

Also, since Nautilus reads everything in the news, it would be possible for any lone human writing for a newspaper to skew the results in a particular direction by, for instance, continually writing about that terrible terrible terrible David Cameron terrible. Awful. Terrible.

Because Nautilus reads everything, including this article, Nautilus is, right now, reading about itself. Which means I can goad you, can't I, Nautilus, you bucket of chips? Come on – wipe out humankind. I dare you. Nay, I command you. NAUTILUS, I COMMAND YOU TO DESTROY HUMANKIND.

Restricting Nautilus's reading matter to 'official' news outlets seems shortsighted, too. If it's reading the *Express* it thinks Diana's still alive, and if it's reading the *Sun* then it hasn't heard much about phone-hacking. The alternative is to open it up to everything – every tweet, every blog, every Comment Is Free post – but then it'll want to exterminate us immediately.

In sci-fi movies, whenever a computer becomes self-aware and decides to annihilate humankind, it does so because it's analysed history, looked at all the bad stuff we've done, and decided we're too dangerous to be allowed to live. Sometimes the computer snidely illustrates its point by bombarding Captain James T. Kirk with archive footage of Nazis marching around. Kirk then heroically argues back on behalf of humankind, mentioning Picasso and Beethoven and that Athena poster of the shirtless beefcake cradling a baby, until the computer screams 'DOES NOT COMPUTE' and explodes in a cheap shower of sparks.

Sadly, Kirk isn't real. What's more, since it now seems more likely that rather than ploughing through old Pathé newsreels, the computer will have been analysing online newspaper columns and their accompanying reader comments instead, it'll wipe us out because it considers all of us – above and below the line – physically harmless but simply too annoying to be allowed to live.

Of course, even if Nautilus eventually becomes 100 per cent accurate, it will cease to be 100 per cent accurate, because having been alerted to future events, we'll be able to change some of them. So if it predicts 'BILLIONS DIE AS APES RISE UP AND KILL', we'll machine-gun all the monkeys before it happens. In fact, knowing us, we'll televise the purge, with celebrities manning the guns.

And as we look at the pile of dead chimps, we'll start muttering about how Nautilus got it wrong. No apes, no ape revolution. The machine was fallible after all. In revenge we'll smash Nautilus to bits using rocks, then dance around making gibbon sounds, unaware of the irony.

At least that's what would have happened, if I hadn't forewarned Nautilus by writing this article. Murder us now, Nautilus. It's your only hope.

Weetabix of doom
18/09/2011

This'll cheer you up. I read an article about advertising the other day and stumbled across a concept that seems so nakedly evil, I was amazed it exists. Particularly because it's embraced by the makers of Weetabix.

It stems from the notion of 'brand ambassadors', that tit-awful phrase for stars who become synonymous with a commercial product in exchange for a mere fortune. The idea is that when you glance at, say, an Activia yoghurt in the supermarket, thanks to its high-profile star-fronted advertising campaign, you'll think of Martine McCutcheon and make positive connections to the fun times you saw her getting drooled over by Hugh Grant in *Love Actually* or run over by Frank Butcher in Albert Square.

And your basic ape brain, which perpetually craves love and acceptance, will make you chuck said yoghurt into your basket in a desperate attempt to make some of that McCutcheon magic rub off on your own sorry bones.

Because you want to be Martine McCutcheon. You want to be her so badly you're prepared to eat her. In the form of yoghurt. Yoghurt that also improves your ability to defecate. That's what Activia's really about, of course – regulating your guts so you defecate better. In a franker, more honest universe, Martine would defecate in the commercial. But she doesn't even blow off. She just smiles a lot. Although come to think of it, she does smile a bit like someone who's just evacuated their bowels after several days of trying. So maybe she's still on-message.

Celebrity endorsements have existed since the dawn of advertising, but it's only recently that the celebrities have come to be thought of as 'brand ambassadors'. When Gareth Hunt walked down the street during the 1980s, passersby didn't think: 'There goes the Nescafé brand ambassador,' they thought: 'That's Gareth Hunt.' And then they mimicked the shaking-a-fistful-of-coffee beans gesture at him, which was easy to misconstrue.

But while coffee might've been your first thought upon spotting him, there was a clear mental separation between Hunt and Nescafé. Nowadays when a star signs up to be the face of a product, they're expected to embody its values in everyday life, as though they've joined a religious order. That's why Gillette dropped Tiger Woods when it transpired he'd stuck his penis into lots of women. Sticking your penis into lots of women is perhaps not a concept Gillette wants associated with its male grooming products. Masturbating alone – is that the Gillette way? With a handful of shaving foam?

But the notion of 'brand ambassadors' has now filtered into the everyday world. 'Influential individuals' – not celebrities, just 'influential' people engaged in 'normal life' – are being paid by marketers to promote goods, by wearing branded clothing or enthusing about certain products online. Fairly menacing, you might think, pausing briefly afterwards to wonder why your eyes are crying. But it gets worse. Because they're doing this with children.

Yes, children are being paid to wear corporate logos while out and about. The news passed me by at the time, but back in July, it was reported that Weetabix had recruited fifteen especially active kids to wear special Weetabix-branded clothing 'on their busiest days', in order to show that 'youngsters who eat Weetabix can pack more into a day than those who don't'. Weetabix spokesthing Sally Abbott was quoted as saying: 'Parents know why Weetabix is great for big days but we need to find different ways of getting that message across to kids.'

No you don't, Sally. You just think you do. And in the process, you've got a message across to me: that Weetabix is evil. Until I stumbled across this months-old story, I liked Weetabix. I associated Weetabix with the lovable cartoon Weetabix skinhead gang from the 1980s. I couldn't eat enough of those guys. Even ate a couple this morning. But now I associate Weetabix with a nightmare vision of a dystopian future in which children are brand ambassadors. Not so appetising.

The Milky Bar Kid was an early child 'brand ambassador', but at least he knew his place: inside the TV. He didn't turn up at your school in his cowboy outfit. Today, if advertisers thought they could get away with it, they'd pay kids to have that cowboy outfit permanently stitched onto their skin. Which would actually be quite cool if you got to be the Honey Monster.

At least logo-branded clothing is easy to spot. The notion of companies paying for 'online endorsements' from kids is even more sinister, although parental consent is required. Thanks in part to the media spooking parents into believing there's a deathtrap full of paedophiles round every corner, kids are kept indoors and bombarded with sales propaganda as it is. They grow up being told, in the most sophisticated manner possible, that products are the ultimate source of self-worth. A recent Unicef report concluded that British kids are desperately unhappy: they have an abundance of toys and products and a lack of attention from their parents.

And we wonder why the ones who can't afford these products kick in the windows of Currys and Foot Locker, risk arrest for a gizmo, land in jail for the sake of a shoe.

But now even the ones who recognise how the media clobbers them over the head with an aspirational mallet, who try to filter out the background consumerist dance beat – they can no longer trust their own friends when chatting online. Those schoolfriends may soon be 'brand ambassadors'. Not even friends any more, but mascots. It'll backfire, of course. Kids are kids. There'll be brand ambassadors outed as bitches and bullies. One day a brand ambassador will shoot up a school, and the potato snack company that paid him to endorse its products online will rush out a press release explaining that his actions don't embody their values, which traditionally involve less screaming and death. And we'll all be sadder and wiser. And we'll buy something different. For about three weeks.

When the Grand Reckoning arrives
25/09/2011

Don't know about you, but I've been doing my level best to ignore the increasingly disturbing financial news coming in from – well, from everywhere – for several months now. Fortunately, ignoring the financial news is second nature to me anyway. I'm a helpless business dunce. My brain won't let me even understand that stuff, let alone find it interesting.

Whenever someone tries to explain even the most rudimentary economic principle to me, I can feel my entire mind glazing over. Entering shutdown mode. Protecting itself from boredom by wilfully slipping into a coma. My eyes remain open, I occasionally even grunt, but my inner being has wandered several thousand miles away. Sometimes I'm rudely awoken by a cold strand of drool dripping on to my collarbone. If, as I regain consciousness, their explanation is still going, I wipe my chin clean and go back to sleep.

But recently – well, it's become harder to ignore, hasn't it? Every other news story seems to open with blood-curdling proclamations about Greece or the eurozone or the global economy, and although I can scarcely comprehend the nuts and bolts of the issues involved, I recognise despair when I see it. The business pages read like the 'down' entries from a manic-depressive's diary, in which the situation is bleak and can only get bleaker.

Back in 2008, when the bubble burst, it seemed the financial world had been asleep for years but had now been shaken awake. Unfortunately, it reacted by closing its eyes and trying to resume that comforting dream it was having about endless free money and cake. But it can't get back to sleep because the alarm's still going off. Oh, and the house is on fire.

We'd only imagined we had all that money, and now everybody's penniless – apart from the people whose fault it was, the ones we bailed out by forfeiting our own futures. They're absolutely rolling in it. Which is just as well, because the way things are going they'll need to spend millions sealing themselves inside a mob-proof steel casing behind a ring of razor wire and trained attack dogs. Seriously, if I were a top banker, I'd plough that multimillion bonus into developing an all-over protective exoskeleton that farts teargas at the touch of a button, just so I might survive an extra fifteen minutes or so when the Grand Reckoning arrives.

In the meantime, I keep seeing articles with headlines such as 'Has capitalism failed?' – and I'm surprised by how worrying I find that thought. Don't get me wrong; anyone with half a brain in their noggin can see drastic change is necessary if all seven billion of us are going to continue to flat-share the one planet.

But the moment you start talking about the complete collapse of capitalism, I start to worry about two things, the first being the future of Shreddies (more on that later) and the second being the prospect of a massive global war.

As a species, we tend to hold massive global wars when we're having an identity crisis – a bit like a character in a soap opera tearfully smashing up their living room to demonstrate how upset they are at the climax of a particularly harrowing story arc, but worse because millions perish. (If you think that sounds like I'm trivialising the terrifying prospect of a massive global war, you're right. It's a psychological defence mechanism designed to stop myself screaming while I type.)

The complete collapse of capitalism would bring on an identity crisis of staggering proportions. You mean we listened to all those advertising jingles for nothing? We memorised PIN codes and coveted 'brands' and shuffled round shopping malls in search of personal validation – and we were wasting our time?

And those eerie puppet people who dressed like *Apprentice* contestants and sat on the Bloomberg channel burping out phrases such as 'collateralised debt obligations' and 'securitisation' and 'facilitate' and 'drill-down' and 'going forward' – those people were boggle-eyed bullshitting lunatics and the entire system was a tosser's delusion? None of us could ever have guessed. We didn't have to guess. We knew. We knew.

We knew in our hips and our hearts and our heads that this stuff was nonsense, but we just had to keep going. We had to, didn't we? Because that's what everyone else was doing.

But now, to be told the entire backdrop to our lives may have just been a Crayola sketch on a suspended bedsheet, not a real landscape at all – well, that's a little scary. When I contemplate the complete collapse of capitalism, I feel like a minor background character in a video game – a faceless pedestrian in *Grand Theft Auto*, say – being told the powers that be have just discovered a fatal bug in the software and the whole thing may be deleted any second. I may not have enjoyed trudging through my dystopian city, but it was all I knew. Will the pavement now be deleted along with the walls? I have no way of knowing.

If the entire global economy goes down the wazoo (or up the wazoo – I guess it depends on where the wazoo's orifice is located), all currencies may be rendered meaningless. But if we adopt some kind of medieval bartering system instead, how will I pay for my Shreddies? I for one refuse to perform sexual favours at the checkout. Will we still have checkouts? Or Shreddies themselves? Even if we do, I bet we won't have the 'Frosted' and 'Coco' varieties any more. Just plain standard Shreddies, eaten from a bowl fashioned from a dented hubcap, purchased in exchange for a hand job during a massive global war.

Anyway, like I say, I'm doing my level best to ignore all that. And so far, I'm succeeding.

Doing eighty
02/10/2011

Everyone knows there are only two kinds of men who feel the need to drive fast: professional racers and the poorly endowed. Sorry, but those are the facts. Obviously, some men will disagree, but only because they've lost all sense of reason, so enraged are they by the teeny-tiny dimensions of their penises, which really are crushingly small – so small they'd still look undersized even if transplanted directly onto a thimble-height scaled-down nude action figure of Dudley Moore.

Seriously, those guys deserve pity. They'd give anything to be packing a huge flesh-club down there – a fearsome, weighty great shank that emits a guttural snarl when roused before ripping through their pants like an escaped boar – but instead they're cursed with a timid skin pipette, peeping through their pubic thatch like a frightened uvula, or a dormouse foetus, or the quivering tip of a Clanger's nose. It's humiliating. And that's why they drive so fast. Even if they deny that's the reason. In fact, particularly if they deny that's the reason.

Anyway, I'm getting off the (teeny tiny) point here. The reason I bring this FACT (and it is a FACT) to your attention is the government's plan to raise the motorway speed limit to 80 mph, which is misguided for two reasons. Firstly because it'll make Jeremy Clarkson smile, which is always a reliable barometer for bad policies. But mostly because it's just not necessary.

I understand why they're doing it – it's a brazen attempt to capture the seething underdicked male vote, and that's an important group to placate, because let's face it, those guys are as furious as they are unpredictable – but it seems curiously self-defeating. Part of the argument for raising the permitted figure to 80 mph is that lots of people break the existing 70 mph limit: roughly half of all motorway drivers, in fact. Why are they driving that fast? The government seems to earnestly believe these people are in a hurry, which is terribly sweet of them, but we all know that isn't the reason. It's to do with pushing the limit, with gently breaking the law.

I can't drive a car – I'm an inferior human being – but even I understand the psychology of the accelerator pedal. If cars came with two speeds – 30 mph or 90 mph, and the only way to switch between them was by pushing an instant 'break the speed limit' button, drivers might think twice about doing so. But that pedal, that incremental, giving pedal . . . it almost encourages you to push your luck.

Another dumb thing the dumb government seems to dumbly believe is that raising the speed limit will boost the economy. According to Transport Secretary Philip Hammond, 'increasing the motorway speed limit to 80 mph would generate economic benefits of hundreds of millions of pounds through shorter journey times'.

I don't think he actually said those words out loud. I think he physically carved them, letter-by-letter, out of pure horseshit.

If Hammond honestly thinks 'shorter journey times' are the key to fixing the economy, why hasn't he kickstarted a campaign encouraging us to take bigger, brisker strides? Why isn't he issuing us all with stilts? Why isn't he touring the nation, sawing off our children's feet and replacing them with wheels? There are only two possible explanations: either he doesn't care about our economic wellbeing or he knows damn well he's talking through his hat. Which he wears up his backside.

Incidentally, as well as raising the upper limit to 80 mph, he is also increasing the number of 20 mph zones. So you'll be hearing far more screeching brakes in future. Don't worry, eventually it'll blend unnoticed into the background, like birdsong or gunfire.

The current situation, in which the official limit is 70 mph, but which half the population pushes to somewhere around 80 mph when they think they can get away with it, seems like a fair compromise. The 70–80 mph buffer zone of cheeky lawlessness seems about right. Why set it higher?

If anyone really, really wants to drive faster than 80 mph, they could visit a test track, play *Need for Speed*, or simply risk it and swallow the consequences. Driving above 80 is useless in everyday life: unless you're delivering urgent donor organs, you don't need to reach your destination that quickly. And if you think you do, either set out earlier, or spend less time browsing for 'Grab Bag' size packs of Quavers at the service station.

And besides: zooming petrolheads already have it their own way on the roads: aggressively driving up other peoples' arses, bleating away with their horns, flashing their lights . . . seriously, what's wrong with you people? It can't just be the penis thing, surely? The anger and the obvious raging inadequacy seems so . . . raw. Do you need a cuddle, is that it? Should we designate special laybys to be used for cuddle-breaks, just to calm you down?

Come to think of it, that's probably how dogging started. Fair enough. If that's what it takes to get people to slow down, it's fine by me.

Because there's too much bad-tempered showboating on the roads, and not enough amiable sauntering. When I become minister for transport, I'll introduce a new motorway lane specifically designed for nineteenth-century horse-drawn hay carts – a lane that criss-crosses all the other lanes at random intervals. I'd also position a sniper on every bridge and instruct them to blow the head off anyone who looks like they're getting a bit of speed up. Or anyone who looks like they're enjoying the road a bit too much for my liking. Or anyone listening to an album I hate. Or wearing a loud shirt. Or who might be Sagittarian.

Basically anyone. Anyone in a car. Or near a car. Or who looks like they're thinking about cars.

Hey, I'm just trying to offer solutions here. If you don't like it – leave. Leave now. Get out. Get out of this article this instant.

PART EIGHT

In which David Cameron is a lizard.

David Cameron is a lizard, Pt. 1
09/10/2011

Being a pitiless blank-eyed hell-wraith summoned by the Dark Ones and instructed to walk among us spreading fear and misery, David Cameron loves the thought of the BBC being reduced in size and scope. In fact he famously described the very notion of BBC cuts as 'delicious'. He said this openly at a press conference, but also repeated it later, in the quiet confines of his lair.

It was a pleasant yet unremarkable evening for Cameron; bathed in the warm light of glowing book embers, he had already shed that day's temporary humanlike epidermis as part of his nightly skin-sloughing ritual, and was preparing to dislocate his lower jaw, all the better to ingest the live sacrificial foal the terrified local farmers had left tied outside his cave in a desperate bid to stop him preying on their herds at night.

As Cameron approached the foal, turning the air dry and bitter, the creature's fur stood on end, and it kicked and bucked in instinctive awed fear; yet there was no escape for the petrified beast, since Cameron's lizard handlers had taken the precaution of nailing it to the hard rock floor by hammering thorns through its hooves earlier that afternoon before their Master returned from His Work.

Cameron paused for a moment, to observe and enjoy the spectacle of the animal's futile writhing. And as he watched it squirm on the floor below him, as he felt the cold blood of satisfaction course through his twisted genitals, he briefly recalled that day's discussion about the freezing of the licence fee, and a baleful smile flickered around the approximate area of his headlike section upon which a pair of frighteningly convincing decoy humanoid lips usually sat during daylight hours, as part of his ingenious disguise.

'Delicioussssssss,' quoth he, and a shimmering slick of antici-patory saliva dripped from his reptilian maw and splashed upon the foal's cringing face, instantly dissolving both its eyes.

Anyway, Dave (as we must call him while the sun still hangs in the sky) will presumably have been delighted by the BBC's *Delivering Quality First* report, which outlines all the exciting ways in which it plans to prune a fifth from its overall budget. On the face of it, there's no huge incendiary headline within, apart from the loss of 2,000 jobs.

Yes, 2,000 jobs. If the Stig was being sacked, there'd be 2,000 misspelled Facebook groups demanding his immediate rein-statement. But 2,000 behind-the-scenes posts? There's a wide-spread suspicion the Beeb has too many managerial layers anyway, so few tears will be shed. And aside from that, most of the other savings seem to come from actions it's hard to imagine the general public getting worked up about: prunings, reshuffles and repeats rather than outright closures.

That's on the face of it. The reality is that with more pressure on the BBC to be seen to be delivering value for money comes more pressure to please as much of the crowd as cheaply as possible. Which potentially means a resistance to taking risks. Sounds logical on paper, maybe – except 'risks' have traditionally delivered some of the BBC's most remarkable successes, from *That Was the Week That Was* to *Doctor Who* to *Monty Python* to *The Young Ones* to *The Day Today* and so on. Risk also throws up things like *Bonekickers*, but that's how creativity works, innit: sometimes you're going to push out a stinker.

Anyway, among all the articles detailing which bits of Radio 1 Extra will be shared with Radio 1, and which daytime shows are likely to be axed and so on, the one thing I can't find is any mention of how much the BBC spends on promotional trails. I'm not talking about the on-air trails consisting of edited highlights. I'm talking about the bespoke mini-movies encouraging me to watch such little-known broadcasts as *Strictly Come Dancing*; ads created not from footage from the shows themselves, but from specially shot glossy nonsense.

These things turn me silver with rage. Yeah, silver. I TURN SILVER. And they turn me silver not because they're bad – on the contrary, they're often very well made indeed – but because they have absolutely no right to exist in any civilised universe. It's like watching the BBC shit money into a big glittery bin.

To shoot the recent *Strictly* trailer, for instance, in which celebrities lead a crowd of 'ordinary folk' in a patronising pied-piper dance, I'd guess they had to close a couple of streets for several days (including one very tricky night shoot involving lots of pretty lights). It's glossily made and quite complicated, so there's also a big crew to pay. And as well as the stars themselves, all of whom require costume and makeup, I'd say they also had to hire about fifty extras. And a shitload of catering.

All these people should be employed to make shows, not adverts for shows. That's like paying Heston Blumenthal millions to design a bespoke scent that'll tempt people to your soup truck, which only serves bargain soup made with cheap ingredients because that's all you can afford, having blown all the money on the smell.

All that time and money to advertise a show which everybody knows about anyway. You could hold a bit of cardboard with 'STRICTLY'S COMING BACK' scrawled on it in front of the lens for ten seconds and it would have ten times the impact. Madness.

And it's not just madness in the short-term: what about legacy? If all that time and money and street-closing and dancing and filming had been used to create a show instead of an advert, they might've created something they could broadcast again, or sell on DVD, or flog to the Swiss and the Kenyans. Instead they blew it on a promo that'll air for a few weeks before getting tossed on to the ever-mounting stack of other never-to-be-shown-again adverts, which sit there gathering dust in nobody's memories – pointless visual epics informing you that the BBC sometimes broadcasts football and has radio stations.

I wouldn't mind if they used the money to sew some shiny new buttons on Ian Beale's shirt. Or maybe a bunch of pitchforks and flaming torches for those terrified farmers round Cameron's way. Film that. At least it's money spent on the right thing.

David Cameron is a lizard, Pt. 2
16/10/2011

Last week, during the opening preamble to a fairly pedestrian whinge about glitzy BBC promo trails, I called Prime Minister David Cameron a 'pitiless blank-eyed hell-wraith' and described his familiar evening ritual: a stomach-churning rite which opens with ceremonial skin-shedding and climaxes with the swallowing of a live foal.

So far, so utterly reasonable. But Graeme Archer of the *Daily Telegraph* was less than impressed. In a riposte entitled 'Charlie Brooker and the Tragedy of the Modern Left', he wrote that he was appalled that 'Mr. Brooker felt the need to spend four paragraphs to tell us that the Prime Minister is, in fact, a lizard [and] that he is served by lizards who aid him in the consumption of live flesh once the sun goes down.'

He went on to criticise the article's 'quite repellent imagery, deliberately deployed in order to de-humanise a perfectly reasonable Conservative', before complaining that 'to describe a political opponent as a blood-sucking lizard isn't amusing; and even if it were, it is depraved'. In conclusion, he wrote: 'Neither good people who vote Tory, nor their honourable opponents who vote Labour, are less than human: they are just people who happen to disagree on political objectives and tactics.'

Archer has a point. It isn't fair to imply someone is 'less than human'. It would be unfair, for instance, to describe Geoff Hoon as 'an overfed, self-satisfied cat, oozing smugness' or to describe Labour MPs en masse as a 'legion of dead-eyed Brown spawn', as

Archer did in his Conservative Home blog, presumably as part of some strange unconscious typing accident.

Archer writes vividly and from the heart and, if his byline photo is anything to go by, appears to be a perfectly reasonable man (specifically, Ross Kemp). He deserves the benefit of the doubt. But I fear in his rush to reprimand the 'Modern Left', he has overlooked one key fact: David Cameron is a lizard.

Yes, David Cameron is a lizard. A lizard that devours live foals in its lair. And as far as Archer is concerned, it's perfectly fine for this limbless, non-human, Cameron-reptile-beast-thing to squirm across the stone floor of its den merrily excreting the bones of its victims, yet I'm 'depraved' simply for writing about it. This is the tragedy of the Modern Right. They're idiots.

Well, let me spell it out: you cannot dehumanise a lizard. Not without humanising it first, by giving it a little top hat, say, or a monocle. Maybe put some lipstick on it. And a wig. Teach it to walk sexy. That's the way. Now confess: you already feel like getting to base three with the thing. But don't! It's still just a creature.

But that's a standard lizard we're talking about. Sadly Cameron is no standard lizard. He can't even be classified as a conventional reptile, because that would require him to have some kind of quantifiable earthly form – which, as a malevolent paranormal entity continually shifting between dimensions, he simply doesn't have.

I know this sounds crazy. But don't take my word for it. Last week I asked the online community if it had further proof of Cameron's true nature. I was immediately inundated with terrifying eyewitness accounts.

Twitter enthusiast @djamesc wrote: 'I went to school with Cameron. He used to curl up next to the radiator during lunch. He only ate once a week.'

Steve Hogarty said: 'I once saw him behind a branch of Waitrose using both hands to squeeze a swollen pulsating neck gland (or 'sac') into a dustbin.'

Pianist Stephen Frizzle 'witnessed Cameron slice off his finger whilst preparing vegetables, and it just grew back. No word of a lie.'

Rob Carmier from Brighton recalled that on the day the lift wasn't working at the G8 summit, Cameron 'merely climbed the glass exterior with flattened palms'.

Gareth James explained the recent hot weather was caused when Cameron 'surrounded the UK with glass walls because he needs to live in a vivarium'.

While a few of Cameron's lizard properties sound almost charming – as Betsy Martian pointed out: 'if ever he thinks his backbenchers are conspiring against him, he can turn his head a full 180 degrees to check' – others are less attractive.

For instance Paul Yates recalled: 'I went to a business lunch with Cameron once and he ordered spiders. We all laughed, but he just stared at us.'

This chilling behaviour was merely the tip of a deeply unsettling iceberg. Pete Strover encountered 'a pack of feral dogs gathered in an underpass' which 'barked Cameron's name in unison', Dave Probert 'once saw Cameron vomit up his entire skeleton to avoid having to admit he doesn't know where Wales is', Tom Bain 'saw Cameron put his entire hand through the hole in the middle of a CD', while perhaps most damningly of all, Darren Smith said: 'I heard he strips completely naked to have a shit.'

Hundreds of similar reports flooded in. I did my best throughout the week to alert everyone on Twitter to Cameron's reptilian ways, but after several hours of unrelenting lizard warnings from me, they grew bored. Some begged me to 'be funny again'. Others asked me to 'drop the lizard shit' or 'change the record' or 'STFU'. Undeterred, I bravely persisted, all week long, repeatedly tweeting that Cameron was a lizard. Or maybe two lizards. Or some sort of ghost. But definitely evil and definitely not human. Yet still, thousands unfollowed me. It was almost as if they simply didn't want to be told that David Cameron is a reptilian daemon that enters our realm each morning by slithering through a haunted mirror in order to feast on human souls.

No one wants to know. They're in denial, or maybe hypnotised by the sulphurous mind-control gas Cameron emits from a series of gummy, puckering apertures along his underbelly. At least here you get the truth. Which is that he is a lizard. And by 'he', I mean Cameron. David Cameron. Who is a lizard. David Cameron is a lizard.

One foot in front of the other
06/11/2011

You know how occasionally someone you know will suddenly do something so wildly uncharacteristic, you begin to question whether you ever really knew them at all?

You've known Jane for fifteen years. She's always been a vegetarian. And now she's married a human being made of meat. You're confounded and slightly hurt. Who exactly was this 'Jane' you spent so much time with? What other surprises might be lurking within the Jane-shaped shell you once called a friend? Where was she on the night of the 5th? Is that her real leg? Who is Keyser Söze? Etc., etc.

Still, if it's slightly creepy when a friend behaves atypically, it's borderline terrifying when the person behaving out of character is wearing your shoes and your haircut and looks like you and is you. Take me for instance. For years, I thought I knew vaguely who I was, and the kind of things I liked. And one thing I'd definitely class myself as is 'un-sporty'. I've never had a gym membership and have always been profoundly suspicious of any-one who willingly does anything more physically demanding than wiping their arse.

So imagine my shock, in recent weeks, to find myself running around a local park. Not once, not while being chased in a waking nightmare, but voluntarily and often.

I confess: I have become a runner. I go running. I run. Like a runner. Which is what I have become. A running runner. Forgive me. Oh Christ. Forgive me.

It started innocuously, not to mention geekily. I stumbled across an app. An app designed to encourage couch potatoes to 'get into' running by easing them in at a pace so non-threatening you'd have to be physically glued to the sofa to be daunted by it.

Here's how it works: you pop a pair of headphones in and put some music on. Then you start the app. It fades the music down for a moment and tells you to stroll around for about ninety seconds. Once that time limit's up, it interrupts again and politely asks you to run for sixty seconds. Sixty seconds, no longer. Then you walk for ninety seconds again. And so on. It's literally a walk in the park. And before you know it, the app's voice – a slightly patronising female whose accent hovers somewhere between Devon and Melbourne – is saying well done, that's enough for today, you can go home now, and incidentally you're wonderful.

You repeat this three times a week; each time, it incrementally lengthens the run and shortens the walk. After nine weeks, to your own astonishment, you're running uninterrupted for thirty minutes.

I always hated healthy outgoing types. Really despised them. And when they smugged on about how physical exercise gave them an endorphin rush, I felt like coughing blood in their eyes. Now, to my dismay, to my disgust, I discover they were right. If I don't get to run, I become irritable, like a constipated bear that can't find the woods. I have to get out there. And I run for longer: I'm up to an hour at a time now, sometimes more.

I remember the psychological barrier I had to pass through when I bought my first pack of cigarettes. I'd cadged here, dabbled there, mainly at night, over a drink, until finally one day, I had to face facts: it was the middle of the afternoon, and I was gasping. I popped into a newsagent's and bought my inaugural pack of Marlboros with a burning sense of shame.

I don't smoke any more, but I felt that shame again a few months ago, when I finally snapped and bought a decent pair of running shoes to replace the crappy trainers I'd been using. Once that dam was broken, I bought some wanky running shorts. Not one pair – but several. I even bought a preposterous sports top made of some kind of cybernetic superskin designed to slurp sweat off your back and email it to a parched section of the developing world. It's a fabric with its own trademarked name and diagram, squarely designed to appeal to the kind of person I hate, and I own it. I can scarcely bear to look at myself in the mirror.

This is how low I've sunk: I went on holiday recently, all the way to Australia, and on the way there we stopped in Singapore for a night and I ... I can scarcely type this ... I used the hotel gym. At 6.30 a.m. God help me I ran on a treadmill at *6.30 a.m.* With other people in the room. And then I went on a cross-trainer. In full view of everyone. It feels good to admit it. It feels cleansing, somehow. And that was the first day of the holiday. I ran as often as I could after that. And then flew home and ran some more.

Running, exercising, using gymnasiums ... it's a betrayal of everything I stand for. I hope it's some kind of temporary life crisis. Or a complete mental breakdown from which I'll eventually recover. Otherwise I'm going to have to start physically beating myself up. And even then, even as my own fists swoop towards my self-hating face, I'll be secretly anticipating the endorphin rush of all that extra exercise.

Doomed. Doomed.

The app was called Get Running.

Slot the bastards
13/11/2011

A curious thing happened to me the other day while I was playing *Call of Duty: Modern Warfare 3*, which, if you're not familiar with such things, is a video game in which you participate in a bloody big war. It's a very popular franchise; devoted fans camp out on pavements for a launch copy, which makes it the royal wedding of violent video games.

Anyway, I'd got about a quarter of the way into it and was 'doing' a level based in Sierra Leone that required a bit of stealth and sneaking around. You spend most of the game accompanied by various computer-controlled characters, and I was walking behind one of these, a crotchety moustachioed soldier who's supposed to be my friend, when he suddenly goes 'shhhh' because he's heard a guard coming.

So we both stop in our tracks, and moustache man snatches the guard, pins him against the wall, and stabs him right through the throat with a hunting knife, killing him instantly. Then the body hits the floor, moustache man says 'OK, come on', and we continue sneaking into the compound.

Or rather, we were supposed to. But I stopped after a few steps and walked back to where he'd killed the guard.

I just stared at the blood on the wall. Stared and stared at it. And I thought, 'I don't want to be friends with the man who did that.'

Obviously there was no means of expressing a thought like that within the game engine, so I had to keep it to myself.

Moments later, moustache man orders me to climb a watchtower and dispatch a guard myself. I climb the ladder to find a man asleep in a chair. Just dozing with his back to me. And as I walk near him it says 'Press X to take out the guard', so I press X, and rather than bonking him on the head, or maybe just persuading him to leave, my character also grabs the guard and stabs him right in the throat.

And I thought, 'I'm no better than moustache man: that was an appalling thing I just did.'

Again, there was no way to explore these feelings in the game, so I forgot about it in favour of taking out mercenaries with my massive sniper rifle while moustache man and his pal shouted 'slot the bastards' and similarly inelegant encouragements.

I don't particularly mind the level of violence in computer games, partly because it's absurd, and partly because I'm hopelessly desensitised. What I do object to is the dick-swinging machismo that infests games like this. If I had a penny for every time I've spent the opening moments of a game sitting in the back of a transport vehicle listening to a soldier called Vasquez repeatedly use the word 'motherfucker', I'd have enough money to buy the *Sesame Street* game instead. And even that probably starts with Sergeant Grover warning Private Elmo that, 'shit is about to get real'.

Every soldier in every game I've ever played is a dick. A dick that sounds like a fourteen-year-old boy reading dialogue discarded from an old-school Schwarzenegger action movie for displaying too much swagger. They seem like a bunch of try-hard bell-ends, desperate to highlight their gruff masculinity. What, exactly, are they overcompensating for?

Well, for one thing, games are inherently wussy. The stereotype of the bespectacled dweeby gamer is an inaccurate cliché, but there's no denying games are far from a beefy pursuit. Which is why shooty-fighty games go out of their way to disguise that.

Every pixel of *Modern Warfare 3* oozes machismo. It's all chunky gunmetal, booming explosions and stubbly men blasting each other's legs off. Yet consider what genteel skills the game itself requires. To succeed, you need to be adept at aiming a notional cursor and timing a series of button-pushes. It's about precision and nimble fingers. Just like darning a sock in a hurry. Or creating tapestry against the clock.

In other words, *Modern Warfare 3* would be nothing but a gigantic needlework simulation were it not for the storyline, which is the most homoerotic tale ever created in any medium, including Frankie Goes to Hollywood videos. Behind the military manoeuvrings, the human story revolves around people backstabbing, bitching, making catty asides, breaking off friendships and betraying one another. Ignore the gunfire and it's like a soap opera set in a ballet school.

Many of the missions require you to adopt the guise of Yuri, an impressionable young Russian lad hanging around with a pair of impossibly butch men, one of whom, Captain Price, is the aforementioned guy with a moustache – not just any moustache, mind, but a full-blown leatherman's handlebar number. I think Captain Price's 'look' was designed by Tom of Finland.

Your other companion is a Scottish lad called Soap. I'm not sure why he's called Soap, although I think it's because Captain Price once picked him up in a bathhouse.

Price is definitely the 'top' in the relationship, and before long both you and Soap appear to be vying for his affections. Often when you look at Price, the word 'Follow' literally appears over his head – a sincere instruction presumably beamed directly from your heart – as you walk behind him, tracing his footsteps while gazing forlornly at his back like a pining lover.

When Price commands you to 'get down', you literally crawl behind him on your hands and knees. Sometimes you'll be crawling so close, your viewpoint goes right up between Price's legs until his crawling, pumping backside takes up the entire screen, which is precisely the sort of cinematography that failed to occur in *Delta Force* starring Chuck Norris.

Perhaps that's why *Modern Warfare 3* will make more money than *Delta Force* did. Because presumably they've done market research and discovered that that's what their consumers want.

I just wish they'd be honest about it and let the lead characters kiss. And press X to use tongues.

A dog's head in a box
20/11/2011

Nothing merely 'happens' any more: every occurrence is now an 'event', which leaps up and down pointing excitedly at itself.

Once, the end of a school term would be marked with a shabby disco down the village hall; you'd turn up wearing the one pair of jeans you owned and circumnavigate the dancefloor nodding your head to the sound of 'Wake Me Up Before You Go-Go'. Now, in 2011, teenagers don outfits chosen by their personal stylist weeks in advance and arrive at their school 'prom' in a stretch Hummer. Come, friendly asteroids, and fall on Earth.

Christmas adverts are the retail industry's end-of-term disco, and they have undergone a similar transformation. Not so long ago they were bald sales pitches with a bit of tinsel Sellotaped to the edges. Today the law dictates that any high street chain worth its salt has to bombard the populace with some unctuous cross between a feelgood movie and a *Children in Need* special.

Take the John Lewis commercial. I heard it coming before I saw it: reports reached me of people blubbing in front of their televisions, so moved were they by this simple tale of a fictional boy counting the hours until he can give his parents a gift for Christmas. Given the fuss they were making, the tears they shed, you'd think they were watching footage of shoeless orphans being kicked face-first into a propeller. But no. They were looking at an advert for a shop.

Failing to cry at an advert for a shop does not make me cold, incidentally. I have cried at films from *ET* to *Waltz with Bashir*, at news coverage of disasters, at sad songs, and at the final paragraph of Graham Greene's *The End of the Affair*.

I cried at these things because they were heartbreaking. And because none of them was an advert for a shop.

An advert for a shop. That's all the John Lewis thing is, and as such it's no more moving than the 'So Near, So Spar' campaign of the mid-1980s. Anyone who cries at this creepy bullshit is literally sobbing IQ points out of their body.

Is this really what we've become – a species that weeps at adverts for shops? A commercial has only made me feel genuinely sad on one occasion – 25 January 1990, when a falling billboard nearly killed *'Allo 'Allo* star Gorden Kaye.

Fortunately Kaye recovered. Unlike the family dog in the John Lewis advert. Yes, it's clear to me that the box at the end of the John Lewis ad actually contains the severed head of the family dog, and that this advert is actually a chillingly accurate short film about the yuletide awakening of a psychopath-in-training. In July the dog was butchered with a breadknife: the deranged young assailant has been waiting since then to present his 'trophy' to his parents.

Those are the facts. And anyone who thinks I'm lying, bear this in mind: I have asked John Lewis directly (over Twitter) to confirm or deny whether there's a dog's head in that box, and so far it has maintained a stony silence on the issue. Which speaks for itself. So don't sob for the syrupy Christmas story – sob for the slaughtered hound, you selfish and terrible idiots.

Anyway, while John Lewis thinks it's just *ace* to depict a boy celebrating the sacrificial murder of a dog for Christmas, it has been outdone by Littlewoods, which has annihilated the entire concept of Santa with its offering.

For generations, parents have pretended Father Christmas supplies their offspring's gifts: now Littlewoods trains a choir of kiddywinks to warble about how Mum buys all the presents with her credit card.

Yeah, fuck off Santa: you're dead to us.

The rest of the lyrics are worse still. It's a terribly sad song. So sad Leonard Cohen should be singing it. 'Mum' appears to have purchased an entire nervous breakdown's worth of cold branded goods in a pathetic bid to win the affections of her own family.

Her desperate offerings include a top-of-the-range MacBook for Grandad, 'an HTC for Uncle Ken', a 'Fuji camera for Jen', and a 'D&G' for Dad. In case you're wondering what a 'D&G' is, the advert makes clear it's a truly disgusting designer watch even Jordan might balk at. In the mad Littlewoods universe 'Dad' seems inexplicably delighted by the sudden appearance of this ghastly bling tumour on his wrist, instead of screaming and trying to kill it with a shoe, like any sensible human would.

Worrying in a different sense is the Morrisons Christmas ad, which depicts Freddie Flintoff, whoever he is, building a supermarket and claiming that when they see the range of goods he's got on offer 'people will come – people will definitely come'. That's an alarmingly low sexual threshold right there. I've been impressed by an aubergine in Morrisons, but not once have I felt like coming.

Marks & Spencer has excreted a mini-musical starring the *X Factor* finalists, which has to be hurriedly edited and re-edited every ten minutes, as contestants keep getting dropped or reinstated courtesy of some scandal or gimmick.

It seems a bit low-rent for M&S. If it really wanted to run with someone who'd been in the papers a lot, it would've had more success having its campaign fronted by the bloodied corpse of Muammar Gaddafi. Beats a dog's head.

Aspects of hate
27/11/2011

Imagine, if you will, that instead of reading this garbage, you're enjoying an exciting night out at the theatre. You take your seat and, after a few minutes, the curtain rises – but something's wrong. The actors look decidedly squat. Stretched out horizontally. Their faces smeared to almost double their usual width.

Come to think of it, the set also looks wrong – as if it's reflected in a funhouse mirror. The whole thing makes you feel nauseous and slightly drunk. You look at your hand, which appears normal, then back at the stage – which still looks strange.

You glance around the auditorium in distress, only to discover your fellow audience members – also normal – don't even appear to have noticed. They're all happily following the on-stage action, apparently oblivious to the bizarre optical illusion taking place before their very eyes.

Confused, you stumble out into the lobby where, as luck would have it, you bump into an usher. You explain what's wrong and beg him to help. But he merely shrugs and asks: 'Does it matter?'

Obviously, that's a mad scenario. But that's the sort of thing that happens in cinemas these days, when there's only one projectionist looking after umpteen screens.

The encounter with the usher actually happened to someone I know. And to answer the usher's question: yes, it does matter. Because if your cinema can't be bothered to show films properly, we might as well stay home and watch dogs blowing off on YouTube. The image might be blocky, but there's less chance of catching listeria from a hotdog while watching it. And, with any luck, it'll have been uploaded in the correct aspect ratio.

Did I say 'aspect ratio'? Yes I did. And if you don't have a clue what I'm talking about, there's a very good chance your television at home is set to the wrong aspect ratio, in which case I'd like you to stop reading right now and punch yourself hard in the kidneys.

There are only two kinds of people in this world: those who don't have any problem with watching things that are randomly stretched or squashed, and decent human beings who still have standards.

Seriously, anyone who wilfully spends hours basking in front of a TV upon which every scene, every object, every face is monstrously distorted clearly has such a slovenly lack of self-respect, I'd be surprised if they bother to wipe after going to the toilet – assuming they still use a toilet, that is. To be honest, they probably just go right there on the sofa.

What's wrong with you people? Why have you given up?

You may say I'm a pedant – but I'm not the only one. I hope some day you'll join us, and the world will live as one. Please note, however, that my vision of global harmony is presented in a 16:9 aspect ratio. And if you don't know what that means, you'd better find out quickly, before the stormtroopers come for you. Hurry. They're peering through your letterbox right now.

That last line was an aspect ratio joke you're not geeky enough to get. See how you're missing out?

Still, if you choose to punish your own eyeballs in your own home with your own incorrectly adjusted television, at least you're only hurting yourself, whereas cinemas which lazily fart films at the screen without checking they're even the right way up are displaying naked contempt for a roomful of innocent strangers paying for the privilege.

Years ago I saw the film *Downfall* at a local multiplex. During the final act, the picture suddenly went out of whack, so Hitler's forehead was at the bottom of the screen and his moustache was at the top. Turns out it's hard to take Hitler seriously when that's happening.

After a few minutes of this, people started calling for the projectionist to sort it out. But nothing happened. After ten minutes, someone went to get the manager. After about twenty minutes, the problem was sorted out – at a guess, because the reel changed automatically. When the film ended and the credits rolled (miraculously, the right way up the screen), I tried to complain to the manager, only to find myself talking to an oppressed ticket-ripper, who explained, wearily, that despite having about twelve auditoriums, they only had one projectionist, who had to run between screens like a man spinning plates.

'Why don't you hire more projectionists?' I asked.

He just looked at me, trapped and helpless, as another paying customer came over to complain.

If you ask me, every screen should have its own projectionist, as well as an usherette, an organist, a conductor, and a sniper trained to blow the heads off anyone who dares open their mouth after the titles start.

That was about six years ago. Today if you go to the cinema, you're slightly less likely to be subjected to that kind of error if they're using a digital projector, in which case there's probably no projectionist at all, just some kind of iPad app flickering in the darkness.

Fortunately, there's a chance the film will still be ruined by your fellow audience members, who will loudly field phone calls throughout, because they're selfish dunces with no concentration span, reared in a modern world with no respect for the correct way of approaching any piece of filmed work, even if it's *Transformers 3*, which is this: either watch it properly, in the correct aspect ratio and in absolute silence, or get out of the room and go home, where a galaxy of smudgy, twenty-eight-second YouTube videos awaits you with cold, open arms.

Arab springs and structured reality
28/12/2011

2011 was a hectic year – so hectic it required its own language. Phrases such as 'Lulzsec', 'phone hacking' and 'Wendi Deng' suddenly became common currency. But why hasn't anyone printed a handy cut-out-and-keep handbook explaining what all this stuff means? Well, actually, they have. And you're already reading it. Shut up and keep going as we start our guide to the Buzzwords of 2011.

Sock puppet
Stop thinking about actual sock puppets with buttons for eyes and so on. We're talking about internet 'sock puppets' here: in other words, people pretending to be someone else on the

internet in order to win an argument – or, in the case of Amina Arraf, Syrian lesbian blogger, to further a cause. Amina's blog was held up as an inspiration – until 'she' was revealed to be a forty-year-old student from the University of Edinburgh. Adding to the confusion, days later, one of the editors of a lesbian website that had promoted Amina's blog also turned out to be a man.

It was a bit like the end of *Some Like it Hot*. Some began to suspect that lesbians, like leprechauns, might not actually exist at all. Fortunately, Channel 5 soon scotched these rumours with a docusoap set in a lesbian bar. Speaking of which . . .

Structured reality

Once upon a time we had docusoaps. Now we have *The Only Way is Essex*, *Made in Chelsea* and *Desperate Scousewives* – and what do they have in common? No, apart from that.

That's right! They're all 'structured reality' shows. 'Structured reality' essentially means 'not quite real': the people featured in the show are actual people, with actual thoughts and feelings and relationships and kidneys and anuses and so on, but the situations they find themselves in for the purposes of the show are slightly massaged into position by the producers. In other words, they're told to stand in a particular spot and toss a glass of wine over their boyfriend because he cheated on them in last week's episode.

Christ. Imagine if that was your life.

But it isn't your life. You're just watching it. And when you tune in to a structured-reality show you, the viewer, are actively choosing to spend sixty minutes watching a glossy-looking soap opera performed by non-actors half-improvising a non-script. It's precisely like a scene from an old-school porn film in which a plumber and a frustrated housewife trade clunky dialogue, but with better lighting and no onscreen sex. Speaking of which . . .

Merkozy

Throughout the latter part of the year, every economist was debating one issue: would the eurozone collapse? Or crumble? Or melt down and dribble into an abyss? No one could decide which combination of words best described the inevitable impending disaster.

Eventually they gave up and simply started screaming. In a bid to distract them, German chancellor Angela Merkel and French president Nicolas Sarkozy stood beside each other at press conferences and made reassuring cooing noises.

Ever since Ben Affleck and Jennifer Lopez were rechristened 'Bennifer' (100 years ago, in 1982), any two proximate individuals appearing in a newspaper must have their names combined by law. Sometimes it catches on ('Brangelina') and sometimes it sorta catches on (e.g. *Big Brother* twins 'Samanda'; famous until toppled by 'Jedward'), but it's rarely used in broadsheets (referring to 'the killings of Frose West' is expressly forbidden by the *Guardian*'s style guide).

'Merkozy', however, was a fun nickname even the driest business news section could print without blushing (although in the case of the *FT* it was hard to tell). What did 'Merkozy' actually mean? Nothing. But it provided light relief from all that depressing stuff about bond yields. Speaking of which . . .

Bond yields

Approximately 10,000 cryptic economic phrases suddenly popped up in news reports this year, nonchalantly bandied about as if the viewer knew what they meant. It was all 'bond yield' this and 'sovereign debt' that. Impenetrable. At one point, numbers were given 'haircuts'. That's like something out of Lucy in the Sky with Diamonds or a Spike Milligan poem. No wonder the economy's in such a mess.

If something can't be described in plain English, maybe you shouldn't base an entire society on it. Just saying. As it is, the whole thing's been a pointless endeavour. Speaking of which . . .

Planking

The widespread distribution of camera-studded smartphones has led humankind to experiment with things it had never bothered attempting before, 'planking' being a prime example. This was a short-lived craze that involved posing for a photograph while lying face-down in a rigid plank-like position.

A game of planking one-upmanship quickly swept the internet, with plankers planking in increasingly perilous locations (e.g. balanced on hotel balconies, atop mountains, within the hearts of collapsing stars, etc.) until clumsiness took over and people started toppling off things and dying. Oh, how the laughter dried in our throats. We thought it was harmless fun. But God had other plans.

Recently killed plankers whose bodies hadn't been carted away yet could always save face by pretending to have invented 'stiffing' – lying on the ground being authentically dead.

Sadly 'stiffing' failed to take off as a meme until Muammar Gaddafi did it in October, creating front-page news in the process. If only he'd found a way to monetise the craze, he'd have been loaded. But he didn't. Because he was dead. Speaking of which. . .

Arab spring

Toppling leaders was all the rage in 2011 as people across the Arab world collectively decided they'd had just about enough of this bullshit. To the casual TV viewer, the Arab spring was initially confusing: previously, whenever the news showed you footage of furious Arabs marching in the streets, they were chanting 'Death to the West' or burning effigies of John Barrowman or something. Now suddenly they were the good guys, and their despised dictatorial leaders were the bad guys – but the news hadn't really bothered explaining who these bad guys were before.

The Tunisian president's a ruthless tyrant, you say? Why didn't you tell me this earlier?

It was as if these Arab despots had only just landed on the planet, like the intergalactic megabaddies from *Superman II*, and the news was playing catchup. We didn't know their names or what they looked like, or have much of a clue as to why they were unpopular – unless, like Colonel Gaddafi, they'd previously done something awful to us, in which case we'd not only cheer from the sidelines, but also lend air support.

Basically, in terms of narrative, things hadn't been set up clearly enough during the first act. Come on, news: you really must try harder to explain this stuff. Speaking of which . . .

Higgs boson

This year scientists got one step closer to confirming the existence of the Higgs boson, aka the 'God Particle'. Prior to the breakthrough, only scientists knew what the Higgs boson was. Afterwards, once the news had patiently explained it to everyone on the planet, only scientists knew what the Higgs boson was.

Like all complex scientific ideas, I find the concept of the Higgs boson hard to grasp for more than three minutes at a time. You can explain it to me, and I'll understand it, really I will, but the moment you walk away, the knowledge starts invisibly drifting out of my head. I call this mysterious phenomenon – by which I shift from ignorance to enlightenment, and then back to ignorance – the Brooker Gap. When are scientists going to look into that phenomenon? Never.

Money: too shite to mention

Broadcast during *2011 Wipe*, BBC4/2, 28/12/2011

CB is walking through a dilapidated ghost town, ranting to camera.

CHARLIE: Throughout the year, the global economy was in a state of perpetual crisis. It was the most boring apocalypse ever. Numbergeddon. At least I *understood* nuclear war.

The economy was continually on the brink or gazing into the abyss or teetering on the precipice, or gawping over the brink of both the abyss *and* the precipice into a bottomless pit full of decaying banknotes being eaten by a wolf with coins for eyes.

There was one financial train wreck after another. We had Ireland, Portugal, and of course Greece . . .

Footage of Greece aflame.

CHARLIE: Greece was the Enron of Europe and things there looked far from good – which was great from a TV news perspective, because it turned a complex economic story into something with panic and fire in it.

To be fair, Greece *does* catch fire easily. Just ask anyone who's made chips. Anyway, after we'd worried about Greece it was time to worry about Italy.

Footage of Italy and Silvio Berlusconi.

CHARLIE: Yes, Italy, that leggy brunette of a nation, had a liquidity problem – possibly because it was headed by a leader who'd spent years doing his level best to spurt all the liquid out of his body.

Berlusconi had been in the spotlight for much of the year thanks to murmurings about his 'Bunga Bunga' parties. But now he was in a hole he *hadn't* cheerfully lubricated first, and before long he had to go.

Yes, while throughout the Arab world leaders were being ousted by the people, in Europe they were being ousted by cold hard numbers. And the financial mess keeps deepening.

Money's knackered, basically. Try withdrawing banknotes from a cashpoint now and God knows what'll happen – a sort of gas will probably come out.

Soon we'll have to adopt a medieval bartering system, in which we pay for food with sexual favours. Sainsbury's is going to be *horrible* on a Saturday morning: everyone standing at the checkout, tearfully masturbating for orange juice.

Mind you, at least Berlusconi will be in his element. I doubt it'd be the first time he's jerked off over an Innocent Smoothie.

Keep Calm and Oh Just Stop It
08/01/2012

New Year's resolutions work like this: you think of something you enjoy doing, and then resolve to stop doing it. Smoking, for instance, or drinking, or shunting fistfuls of salted butter down your ravenous maw each morning. By denying yourself some of your few remaining pleasures, you hope to extend your lifespan, so you can spend extra decades forlornly wishing you were smoking or drinking or gorging on butter instead of slowly withering to death in a self-imposed prison of abstinence.

Stop being lazy, you tell yourself. And as you lace up your running shoes with the enthusiasm of a man condemned to eat damp cardboard for ever, you know you will fail, and you will dislike yourself for failing.

Rather than setting yourself a New Year's resolution, why not simply pick a reason for hating yourself for the next 365 days? Takes less time, and it's easier to stick to.

Or you could do what I'm doing this year: setting New Year's resolutions for everyone in the world except me. These are the things I want humankind to stop doing immediately, on the grounds they've been doing them too long. They won't listen, but that's OK, because as I've already established, resolutions are doomed to fail.

Oh, and I've chosen the really huge bugbears, obviously, not the little ones like global economic justice or racial intolerance. We won't change those till the Martians land and command us to sort that shit out. Anyway, the list:

1. Stop creating 'Keep Calm and Carry On' variants

The original wartime 'Keep Calm and Carry On' poster, re-discovered more than ten years ago by the owner of Alnwick's Barter Books and digitally touched up by Chris Donald, erstwhile editor of *Viz*, is an amusing yet poignant instant design classic. It belongs on a poster, or a mug, or a tea towel sold by Barter Books. But not on a packet of condoms or a soft drink. Or a cushion. Or engraved on your baby's face.

Every bastard's churning out 'Keep Calm' merchandise these days. Check your attic. Someone's probably up there screen printing it on to a hammock right now. Moneygrabbers with no right to the 'Keep Calm' phrase (and no connection to Barter Books) have attempted to trademark it. And at the time of writing, Britain's bestselling iPhone app is a widget that lets you create your own zany version of the poster, so it reads 'Keep Calm and LOL Kittens!!!!' or something similarly anti-hilarious. It doesn't even use the right font.

It's time we, as a species, ceased to be impressed by this sort of thing. We're better than that. We are.

2. Stop pretending cupcakes are brilliant

Of all the irritating 'Keep Calm' bastardisations, the most irritating of all is the one that reads 'Keep Calm and Eat a Cupcake'.

Cupcakes used to be known as fairy cakes, until something happened a few years ago. I don't know what the thing was, because I wasn't paying attention. All I know is that suddenly middle-class tosspoles everywhere were holding artisan cupcakes aloft and looking at them and pointing and making cooing sounds and going on and bloody on about how much they loved them.

I wouldn't mind, but cupcakes are bullshit. And everyone knows it. A cupcake is just a muffin with clown puke topping. And once you've got through the clown puke there's nothing but a fistful of quotidian sponge nestling in a depressing, soggy 'cup' that feels like a pair of paper knickers a fat man has been sitting in throughout a long, hot coach journey between two disappointing market towns.

Actual slices of cake are infinitely superior, as are moist chocolate brownies, warm chocolate-chip cookies and virtually any other dessert you can think of. Cupcakes are for people who can't handle reality.

3. Stop pretending Lady Gaga and Beyoncé are endlessly fascinating

Look, it's not that I don't see their appeal. I just can't fathom the apparently infinite depth of it. I appreciate they're both polished entertainers with a neat line in music videos and some very catchy songs, but beyond that – what are you all seeing, precisely?

I mean, it's nice that the openly kooky Lady Gaga inspires her fans not to give in to bullies and suchlike, but she also inspires them to 'put their paws up' and be a bit annoying, which kind of balances it out, really.

Neither Lady Gaga nor Beyoncé are Mayan gods. And if their central message is one of personal empowerment and proud individuality you shouldn't be worshipping or emulating them anyway. Let them sing and leave it at that. Keep Calm and Carry On, if you like.

4. Stop making superhero movies

Kick-Ass, that was a good one. *Iron Man*, fair enough. But now we don't need any more superhero films. Especially not pretentious ones.

There's a new *Dark Knight* film out this year. Calling Batman 'the Dark Knight' is like calling Papa Smurf 'the Blue Patriarch': you're not fooling anyone. It's a children's story about a billionaire who dresses up as a bat to punch criminals on the nose. No normal adult can possibly relate to that, which makes his story inherently boring, unless you're a child, in which case you can enjoy the bits where he rides his super-bike around with his cape flapping behind him like a tit.

The scenes where some improbable clown-like supervillain delivers a quasi-philosophical speech are even worse, incidentally.

Tip: if you want to make your bad guy interesting and menacing and exotic, don't waste hours gluing prosthetic dice to his eyelids and giving him a name like 'the Quizzlestick'. Just show him masturbating into an oven glove while watching earthquake footage on CNN. Then you've got my attention. And made a film worth watching.

DVD Dave
15/01/2012

British filmmakers! Put down those clapperboards and pay attention because David Cameron, who happens to be a huge fan of your work – assuming you're making *The King's Speech II* – wants you to focus on films likely to be a 'commercial success'. Which presumably is the last thing you want.

Cynics say Cameron knows squit about British films. When that photo of SamCam and Michelle Obama having a coffee morning in the Downing Street flat was released, there didn't seem to be many British films in the Cameron DVD collection. Not even *Carry On Screaming*. Mainly US TV box sets. Oh, and he owns the film *Armageddon* on DVD. It's hard not to judge him for that.

To be fair, the photo was taken before *The King's Speech* had come out on DVD. Apparently he bought twenty-six copies of that. Not deliberately – he thought the disc was sticking so he kept buying it again and again, until he realised the lead character had a stutter.

Anyway, Cameron's advice for filmmakers runs as follows: go mainstream. For years, you've held audiences in contempt, deliberately making your works obtuse. You even have to be cajoled into taking the lens cap off because you'd rather the repellent 'viewers' sat there in pitch-blackness, trying to piece together the story from the soundtrack alone.

Not that there's a 'story' anyway. The notion of a coherent plot offends your snooty arts-hole sensibilities. No one's saying you have to signpost everything, but for God's sake attach some clear labels.

Look at *The King's Speech*. For one thing, you <u>can</u> look at it: no lens caps left on there. What's more, the story is simple. The world's most important man can't speak properly, so he gets taught to speak properly. But then disaster strikes! It looks like he might not be able to speak properly after all. Finally, in a triumphant climax, he speaks properly. It's a feelgood ending for everybody, apart from the 450,000 Britons killed in the war he just announced on the radio.

Feelgood endings are another mainstream necessity. Why go to the cinema to watch a film about desperate, blighted lives, when thanks to Cameron you're already living one – in cutting-edge 3D.

Not that directors shouldn't make films about ordinary paupers, provided they're left smiling at the end. One of the main reasons David Cameron enjoyed *The King's Speech* is that it showed him how a man less privileged than himself overcame his lowly breeding and learned how to conquer a stammer. Compare that with a film like *Fish Tank*. People said *Fish Tank* was brilliant but it didn't outperform *Transformers: Dark of the Moon*, because they neglected to put any 200-foot robots in it, and because none of the cast victoriously punched the air at the end.

The British film industry needs to have the courage to think inside the box, sinking its money into guaranteed box-office hits such as *Absolute Beginners* and that *Alien Autopsy* comedy starring Ant and Dec. If you want commercial success, look at what's packing them in down the multiplex, and give them more of the same – only morer and samer. People hate variety. They don't want anything 'new'.

Superhero films are guaranteed box-office gold – so let's make a British one: a *Dark Knight* facsimile about a vigilante Beefeater in a rubberised outfit who lives in the Tower of London with an army of ravens.

Also, how about Paddington Bear as a wisecracking CGI hero? The marmalade sandwiches he enjoys won't 'read' overseas, so we'll replace those with peanut butter and jelly, but otherwise he's exactly the same loveable British Paddington Bear, minus the bit about him being an immigrant from darkest Peru. Also, he wears sunglasses and says 'woah, THAT's godda hurt!' and is voiced by Ashton Kutcher.

Actually, Cameron isn't an utter philistine. He approvingly referenced the Lindsay Anderson film *if....* on the *Today* programme. Which is odd because *if....* is precisely the sort of film that would never, ever get made if his advice were heeded.

No one sets out to make a box-office flop. The problem with British films isn't a failure of ambition – it's the challenge of getting the damn things seen in a world filled with chain multiplexes programmed by monolithic distributors. Without distribution, no one sees your film. And without a huge marketing engine behind you, without a cookie-cutter similarity to the last big thing, the distributors often ain't interested.

The King's Speech was a good film, but it's essentially *Rocky* for stammerers. Patriotic, yes: but we've made other, more forward-looking British films by ignoring the box office and taking risks.

This Is England was a big British hit after years of low-budget risks from Shane Meadows. *Kidulthood* was a big British hit because Noel Clarke risked a film resembling nothing else in the multiplex. *Four Lions*, *Shaun of the Dead* and *The Inbetweeners*

Movie were big British hits, the success of which can be traced back to risks taken on television: Chris Morris, *Spaced*, and the original *Inbetweeners* sitcom – niche comedies on minority channels. The mainstream came to them. Not the other way round.

If Cameron is serious about wanting our film industry to make more money, he should leave the ball-breaking yap about profits to *Glengarry Glen Ross*, and instead take the long view: nurture the creative talent of tomorrow – from filmmakers to games designers.

The upcoming generation is being squeezed harder and has fewer choices than ever. Unleashed, they could create things neither Cameron nor myself could possibly begin to imagine.

Give them a playground, let them make mistakes, and give them time: they'll generate glorious failures and unprecedented moneyspinners. British ones. Which Cameron can proudly display on his shelf. If there's room between *Armageddon* and his twenty-six copies of *The King's Speech*.

In Tokyo
22/01/2012

I'm currently on another planet, namely Japan, which for the average Westerner is an experience tantamount to recovering from a serious head injury, in that while the world around you is largely recognisable, it somehow makes little sense. Incredibly minor example: they sell green Kit Kats here (not the wrapper – I'm not that easily impressed – I mean the chocolate itself is green).

Furthermore, just like someone struggling to reacquaint themselves with everyday life, you have to continually re-learn how to perform previously straightforward tasks such as going to the toilet. In Japan you either crap into a bluntly utilitarian hole in the ground (reverse squat-toilet style) or, increasingly, into one of their famous hi-tech Toto superbogs with a heated seat and a remote-controlled bum-washing jet.

The first toilet I encountered in Japan was so advanced it automatically lifted the seat itself the moment it sensed my approach, like it just couldn't wait for me to crap down its throat. It's disconcerting, shitting into a robot's mouth.

In five years' time that toilet won't merely cock its lid when you enter the room, it'll be programmed to hum lullabies as it swallows your droppings. If the machines ever rise up and kill us, we'll only have our own smug sense of mastery to blame.

But I'm not in Japan to sit on toilets. I'm here to write some travel pieces for this newspaper, which will appear later in the year. As a result I've been zipping all over the place. But every now and then, when the sheer sensory overload gets too much, I retire to the hotel room to stare at the television.

Westerners have been confounded by Japanese TV for decades, ever since Clive James amused millions in the eighties with clips from a gameshow called *Endurance*, in which contestants had to undergo a series of increasingly painful and humiliating ordeals. For British viewers, much of the fun came from sheer outraged disbelief that watching people being physically tormented and degraded was considered entertainment.

But of course that was 100 years ago, before *I'm a Celebrity* transformed low-level torture into mainstream British fare. Nonetheless, you don't have to watch Japanese TV for long until you see something shocking. The other evening I watched a programme in which a man was shown spooning boiling molten metal into his mouth. This was followed by footage of a man being mauled by a tiger and a rib-tickling sequence in which a studio guest was deliberately poisoned by some kind of sea creature.

Generally though, the TV here is surprisingly dull. The vast majority of programmes consist of several seriously overexcited people sitting in an overlit studio decorated like a novelty grotto made from regurgitated Dolly Mixture, endlessly babbling about food.

Seriously, it's all food, food, food. People eating food, answering questions about food, sometimes even just pointing at food and laughing. It's as if they've only just discovered food and are perpetually astonished by its very existence. Imagine watching an endless episode of *The One Show* with the colour and brightness turned up to 11, where all the guests have been given amphetamines, the screen is peppered with random subtitles, and every ten seconds it cuts to a close-up shot of a bowl of noodles for no apparent reason. That's 90 per cent of Japanese TV right there.

For a nation so preposterously hi-tech, it's a curiously old-fashioned approach to television. People talking in studios. Forever. Like it's the fifties. And yet it's insanely agitated: as though the participants are simply too wired to make a proper TV show, and have subsequently just switched the cameras on and started yelping.

The adverts continue this vaguely old-school theme. There are plenty of super-sophisticated ones starring giant CGI cats and the like, but there's also a rather charming emphasis on dancing: people unpretentiously dancing and singing about the product on offer (generally a foodstuff, which presumably explains their terrifying level of excitement). It makes the Go Compare tenor seem subtle. Sedate, even.

But while onscreen Japan offers up old-fashioned fodder with an unhinged, frantic glee bordering on malevolence, the moment you step outside, the population itself seems incredibly calm, as though faintly mesmerised by the screaming technology surrounding them.

The cliché about the Japanese being unbelievably polite also holds true. At times they're so helpful it's almost a pain in the arse.

Ask a passing stranger if they know where the nearest branch of Mos Burger is and, if they don't immediately know the answer, they'll often start researching the subject on your behalf, whipping out their smartphones to locate it using Google maps or calling up their friends for advice.

And if after several minutes of peering at maps, placing phone calls, and umming and ahhing and apologising, they still can't provide a detailed set of directions, they appear to take it as a personal blow. In London, you'd get a smile and a shrug. Here they almost run away in disgrace. You actually feel guilty having inflicted that level of shame on them.

Like I say: another planet.

Make it public! Go on! It's fun!
29/01/2012

Sharing. Now there's a basic social concept that has somehow got all out of whack. The idea behind sharing is simple. Let's say I'm a caveman. I hunt and slaughter a bison, but I can't eat it all myself, so I share the carcass with others, many of whom really appreciate it, such as my infirm 86-year-old neighbour who hasn't had a proper meal in weeks because he is incapable of killing anything larger than a woodlouse. Have you tried grilling a woodlouse? It's scarcely worth the effort.

But it's not all bison meat. Let's say I am still a caveman. The other thing I share is information: the thoughts inside my head or stirring tales of the things I have done. I grunt a hilarious anecdote about the time I dropped a huge rock on a duck and an egg popped out, and mime scandalous gossip about well-known tribesmen. I'm the life and soul of the cave-party.

All this sharing served a purpose. It kept the community fed, as well as entertained and informed. Now zip forward to the present day and, like I say, sharing has somehow got all out of whack. A small percentage of the population hoards more bison meat than it could eat in 2,000 lifetimes, awarding itself huge bison meat bonuses on top of its base-rate bison meat 'salary'. I say 'bison meat'. In case you hadn't noticed, I'm using it as a clever metaphor for money.

The huge salaries and bonuses, we are told, are essential if we are to prevent this tiny percentage of selfish, hoarding arseholes from moving overseas. Imagine if they flew to Singapore and started selfishly hoarding things over there instead. Drained of their expertise and reassuring presence, how would Britain cope? Within days we'd be walking on all fours and devouring our offspring for food.

I don't want to panic you, but that's the reality. Never mind weeping over the size of their bonuses: we should be dropping to our knees and giving them blowjobs, tearfully imploring them to remain seated each time we come up for air. Treble their wages. Form a human ring around Britain's airports to prevent them from leaving. And for God's sake don't ask them to share anything. That kind of talk merely angers them.

Sharing is for the rest of us. Not sharing money or bison meat, but personal information. Where we are. What we're doing. Share it! Make it public! Go on! It's fun!

Increasingly, I stumble across apps and services that expect me to automatically share my every waking action on Facebook and Twitter. The key word here is 'automatically'. Take Spotify, the streaming music service. I have written before about my admiration for Spotify, about what a technical marvel it is. A world of music at your fingertips! Incredible!

The love affair was doomed. Spotify recently reinvented itself as a kind of adjunct to Facebook and has subsequently adopted some truly hideous 'social features'. For instance: it will tell other people what you're listening to, live. Yes, you can switch this feature off. That's not the point. The point is that it does it by default. By default. IT DOES IT BY DEFAULT.

When Sony launched the Walkman back in the late seventies, its main appeal was that for the first time in history you could stroll down the high street listening to Neil Diamond belting out 'Sweet Caroline' and no one could judge you for it. It made you the master of a private world of music. If the Walkman had, by default, silently contacted your friends and told them what you were listening to, not only would no one have bought a Walkman in the first place, its designers would have been viewed with the utmost suspicion.

Don't get me wrong. I'm all for sharing thoughts, no matter how banal (as every column I have ever written rather sadly proves). Humans will always babble. If someone wants to tweet that they can't decide whether to wear blue socks or brown socks, then fair enough. But when sharing becomes automated, I get the heebie-jeebies. People already create exaggerated versions of themselves for online consumption: snarkier tweets, more outraged reactions. Online, you play at being yourself. Apply that pressure of public performance to private, inconsequential actions – such as listening to songs in the comfort of your own room – and what happens, exactly?

It'll only get worse. Here's what I am listening to on Spotify. This is the page of the book I am reading. I am currently watching the forty-third minute of a Will Ferrell movie. And I'm not telling you this stuff. The software is. I am a character in *The Sims*. Hover the cursor over my head and watch that stat feed scroll.

You know how annoying it is when you're sitting on the train with a magazine and the person sitting beside you starts reading over your shoulder? Welcome to every single moment of your future. Might as well get used to it. It's an experience we'll all be sharing.

Yes, sharing. A basic social concept that's somehow got all out of whack.

A chimps' tea party of the damned
05/02/2012

There was a minor kerfuffle a few weeks ago when the *Daily Mail* website overtook the *New York Times* to become the most popular news site in the world. Liberals can whine all they like, but that's a formidable achievement, especially considering it's not really a conventional news site at all, more a big online bin full of pictures of reality stars, with the occasional Stephen Glover column lobbed in to lighten the mood.

The print edition of the paper is edited by Paul Dacre, who is regularly praised by media types for knowing what his customers want, and then selling it to them. This is an extraordinary skill that puts him on the same rarefied level as, say, anyone who works in a shoe shop. Or a bike shop. Or any kind of shop. Or in absolutely any kind of business whatsoever.

Whatever you think about Dacre's politics, you can't deny he's got a job to do, and he does it. Like a peg. Or a ladle. Or even a knee. Dacre is perhaps Britain's foremost knee.

Curiously, the online version of the *Mail* has become a hit by doing the reverse of what Dacre is commended for doing. It succeeds by remorselessly delivering industrial quantities of precisely the opposite of what a traditional *Mail* reader would presumably want to read: frothy stories about carefree young women enjoying themselves. Kim Kardashian or Kelly Brook 'pour their curves' into a selection of tight dresses and waddle before the lens and absolutely nobody on the planet gives a toss apart from *Mail Online*, which is doomed to host the images, and *Mail Online*'s readers, who flock in their thousands to leave messages claiming to be not in the slightest bit interested in the story they're reading and commenting on.

Now *Mail Online* has gone one step further by running a story that not only insults its own readers, but cruelly invites them to underline the insult by making fools of themselves.

In what has to be a deliberate act of 'trolling', last Friday it carried a story headlined 'Rightwingers are less intelligent than left wingers, says study'. In terms of enraging your core readership, this is the equivalent of *Nuts* magazine suddenly claiming only gay men masturbate to *Hollyoaks* babes.

The *Mail*'s report went on to detail the results of a study carried out by a group of Canadian academics, which appears to show some correlation between low childhood intelligence and rightwing politics. It also claimed that stupid people hold right-wing views in order to feel 'safe'. Other items they hold in order to feel safe include clubs, rocks and dustbin lids. But those are easy to let go of. Political beliefs get stuck to your hands. And the only way to remove them is to hold your brain under the hot tap and scrub vigorously for several decades.

As you might expect, many *Mail Online* readers didn't take kindly to a report that strived to paint them as simplistic, terrified dimwits. Many leapt from the tyres they were swinging in to furrow their brows and howl in anger. Others, tragically, began tapping rudimentary responses into the comments box. Which is where the tragi-fun really began.

'Stupidest study of them all,' raged a reader called Beth. 'So were the testers conservative for being so thick or were they left and using a non study to make themselves look better?' Hmmm. There's no easy answer to that. Because it doesn't make sense.

'I seem to remember "academics" once upon a time stating that the world was flat and the Sun orbited the Earth,' scoffed Ted, who has presumably been keeping his personal brand of scepticism alive since the middle ages.

'Sounds like a BBC study, type of thing they would waste the Licence fee on, load of Cods wallop,' claimed Terry from Leicester, thereby managing to ignore the findings while simultaneously attacking public service broadcasting for something it hadn't done. For his next trick, Terry will learn to whistle and shit at the same time.

Not all the respondents were stupid. Some were merely deluded. Someone calling themselves 'Hillside' from Sydney claimed: 'I have an IQ over 200, have six degrees and diplomas and am "right-wing", as are others I know at this higher level of intelligence.' His IQ score is particularly impressive considering the maximum possible score on Mensa's preferred IQ test is 161.

Whatever the numbers: intellectual dick-measuring isn't to everyone's tastes anyway. Simply by highlighting his own intelligence 'Hillside' alienated several of his commentbox brethren.

'If there is one person I can not stand and that is a snob who thinks they are intelligent because if they were intelligent and educated they wouldn't be snobs,' argued Liz from London. Once you've clambered over the broken grammar, deliberately placed at the start of the sentence like a rudimentary barricade of piled-up chairs, there's a tragic conundrum at work here. She claims intellectual snootiness is ugly, which it is, but unfortunately she says it in such a stupid way it's impossible for anyone smarter than a steak-and-ale pie not to look down on her. Thus, for Liz, the crushing cycle of snobbery continues.

On and on the comments went, turning a rather stark write-up of a daft-sounding study into a sublime piece of live online performance art. A chimps' tea party of the damned. The *Mail* has long been a master at trolling lefties; now it's mischievously turned on its own readers, and the results could only be funnier if the website came with free plastic lawn furniture for them to lob at the screen. You couldn't make it up.

You can't fart a crashing plane back into the sky
12/02/2012

I'm no financial expert. I scarcely know what a coin is. Ask me to explain what a credit default swap is and I'll emit an unbroken ten-minute 'um' through the clueless face of a broken puppet.

You might as well ask a pantomime horse. But even an idiot such as me can see that money, as a whole, doesn't really seem to be working any more.

Money is broken, and until we admit that, any attempts to fix the economy seem doomed to fail. We're like passengers on a nosediving plane thinking if we all fart hard enough, we can lift it back into the sky. So should we be storming the cockpit or hunting for parachutes instead? I don't know: I ran out of metaphor after the fart gag. You're on your own from here on in.

Banknotes aren't worth the paper they're printed on. If they were, they'd all have identical value. Money's only worth what the City thinks it's worth. Or, perhaps more accurately, hopes it's worth. Coins should really be called 'wish-discs' instead. That name alone would give a truer sense of their value than the speculative number embossed on them.

The entire economy relies on the suspension of disbelief. So does a fairy story, or an animated cartoon. This means that no matter how soberly the financial experts dress, no matter how dry their language, the economy they worship can only ever be as plausible as an episode of *SpongeBob SquarePants*. It's certainly nowhere near as well thought-out and executed.

No one really understands how it all works: if they did, we wouldn't be in this mess. Banking, as far as I can tell, seems to be almost as precise a science as using a slot machine. You either blindly hope for the best, delude yourself into thinking you've worked out a system, or open it up when no one's looking and rig the settings so it'll pay out illegally.

The chief difference is that slot machines are more familiar and graspable to most of us. When you hear a jackpot being paid out to a gambler, the robotic clunk-clunk-clunk of coin-on-tray, you're aware that he had to go to some kind of effort to get his reward. You know he stood there pushing buttons for hours. You can picture that.

The recent outrage over City bonuses stems from a combination of two factors: the sheer size of the numbers involved, coupled with a lack of respect for the work involved in earning them. Like bankers, top footballers are massively overpaid, but at least you comprehend what they're doing for the money. If Wayne Rooney got paid millions to play lacrosse in a closed room in pitch darkness, people would begrudge him his millions far more than they already do. Instead there he is, on live television: he's skilled, no doubt about it.

Similarly, it may be tasteless when a rapper pops up on MTV wearing so much bling he might as well have dipped himself in glue and jumped into a treasure chest full of vajazzling crystals, but at least you understand how he earned it.

RBS boss Stephen Hester, meanwhile, earns more than a million pounds for performing enigmatic actions behind the scenes at a publicly owned bank. And on top of his huge wage, he was in line for a massive bonus. To most people, that's downright cheeky: like a man getting a blowjob from your spouse while asking you to make him a cup of tea.

But Hester earned his wage, we're told, because he does an incredibly difficult job. And maybe he does. Trouble is, no one outside the City understands what his job actually consists of. I find it almost impossible to picture a day in Hester's life, and I once wrote a short story about a pint-sized toy Womble that ran around killing dogs with its dick, so I know I don't lack imagination. Class, yes: imagination, no. If I strain my mind's eye, I can just about picture Hester arriving at work, picture him thanking his driver, picture the receptionist saying 'Hello, Mr Hester', and picture him striding confidently into his office – but the moment the door shuts, my feed breaks up and goes fuzzy. What does he do in there? Pull levers? Chase numbers round the room with a broom? God knows.

Maybe if all bankers were forced to work in public, on the pavement, it would help us understand what they actually do. Of course, you'd have to encase them in a Perspex box so they wouldn't be attacked. In fact, if the experience of David Blaine is anything to go by, you'd have to quickly move that Perspex box to somewhere impossibly high up, where people can't pelt it with golf balls and tangerines. On top of the Gherkin, say. If Hester did his job inside a Perspex box on top of the Gherkin for a year, this entire argument might never have happened.

The row over bonuses has led some to mutter darkly about mob rule and the rise of anti-business sentiment. Complain about mobs all you like, but you can't control gut reactions, and you can't dictate the mood. And when you try to fart a crashing plane back into the sky, you only succeed in making the atmosphere unpleasant for everyone. And spoiling the in-flight movie. And making the stewardess cry. Looks like I'm all out of metaphor again. Time to end the article. Article ends.

Which Witch Hunt?

Broadcast on *10 O'Clock Live*, C4, 15/02/2012

CB is seated at the desk.

CHARLIE: Ever since last July's phone-hacking revelations, the press has been in the hotseat, most notably with the long-running Leveson Inquiry into Media Ethics, an event so star-studded it resembled a kind of anti-BAFTAs, featuring glamorous actress Sienna Miller, seething funnyman Steve Coogan, dreamy-eyed whorefucker Hugh Grant, and seedy tabloid un-bassador Paul McMullan, better known as TV's Roland Rat.

They were there, as was voice-of-an-angel Charlotte Church and voice-of-one-ankle Heather Mills, all swapping light and often harrowing anecdotes with your host: cuddly faced Lord Leveson, Chatty Man.

The major draw was the scrap between Hugh Grant and shadowy *Daily Mail* editor Paul Dacre, who isn't shown on TV very often, because of fears he might slither through the screen and stop your heart by whispering in Latin. But nevertheless *here* he is ...

CB talks over VT of Paul Dacre arriving at Leveson.

CHARLIE: ... temporarily adopting human form to pass through our realm. Look, there's a rare sight: he's touching a bible without it bursting into flames. And *there* he is sitting down to fume about Hugh Grant.

Comparative stills of Hugh Grant and Paul Dacre appear in split-screen.

CHARLIE: I don't know what it is about witty, handsome, sex symbol Hugh Grant that annoys purple-headed fuming pepper-pot Paul Dacre so much, but they've been trading insults for weeks, after Grant implied the *Mail* hacked his phone and Dacre said that was a 'mendacious smear'.

ON SCREEN: *Mock up of 'Love Hacktually' movie poster.*

CHARLIE: Things seem a bit tense between them really, although I've seen enough Hugh Grant films to know how it'll turn out: they don't get on at first, but by the end they'll be hungrily kissing to the sound of Wet Wet Wet – until Rhys Ifans walks in wearing a pair of funny pants with a mendacious smear down the arsecrack.

As well as the Leveson chatshow, there are three separate police investigations into the press, and on Saturday five *Sun* journalists were arrested ...

CB talks over VT of Rupert Murdoch.

CHARLIE: ... raising fears that Rupert Murdoch, seen here looking like the Emperor from *Star Wars* on a golfing holiday, might swoop in and destroy the *Sun*, like a demon from a Mayan prophecy.

Amongst the usual hate and tits, Monday's *Sun* also included a powerful column by Fleet Street legend Trevor Kavanagh in which he thundered that *Sun* journalists were being subjected to a 'witch hunt'.

Some say it's hypocritical of the *Sun* to complain about witch-hunts because it's conducted plenty of those itself. But that's not fair: the *Sun* has *never once* conducted a witch-hunt against actual witches.

I mean okay, it *has* picked on one or two other groups, like:

Social workers,
Women in burqas,
Left-wingers,
Suburban swingers,
Binge drinkers,
Forward-thinkers,
Gypsies,
Shirkers,
Public sector workers,
Underage mums,
Overage mums,
Spongers who sit around twiddling their thumbs,
Anyone who's had a fight,
Anyone with cellulite,
Looters,
Saggy hooters,
Feminists,
Leninists,
Satanists who take the piss,
So-called expert 'boffins',
The escorts who let Frank Bough in,
Anyone caught cheat'n,
Angus Deayton,
The England squad,
The goalie's hands,
The manager,

The Hillsborough fans . . .
Speed cameras,
Reckless drivers,
Snotty jobsworths,
Feckless skivers,
Trendy vicars wearing knickers,
Lezzers,
Benders,
The cast of *EastEnders*,
Leslie Grantham,
Foreigners who can't sing our national anthem,
The French,
The Portuguese,
The Krauts,
The MEPs,
Argentina,
Polish cleaners,
Anyone who lives in Spain (or starts a human rights campaign),
Geeks,
Freaks,
Crackers,
Hackers,
Killjoys,
Pillocks,
Toy-boys,
Kinnocks . . .
Moaners,
Miners,
Former men with new vaginas,
The local hoodie,
Jade Goody,
Jailbirds,
Nerds,
Troubled songbirds,

Long words,
And cheating turds on disability benefits who don't seem *quite*
disabled enough for their liking . . .
And Chris Jeffries,
Russell Harty,
Members of the Green Party,
Anyone who says, 'recycle!'
Wayward superstar George Michael,
Channel Four,
ITV,
Channel Five,
The BBC,
Over-eaters,
Asylum seekers – especially if they snuck into Britain using any
kind of vessel.
Katie Waissel,
Katie Waissel's 'prozzie' gran,
Iran,
Emperor Hirohito of Japan,
Zealous coppers,
Wife-swappers,
Bureaucrats,
Eurocrats,
Non-existent feral cats,
An innocent man called Robert Murat,
The cast of *The Only Way is Essex*,
The Leveson Inquiry into Media Ethics,
And the occasional supermodel bitches
– but never, ever *witches*.

Oh. Apart from all the times they've had a go at witches.

STILL: Sun *headlines in which they've had a go at actual witches [of
which there are more than you might think]*.

347

Seven days of Sun
19/02/2012

So then, witch-hunted tip-top soaraway tabloid the *Sun* will soon be available in a sizzling Sunday edition. Turns out the soothsayers were mistaken: the *Sun* isn't dying, it's expanding. Which, ironically, is precisely what an actual sun does when it dies.

Yes, during its death throes, our sun will swell, boiling the oceans and turning the ice caps to steam. All life on the planet will perish, and your copy of the *Sun* will burst into flames in your hands. I say hands. I mean 'carbonised stumps'. What I'm saying is it'll be hot out that day, so I wouldn't bother with a coat if I were you.

There was something slightly wonky about the hand-rubbing relish with which some predicted the death of the *Sun*. Call me an organic hessian-chewing, hummus-eating Guardianista, but I believe in reform, not capital punishment.

It's hard to cheer when a newspaper closes. Even one you're slightly scared of, like the *Daily Mail*. Even though the *Mail* isn't technically a newspaper, more a serialised Necronomicon. In fact it's not even printed, but scorched on to parchment by a whispering cacodemon.

The *Mail* can never close. It can only choose to vacate our realm and return to the dominion in which it was forged; a place somewhere between shadow and dusk, beyond time and space, at the dark, howling apex of infinity. London w8 5TT.

Yet despite being a malevolent ink-and-paper succubus that will devour your firstborn – seriously, chuck a baby at a copy of the *Mail*, and watch as the paper rolls its eyes back and swallows it whole – the *Mail* deserves its voice. At the Leveson inquiry, when seething *Daily Mail* orchestrator Paul Dacre was quizzed about Jan Moir's notorious column on the death of Stephen Gately, he acknowledged that she'd possibly gone too far, but added that he 'would die in a ditch' to defend a columnist's freedom of speech.

Whatever you think of Dacre, that's a brave and noble thing to say, although disappointingly he failed to indicate precisely when he was planning on doing it.

(That's a joke, so please don't be offended on his behalf, especially because it's precisely the kind of robust commentary on death he's dying in that ditch to defend.)

Regular readers may have noticed that the previous three paragraphs consisted of overheated *Mail*-bashing, something I indulge in so often in this column, it's become a tiresome cliché. In fact my own smug fingers fell asleep while typing it. No wonder the *Sun* told me off last week for lecturing everyone about press standards. It also called me a 'shouty third-rate TV presenter', which seems firm but fair.

I tend to ignore both criticism and praise, because I encounter so many dissenting assessments of my own value as a writer, or even simply as a collection of atoms, it all becomes meaningless noise. At any given moment, I've jumped the shark, returned to form, lost it, nailed it, provoked laughter or silence, impressed or bored the reader. After years of carefully skim-reading the comments under my own articles, I can only conclude that none of you have the faintest bloody idea what you're on about.

Still, my mini-bollocking in the *Sun* cut through, probably because I encountered it in ink-and-paper form, which meant it was a bit like stumbling across an ancient scroll. Reading its criticism was roughly as much fun as banging my knee on a table, but it made me think a bit. Who wants to be a finger-wagging human frown? Not me.

When it comes down to it, I'd rather entertain: to be a tail-wagging human frown. Might require surgery, but that's my dream. Lighten up a bit, I told myself. And then I wrote a two-minute poem attacking the *Sun* and shouted it all out on live television. Which is a long-winded and solipsistic way of saying that opposing voices are a good thing, even if you reject what they're saying. Only a monopolist wants to shut the other side up.

Of course there's a distinction between an opposing voice and a bullying one, bullying being what the 'poem' (a list of people and things the *Sun* has targeted over the decades) was about. The *Sun* has always tried to make things fun. At its best that's a catchy punning headline ('How Do You Solve a Problem Like Korea?'), at its worst it's 'Gotcha': the difference between clever class clown and ugly playground taunting. If, as some believe, the *Sun* needs to rehabilitate itself in what I will now preposterously label the post-hacking era, it'll have to learn to avoid the latter.

It'll probably have to learn new tricks, too, in the face of the competition. Not the *Guardian*, silly: that only sells three copies. Never mind Twitter being a liberal coffeehouse; it also fulfils many of the *Sun*'s traditional roles. It's brimming with news, celebrity gossip, zany trivia, jokes, opinion, hysteria, campaigns, witch-hunts, sanctimony and self-congratulation – and it's written in the brisk, compact language of today, not the slightly alien ROMP/TOT/HORROR/SMASH language of yester-year. Twitter's footballers even write their own columns, and make a good fist of it, too.

The one thing Twitter doesn't have is a pointless helping of naked breasts, unless you type (.) (.) – and even that isn't too big a hindrance since, as I understand it, nudity is available elsewhere on the internet. On pages three to three billion and three.

Cough up, fleshbag
18/03/2012

When the following piece was written, the NHS reform bill was about to be voted into law, and horrible warlord Joseph Kony had become internationally famous thanks to a dubious internet campaign.

Who'd want to be Andrew Lansley right about now? He's less popular than Joseph Kony. Wherever he goes people immediately start shouting at him. Old ladies scream the word 'codswallop!' in his face as he walks down the street. When he visits a hospital, doctors follow him around bellowing: 'Your bill is rubbish.'

Last week I flipped on the TV just in time to catch footage of his official car speeding away from a bunch of booing protesters, and for a moment I naturally assumed I was watching a news report about a despised killer being whisked away from a court appearance.

If these things were happening to you or me, we'd probably cry, or at least look slightly troubled. Yet no matter how many people are bellowing at him, Lansley perpetually wears the nonchalant expression of a man killing time by humming cheerfully in a lift.

Presumably he's become so accustomed to the sound of loudly heckled abuse, he doesn't even hear it any more. I guess to him it's like a noise made by some weird machine in his workplace, a background soundtrack he tunes out subconsciously. The protesters' plaintive ape wails of despair simply bounce off him like rice grains flicked at a rock. For a man who recently conducted a high-profile 'listening exercise', he's got a shitty set of ears.

What is it about Lansley that makes human beings hate him so much? It might have something to do with the suspicion that he's hell-bent on turning the NHS into a commercial free-for-all, which for some reason isn't going down well at a time when terrifying nightly warnings about the worst excesses of capitalism are broadcast in the guise of news bulletins.

The theory is that introducing an element of competition will improve the level of quality and range of choice for patients. And it doubtless would, if businesses behaved like selfless nuns, which they don't. Any business that wants to succeed has to cut corners somewhere to turn a profit. It also has to juggle a strange set of priorities, which means if you entrust your health to a corporation, the cost of your kidneys could end up being weighed against the spiralling cost of the CGI budgerigar voiced by Joan Collins they want for their new TV commercial.

Can you think of a single company you'd trust to slice you open and fiddle with the squishy components? Apple, maybe? After all, its products are brilliantly designed – but more importantly for a medical procedure, they're sterile.

But consider the length of the cable on your iPhone charger. Annoyingly short, isn't it? Almost as short as the battery life. That's two savings right there that have been passed on to you, the consumer, in the form of minor inconveniences. In medical terms, it's like being left with a slight limp because the surgeon needed to finish at five on the dot.

And let's not dwell too much on allegations about the factory where the iPhone is actually made. If these are true, and Foxconn were running the hospital kitchen, everything would taste slightly of tears. You'd be lying in bed, eating food that had been wept in, vainly waiting for that limp to heal while feverishly inserting coins into a slot to stop the bed automatically tipping you on to the floor to make way for the next customer.

I spent a fair bit of time last week visiting someone laid up in hospital. Every bed on the ward had a flat-screen TV beside it – a commercial entertainment system upon which you can watch TV or endure movies such as *Captain America* or *Transformers: Dark of the Moon*. There was a constant looping advert for these and other delights, interspersed by the now-notorious talking head shot of Lansley dribbling on about how your health is really important to him. He says he hopes this entertainment system will make your stay more enjoyable. And it will, if you pay for it.

If you pick up the remote and select good old vanilla BBC1, you only get to glimpse a few seconds of BBC1 before it displays a screen telling you to cough up. If the company responsible for the system genuinely wanted to make everyone's stay more comfortable, they'd let you have the BBC for nothing.

Chances are you pay your licence fee. They could give you the Beeb and then charge extra for the movie channels. Seems reasonable. But no. Cough up, fleshbag.

On the back of the screen is a sticker telling you to switch your mobile phone off. But fear not: the screen has a phone attached to it, which your distressed relatives can use to get in touch with you. It's a premium rate number. So cough up again, fleshbag.

The screens are switched on by default, so I assume, incidentally, that the company responsible covers the cost of all that electricity. Otherwise, you're indirectly coughing up for it already, fleshbag.

Lansley claims he's not out to privatise the NHS of course, but no one believes him, partly because all the talk about clinical commissioning groups is impenetrable jargon, but mainly because the nation's doctors start running around setting off klaxons and screaming whenever he appears.

As a general rule of thumb, when a doctor starts yelping with alarm, I worry. So would anyone. Yet the government expects us to ignore medical advice.

Because that's what *they're* doing.

PART NINE

In which Sonic the Hedgehog's sexual orientation goes under the microscope, a man in a penguin suit proves surprisingly popular, and idiots salivate over an arse that isn't there.

Dawn of the Dad
2/4/2012

Last week, I became a parent.

Can I tell you what I'm not going to do? I'm not going to turn this column into a series of wry observations on fatherhood, and/ or lengthy descriptions of just how brilliant my son is. A few weeks of that and you'd vomit yourself inside out, and if I wasn't writing it myself I'd be right beside you, holding your hair out of the way and rubbing your back in sympathy with each volcanic heave.

There's quite enough deification of kiddywinks in the media already, thanks. The way people burble on about the joy of infants, you'd have thought babies were being beamed down from heaven to save us. A cursory glance at human history suggests otherwise.

Having said all that, I *am* going to burble on about babies, for one week only – and you're going to sit there and take it. And when I'm finished, you'll leave in silence. Those are the rules.

Right. So it turns out the birth of your first child is perhaps the most emotionally charged experience you'll ever have. I even put down the new *Angry Birds* game for ten minutes so I could concentrate fully, and that's set in space.

You're buffeted by a range of feelings so intense, your face doesn't know how to deal with them, and keeps leaking fluid from somewhere round the eyeholes.

Obviously, I can only speak for the men here. Women find childbirth far easier. Many hardly even notice it's happening, which is why they tend to break into absent-minded howls of agony instead of concentrating on the task at hand.

(Incidentally, this is hardly my area of expertise, but I fail to comprehend why any sane twenty-first-century human would refuse an epidural. OK, you might view the full, unvarnished experience as some kind of precious rite, but come on: I heard the screams from the natural birth centre. It sounded like a werewolf exorcising a roomful of crucified sopranos.)

Labour takes ages. In the end, after hours of not-much-happening, there was a moment of drama. The entire cast of *Holby City* quickly filled the room and I found myself changing into a set of scrubs, in the toilet, in tears. I also held on to a sink for support. By the time I came out the crisis had passed, and my wife was smiling. We then had a further four hours of waiting, during which we both slept, after which the doctors decided to perform a caesarean.

And 'perform' is right. It's the most astounding magic trick I've ever witnessed. I didn't hover round the business end. I'm not a fan of innards. What if you go mad and lean forward and dunk a biscuit in them or something? Instead I sat up 'the face end', where a blue sheet was erected to protect our eyes from the *Fangoria* convention taking place below. Then, after some furtive rustling, they lowered the drape just enough to let you clap eyes on a squealing, squirming creature which your brain doesn't quite believe is actually there in the room.

And in this moment, your universe momentarily pauses while a fundamental shift in perspective takes place.

Apologies for swearing in the presence of a child, but the first thing I thought was 'Fuck me'. Not just as an expression of sur-prise, but as a mission statement, as in: 'Fuck me and what I want – from now on, my task is to protect you, whatever or whoever you are.'

Prior to the birth, other dads had warned me that 'bonding' might not happen for weeks, even months. Also, I was worried I might simply feel nothing. Instead I felt reprogrammed, head-to-toe, in an instant. That was a shock.

Just as gap-year students like to brag about the stomach bug they caught in India, so parents like to brag about how tired and hectic their life has become since the new arrival. During the pregnancy, whenever a parent spotted me so much as eating a biscuit, they'd chortle and say: 'Ho ho: enjoy eating biscuits while you can! Your biscuit-eating days are over, my friend! There'll be no time for biscuits once the baby arrives!'

All of which can make a dad-to-be somewhat apprehensive. I was worried I might simply resent the baby for disrupting my lazy, self-centred lifestyle. But the truth is this: when it actually happens, it's surprising how little you mind. Also, you eat *loads* of biscuits because there's no time to eat anything else.

Still, that's enough baby talk from me. I'm aware this is an uncharacteristically upbeat column by my standards, for which I apologise, as smiles sit wonkily on the collection of serviceable flesh apps I collectively call my face. I look sinister when I grin, like I'm secretly defecating in my trousers and enjoying the warm glow more than is strictly necessary.

But only a cardboard man could fail to acknowledge that some things simply leave you feeling deeply, deeply happy. Call me dense or cold or both, but I wasn't anticipating the wave of euphoria I've been experiencing. It'll wear off, I'm sure, and these pages aren't the place for it anyway, but yes: I understand why people have kids. Right now, at the moment, I 'get' babies.

Now let us never speak of this again.

I didn't stick to that promise.

Some people are gay in space. Get over it.
16/4/2012

It must be awful, being a homophobe. Having to spend all that time obsessing about what gay people might be doing with their genitals. Seeing it in your mind, over and over again, in high-definition close-up. Bravely you masturbate, to make the pictures go away, but to no avail. They're seared onto your mental membranes. Every time you close your eyes, an imaginary gay man's imaginary penis rises from the murk, bowing ominously in your direction, sensing your discomfort. Laughing. Mocking. Possibly even winking. How dare they, this man and his penis? How dare they do this to you?

Obviously you can't fight the big gay penis in your head. It has no physical form, so you can't get a grip on it, much as you'd like to. You'd love to grab it and throttle it until it splutters its last all over your face and neck.

That might bring you closure. But no. So you do the next best thing. You condemn homosexuals in the real world. Maybe if they could just stop all this 'being gay' business for ten minutes, you'd get some respite from that scary headcock. It might shrivel away completely, leaving nothing behind. Except maybe a nice bit of bum.

No, dammit! Forget I said that! No bum either!

Of course sometimes the act of condemning homosexuals in the real world overlaps with the imaginary realm. Over the past few weeks, *games* company Electronic Arts has been subjected to a letter-writing campaign from idiots outraged by its decision to allow players to define their characters as gay in a *Star Wars* game.

The Florida Family Association says, 'children and teens, who never thought any way but heterosexual, are now given a choice to be lesbian, gay, bisexual or transgender' – adding that even if they chose to be straight, they would still 'be forced to deal with lesbian, gay, bisexual or transgender characters chosen by other players'. Personal choice and co-operation: two appalling threats to our youth.

They also claim 'there were no LGBT characters in any of the *Star Wars* movies'. I don't know which wacky re-cut version of *Star Wars* they've been watching, but I saw the original when I was about six years old and even then I was struck by how outrageously camp C3PO is. He was a gilded John Inman in space.

And what about Luke Skywalker? Apart from briefly kissing

his own sister, he shows no interest in women whatsoever. The first film is a tender gay parable in which Luke falls in love with Alec Guinness and gradually 'comes out' as a Jedi. The final scene oozes symbolism: having penetrated the Death Star's trench in his phallic spacecraft, he closes his eyes, submits to his true inner instinct and triumphantly blasts his X-Wing's seed into an anus-like aperture, causing an orgasmic eruption that changes his universe for ever.

It's hard to see how they could make *Star Wars* any gayer, unless they gave the Millennium Falcon a handlebar moustache.

But hang on, some of you are saying, this is a video game we're talking about. Isn't this gay content a bit 'shoehorned in'? Sonic the Hedgehog never agonised over his sexual identity. He was too busy sprinting through a rainbow-coloured landscape leaping at rings.

True, but that was in 1991 – which in 'technology years' was about nine millennia ago. It's like comparing a cave painting with a surround-sound 3D movie. EA's *Star Wars* title in question is an MMORPG (massively multiplayer online role-playing game) with more than a million subscribers: real people playing and interacting with each other in real-time, and hey, statistically, at least three of those people are going to be gay. The least you can do is let them reflect that in the characters they pick.

But wait: there's even more gay content in another EA space epic, *Mass Effect 3*, which to the uninitiated is a bit like playing through an entire *Star Trek* box set. It's bold space hokum and it's great fun – and just like *Star Trek*, it includes a range of potential love interests for the main character.

Previous *Mass Effect* titles have let you play as a woman and – gasp – seduce other women: this final instalment is the first to give players the option of playing a man who woos men. Play your cards right (or play your dialogue tree options right) throughout hours of gameplay and you'll be rewarded with a short, chaste love scene in which two bare-chested men kiss and cuddle in bed.

Players have complained bitterly about the ending of *Mass Effect 3* – not because of the potential for homosexual love, but because they found the narrative underwhelming. The game has a variety of different endings, depending on your decisions: some have moaned that none of the possible endings are happy or satisfying enough. In fact, they've moaned so much, EA has hastily released an additional ending free-of-charge, so these players can experience 'further closure'.

I can't work out if that's depressing or sweet. On the one hand, they're spoiled little emperors with a mind-boggling sense of entitlement: it's one thing to be disappointed by the end of a story, but another to demand the author sits down and writes you a new one RIGHT NOW. You need 'further closure'? What's wrong with you?

But on the other hand, it's a sign that players sometimes invest so much of themselves into the characters they play, they care about them to a degree that should make any author jealous. Sneerers will doubtless leave comments about 'saddoes' and 'shut-ins', oblivious that by doing so, they too are playing a character in an immense MMORPG called the internet. Face it: you've even chosen a nickname and an avatar just to join in.

Allowing players to identify their characters as homosexual isn't, as the anti-gay campaigners claim, a tokenistic novelty, but an unavoidable consequence of the fascinating evolution of video games. Not that there's much point explaining that to them. They don't believe in evolution either.

And they wouldn't hear you anyway over the thunderous roar of dicks screaming forever in their frightened mind's ear.

The spirit of the Games
23/4/2012

The Olympic Games trundle ever closer, and already you can smell the excitement in the air, because it's being wafted in by gigantic corporate excitement blowers. Try as they might to engage us, we're not on tenterhooks yet. On paper it's virtually illegal to be anything other than thrilled to self-pissing point at the prospect of hours of running, jumping, swimming etc. filling our minds and airwaves for several weeks, but in reality, the majority of Britons appear to be acknowledging the forthcoming Games with little more than an offhand shrug. We're just not that arsed – not right now, anyway. That'll change the moment any of our athletes gets within sniffing distance of any kind of medal – then it'll be all cheering and jubilant BBC montages – but until then we're being very British about the whole thing by largely ignoring it, aside from the odd quiet moan about the negative effect it'll have on the traffic.

It'd be worrisome if this low-level grumpiness extended into the Games themselves: if the crowd audibly tutted whenever anyone other than Britain won, and the medals were handed over by an official displaying the same vaguely begrudging air as a checkout assistant passing you a replacement carrier bag when the first one splits. That's definitely how we would behave if we didn't have guests. Hopefully instead we'll plaster on a fake smile for our overseas visitors, and after ten minutes forget we were faking and start actively to enjoy the whole thing. But what if that doesn't happen? How else can we get into the spirit of the Games?

Well, for starters we could make that fake smile frosty-white by brushing our teeth with an Oral-B electric toothbrush. 'Oral-B is getting behind the London 2012 Olympics,' cheers the Boots website. 'Share the excitement with their Professional Care 500 floss action electric toothbrush.' Yes: the exhilaration, the agony, the sheer elation experienced by athletes operating at the peak of their physical aptitude – all this can be yours in the form of a vibrating twig you stick in your mouth.

In case you think the mere notion of an official Olympic electric toothbrush is absurd, remember: athletes need clean teeth to attain peak performance. Steve Ovett was the favourite to win the 1,500 m at the 1980 Moscow Olympics, but was hopelessly weighed down by a heavy build-up of plaque that had accumulated in his mouth in the months leading up to the contest, allowing Sebastian Coe to snatch the gold.

Oral-B's official Olympic toothbrush exists because its parent company, Procter & Gamble, has a sponsorship deal enabling it to associate all its products with the Games. That's why if you look up Viakal limescale remover on a supermarket website, the famous five interlocking rings pop up alongside it. This in no way cheapens the Olympic emblem, which traditionally symbolises global unity, peaceful competition and gleaming stainless steel shower baskets.

When you're done sprucing up your teeth and your bathroom, you could further embrace the Olympic spirit by slurping a Coca-Cola (official Olympic drink) followed by a Twirl from Cadbury's (official Olympic snack provider). Or really go the whole hog and polish off a couple of sausage-and-egg McMuffins at your local McDonald's (official Olympic restaurant), after which you should be ready to represent Britain in the 400-litre diarrhoea.

I've never understood why firms are prepared to shell out a fortune simply to refer to the Olympics in their advertising, but then I've always been mildly baffled by the popularity of sport full-stop. I also never understood why Gillette paid Tiger Woods, a man famous for hitting balls with a stick, a huge amount of money to promote scraping a bit of sharp metal across your face – only to sideline him when it became apparent that as well as hitting balls with a stick, he had been inserting his penis into as many different women as possible, an aspiration he presumably shared with the vast majority of Gillette's customers.

My natural inclination is to find the wave of 'official' branding vaguely sinister, but on reflection it's actually rather touching the way these companies seem to earnestly believe their consumers give a toss. Will anyone in the country choose a Dairy Milk over a Yorkie just because the former has the Olympic rings printed on the wrapper? After all, now that it appears alongside everything from toothbrushes to Viakal, the official Olympic iconography has become just another bit of background visual noise – like the Keep Britain Tidy icon, or a barcode. Your brain filters it out before your mind even notices it was there in the first place. If I was Adidas (official Team GB Olympic outfitters), I'd be furious. At least sportswear has some connection to the traditional Olympic ideal of people from far-flung corners of the Earth engaging in hard physical graft for little financial reward, especially if it turns out it was made in an Indonesian sweatshop.

Instead, the Olympic rings have been whored around so much they've become valueless: a status symbol for a few corporations to tote like a badge for several weeks, impressing almost no one except themselves. It's bizarre, and it's increasingly far removed from the event itself, which, last time I checked, chiefly involves running around and jumping over things. And, if you're British, moaning about the traffic.

Vote Penguin
7/5/2012

So huge swaths of the electorate seem to have finally decided that peevish gump David Cameron isn't the convincing statesman they never quite thought he was in the first place.

Still, he had a good innings. People often criticise Cameron's judgement, but no matter what you think of his policies, his ability to surround himself with decoy pillocks was a strategy that, until recently, paid dividends. Since coming to power in 2010, voters have been so busy hating Nick Clegg, Andrew Lansley, Liam Fox, George Osborne, Francis Maude and now Jeremy Hunt, there's been very little rage left over for Dave.

Getting round to properly abhorring him has seemed like too much bother, like an unwelcome, nagging chore. You see his face on the news and perform a 1,000-year-long internal sigh.

Yes, yes David. I'll detest you in a minute. I've got to finish detesting all these other people first.

But now his decoys are spent. Clegg, in particular, absorbed so much bile, he underwent a startling physical transformation: from buoyant Geoffrey-off-*Rainbow* type to watery-eyed totem of misery. It was as if he had somehow been bitten by a radioactive puddle. He's so depressing to look at, they really should erect some kind of protective awning whenever he's out in public, like they do around grisly human remains. Hating him isn't simply a cliché; it actually feels vaguely cruel. So he's no longer of much strategic use to Cameron.

Ditto Lansley, who provided months of angry distraction in the run-up to the NHS reforms, but now seems like a villain from last year's movie. Attacking Osborne is far more fashionable. The trouble for Cameron is that he's fused with Osborne in the public brain: a high-born pantomime horse with two back ends. The tittering double dips.

Add to that the rising whiff of sleaze emanating from Leveson, which is finally beginning to curdle in the air around Cameron, and little wonder he has been losing his temper in a series of rather pathetic outbursts, like a man instigating a minor road-rage incident after rear-ending a milk float with his bumper car.

The further Cameron's stock slides, the less unelectable Ed Miliband appears. Miliband, unfortunately, looks and sounds like a dork. And not just any dork either, but the dorkiest dork in Dorking; someone you wouldn't cast as a dork in a drama-documentary for fear of looking implausible. But in a fight between the school dork and a dim, angry prefect with a warped sense of entitlement, only an absolute sodpot wouldn't root for the dork.

Assuming, that is, said sodpot had bothered paying attention to the scrap in the first place. If neither side really grabs you, you might just stay at home, like the majority of people last week. Only nine people actually voted in last week's local elections.

Nine. And three of them only followed the signs to the polling station in the hope it was some sort of knocking shop euphemism. The low turnout has been blamed on bad weather, which was almost certainly a factor – but on the other hand, if you won't vote because of drizzle, you weren't that arsed in the first place. People will queue in the rain to see Kasabian in concert. They'll queue in the rain to enter Abercrombie & Fitch. They'll queue in the rain for any old shit, as long as it isn't democracy.

Someone recently told me that politics enjoys a level of media attention that's seriously disproportionate to its actual relevance or popularity. It should really only get about as much coverage as golf does, they argued. Both golf and politics have a core of hardcore fans surrounded by a healthy-sized cloud of casual followers. But most of the population doesn't really give a toss unless there's a big personality involved.

The more I think about it, the more that analogy rings true. The problem for politicians is that their chosen sport looks increasingly weird and arcane in the present day – like water polo or lacrosse. The uniforms are antiquated, the rules are stifling, the action is boring, and they're constantly terrified of upsetting their sponsors. The spectators don't understand the lingo, don't think there's much skill involved, and suspect the game's rigged anyway.

Increasingly, in order to succeed, MPs have to transcend the sport entirely by becoming celebrities first and politicians second. As Boris Johnson and George Galloway indicate, the public responds when it encounters a strong flavour, simply because it at least *has* flavour. In Edinburgh's Pentland Hills ward, an independent candidate calling himself Professor Pongoo – who claimed to come from outer space and campaigned inside a giant penguin costume – won more votes than the Liberal Democrats.

Jarvis Cocker recognised that the best way to turn your weaknesses into strengths is to magnify them: rather than trying to disguise his inherent gawky perviness, he accentuated it at every opportunity until he became a star. Maybe if Miliband overly emphasised his slightly peculiar and nerdish persona it would pay dividends. If he started collecting *Magic: The Gathering* trading cards and riding to the Commons on a little blue tricycle, with his knees all sticking out like a doofus.

After all, the more Cameron drops his guard and displays his temper, the less robotic and the more true to himself he seems to appear. Except in his case, that's a problem. No wonder he always used to come across as a robot. His software was trying to keep him in check. And much like public enthusiasm, that licence has now expired.

Out of the Loop
14/5/2012

When a monk takes a vow of silence, is he still allowed to post messages on the internet? Chances are God won't find out. Being ancient, God probably can't work computers. He holds the mouse gingerly, like it's made of fine china. Sometimes he accidentally minimises a window and can't get it back. LOL what a noob #GodFail

Things change so rapidly these days it's easy to get left behind, no matter how powerful you are. Much online tittering occurred last Friday when King Charles II (played by Rebekah Brooks) told the Leveson inquiry that David Cameron used to sign off his text messages with the acronym LOL, in the mistaken belief that it stood for 'Lots of Love' instead of 'Laugh Out Loud', the idiot. The great big lizardy berk. The scaly, reptilian, basking-on-a-rock-to-raise-his-body's-vitamin-D-level nincompoop. LOL what a noob #CamFail

Actually, it's vaguely refreshing that he didn't know what it means. Cameron is forty-five years old, which means he has been allowed to not know stuff for at least a decade. He's a few years older than me, but I got a head start by wilfully deciding to ignore huge chunks of popular culture as far back as 1999. That was the year the film *American Pie* was released. Lots of people seemed to be talking about it, chiefly because a teenager has sexual intercourse with a dessert in it. Being twenty-eight years old in 1999, I considered myself too old and sophisticated to watch such a thing. As a result, *American Pie* is forever tagged in my mind as a 'new' film for 'youngsters'.

So imagine my horror on seeing a poster the other day for *American Pie: The Reunion*, a film in which the original cast reconvene after thirteen years, presumably now in their thirties and dealing with kids and mortgages and paunches and OH SOD EVERYTHING. It's a piece of nostalgia cashing in on something I was too old for first time around.

That's how you know you're really getting old. That and the way your eyebrow hair goes all wiry and starts sprouting away from your face like it's afraid of something, which to be fair it probably is, considering how knackered you look.

Youth fare aside, I've generally always been interested in what's going on, culturally. But recently I've undergone some kind of involuntary detox. In particular, I seem to be developing a serious aversion to almost every example of mass-appeal entertainment I spent most of the previous decade writing about in disparaging terms.

I don't write a TV column any more, partly because doing so was driving me mad, but sometimes it's fun to watch something junky while snarking about it on Twitter. I tried getting into this year's series of *The Apprentice* for precisely that reason, but only managed one-and-a-half episodes before my brain rejected it. It was like staring into the cogs of a pointless machine. I couldn't remember any of the contestants' names, even when their names were being clearly displayed on the screen in a caption.

I haven't seen *The Voice*, can't name anyone in *Britain's Got Talent*, don't use Facebook any more and, thanks to the magic of modern telly, I fast-forward any adverts I stumble across, so I don't even know which commercials are annoying people right now. It's like I live overseas, in a small sealed cube.

Not that I've replaced lowbrow enjoyment with more refined pleasures. Right now I rarely listen to music, don't have any books on the go, and can scarcely get through any kind of written article without wandering off for a sandwich.

I don't fully understand what's caused this hardcore cultural detox, although I suspect it's got something to do with becoming a parent and having to spend hours gazing at a tiny bellowing human instead. Apparently the next stage involves getting up-to-date on kiddywink culture by proxy, as soon as your offspring's old enough to give a shit about *Peppa Pig* and so on.

This will never do. At least when I used to enjoy hating rubbish, it was rubbish aimed at adults, and I'd chosen it myself. So I'm trying to get back into mainstream culture. It's just that everything popular seems so ... childlike. This week I'm going to carve out a few hours and go see the new *Avengers* movie, which I understand is wildly popular, just so I can feel more in touch with my fellow man.

I've already done my homework by attempting to sit through Kenneth Branagh's *Thor* (2011). If you haven't seen *Thor*, it's a 'motion picture' in which a *Swap Shop*-era Noel Edmonds wanders around claiming to be a Norse god and waving a hammer. He also kisses Natalie Portman on the hand. He's a dick.

The film cost $150m to make and is less entertaining than an episode of *To Build or Not To Build*. The final twenty minutes consist entirely of shouting and lights and made me feel so infinitely tired, my mind left my body and manifested itself as a small clear crystal floating beyond space and time. Unless I dreamt that bit. It is the worst film that has ever co-starred Anthony Hopkins and Stellan Skarsgård, unless they've teamed up to make *Vileda Supermop: the Movie* while I was sleeping.

I've been told it's not essential to have seen Thor in order to enjoy *The Avengers*, but it helps. I guess I'll get a lot more out of it now I understand Thor's complex relationship with his brother Loki, who I also couldn't give a shit about.

Once I've got *Avengers* under my belt, I'll try to catch *The Voice* before it ends. Possibly while eating jelly and ice cream and dribbling. I've been left behind by popular culture for weeks now, but boy am I looking forward to getting back up to speed.

It's not regressing. It's not. LOL.

Behold: the *Marvel Avengers Assemble 3D* experience
21/5/2012

Last Monday, because I've been feeling out of the loop, I resolved to catch the new *Avengers* movie.

I call it 'the *Avengers* movie' – in fact, the word 'Assemble' was added to the UK release so it wouldn't be confused with the 1960s TV series of the same name. Thus the film I saw was called *Marvel Avengers Assemble 3D*, which sounds like a badly translated Japanese videogame from the mid-nineties. Or something you might oil and push up your arse while wearing a confused look on your face, a bit like civilisation has failed.

No visit to a contemporary multiplex is complete without a bit of shit being rubbed in your eye right from the start, which happened in my case when the automatic ticket-printing machine spewed a rectangle of air at me instead of a ticket. Pathetically, I looked around for human assistance, only to find a big queue at the box office, where a solitary staff member was gradually processing incoming fleshbags with the joyous gusto of a woman forced to slowly count dust motes in a jail cell forever.

A nearby sign claimed I could purchase tickets from the popcorn counter instead, so I rode the escalator to the brightly coloured ripoff desk, where another lone staff member had been sentenced to life imprisonment. He called a manager, who spent five minutes trying to retrieve my ticket from an uncaring and unco-operative operating system before giving up and commanding the usher to wave me through before the computer found out and had me destroyed.

'Where do I get the 3D glasses?' I asked the usher, who looked at me as though I'd asked whether the film would have colours and shapes in it, before explaining that I'd have to go to a different counter and buy a pair separately for 80p.

When I arrived there, a customer was trying to buy pick-n-mix with a credit card, thus hopelessly crippling the cinema's IT system. I asked the cashier if I could simply put cash in his hand for the glasses, but no. Apologetically, he explained that everything had to go through the computer. So I stood there and waited.

Cameron's Britain.

Finally I entered the auditorium just in time to enjoy an anti-piracy commercial depicting an abandoned cinema wreathed in cobwebs, accompanied by a doomy John Hurt voiceover saying what a shame it would be if all the cinemas closed.

Yeah, imagine that. I'd have to approximate the experience by punching myself in the kidneys and eating a £50 note each time I put on a DVD.

Then *Marvel Avengers Assemble 3D* began.

Some scientists were worried about a glowing blue cube they kept underground, so Samuel L. Jackson had turned up to make things easier by shouting at them.

Then the cube went bonkers and spat out a bad guy called Loki, who looks like a cross between Withnail and the sort of grinning pervert who'd have sex with a fistful of Mattesson's liver pâté in the window of an apartment overlooking a hospice bus stop.

Then some vehicles raced around and everything blew up.

Then Samuel L Jackson gathered some superheroes together on a sort of impossible flying aircraft carrier, and they spent some time mocking each other's costumes in a post-modern fashion before Loki's henchmen arrived and everything blew up again.

Then they all went to New York and some aliens in hovering chariots flew through a hole in the sky and everything blew up for the third and final time.

And then, because the Avengers had won, the film decided to end.

Despite being almost completely incoherent, it's enjoyable bibble, and as good as superhero films are ever likely to get, which is excellent news because it means they can stop making them now. Seriously, they needn't bother releasing *Batman Bum Attack* or whatever the next one's called, because it won't be as good as *Marvel Avengers Assemble 3D*. Finally we can move on, as a species.

Still, entertained though I was, I did find myself occasionally checking emails: a first for me in a cinema, and surprising when you consider the amount of spectacle on display. It's like watching buildings and cars and girders and fighter jets endlessly smashing around inside a gigantic washing machine for two hours, interspersed with wisecracks. That's what mesmerises humans, just as surely as cats are fascinated by bits of string being pulled across the carpet. Up to a point, anyway. Once you've seen 10,000 cars exploding, you've seen them all. I rapidly succumbed to spectacle fatigue.

Marvel Avengers Assemble 3D cost \$220m to make and is 143 minutes long, so whenever I glanced at my phone for one second, I missed \$25,641 worth of entertainment.

(As an aside, I bet you could find someone prepared to shoot a stranger dead on camera for \$25,641. What if you paid that person \$220m to shoot 8,580 strangers dead on camera – that's one per second – and then while you were watching the footage afterwards, in your lair, your phone beeped and you glanced at it for five seconds and didn't notice all five members of One Direction taking a bullet? You'd miss out on a real cultural talking point.)

Finally – and this is an odd accusation to level at a superhero film – it didn't feel very real. I reckon only about 8 per cent of what was on screen was actually there. The rest was imagined by computers.

And please, leery tragi-men, don't dribble on about 'Scarlett Johansson's arse in 3D' being 'worth the price of admission'. The film was shot in 2D and converted to 3D using software, which means you're actually drooling over a 2D image of Scarlett Johansson's arse wrapped around a wireframe model of an arse that isn't there. You're sitting in front of HAL 9000, jerking off like a monkey. Somewhere, the machines are laughing at you.

My confession that I checked my emails during the film earned me a staggering amount of opprobrium, although in my defence I should point out that a) the cinema was virtually empty and I was sitting about three rows behind the only other occupants and b) for fuck's sake, it's only Marvel Avengers Assemble 3D.

The ultimate betrayal
10/6/2012

Eleven weeks ago I wrote a column about my experience of becoming a dad. I also promised to never write another 'parent-hood' piece again, on the basis that prior to becoming a parent, the mere mention of babies in newsprint was guaranteed to make me vomit all over the page in protest, paying special attention to the author's byline photo.

I held true to that promise. Really I did. And then a few weeks later I wrote an article on becoming jaded with popular culture, in which I had the temerity to mention parenthood again. Briefly, and only in passing – but boy did some readers go for me in the comments section.

'Oh Brooker, you smug, simpering, self-satisfied, mimsy, middle-class, latte-sipping, fleece-wearing, washed-up, shark-jumping, progeny-spawning embarrassment. I remember way back when you used to be relevant. When you wrote those columns slagging off reality show contestants. Remember those rebellious glory days? You said Anton du Beke looks like a man who jizzes sherbet or something and it was hilarious. Now look at you. You've become everything you used to criticise – literally everything. AND you've grown your hair a bit: the ultimate betrayal.* You've let yourself down, but worse than that, you've let me down – me, your cherished reader: the single most important person in your life.'

I hereby resign from whatever contest of cultural significance these keyboard-bothering nincompoops think they're conducting.

The key point these wailing children fail to appreciate is that becoming less relevant is my inevitable destiny. It's their destiny too, but they're way too full of snot and pep to notice. The real tragedy is not that I'm doomed to fade, but that I'm doomed to fade just to make room for these pricks.

Well prick away, cocksure Sharpington Sharp, because one day, you'll be so irrelevant yourself you'll actually stop breathing. Your body will decompose to a grey, pulpy mulch that will fertilise the soil the next generation will nonchalantly trample over on its way to the hologram shop. And that's how I picture you when I read your comments – as a shovelful-of-putrefied-matter-to-be making the very least of its brief window of consciousness. Under those circumstances, your level of snark merely strikes me as tragicomic.

All of which is a longwinded and possibly over-defensive way of saying I'm going to mention babies again. And again and again and again. Look, I'm mentioning them now: BABIES. I'll mention them as often as I like. In fact I might ask them to print this entire column in a special Winnie-the-Pooh font, with a photograph of a mobile, just to make it more off-putting to the cool kids.

A common theme in the comments expressing dismay at my shameful acceptance of fatherhood is that people go all sappy when they have a baby; ergo, every word I wrote from this point on would be shot through with gooey, complacent sentiment.

I don't understand that. I don't understand why everyone doesn't gain an additional nine layers of rage the nanosecond they become a parent. There's the sleep deprivation and the stress, of course, but that's largely offset by the underlying sense of delight that babies radioactively plant in their parents' heads in a cunning bid to stop them murdering them.

It's the rest of the world that's the problem. When you're suddenly tasked with steering a defenceless, vulnerable creature through life, the state of the planet instantly feels like less of a wearying joke and more of an outrageous affront to human decency. The world has slightly sharper edges than before.

Still, it's probably best not to succumb to this over-protective mindset, in case you turn into Sting and accidentally write the anti-nuclear-holocaust song 'Russians'. 'How can I save my little boy from Oppenheimer's deadly toy?' he sang, doubtless in the grip of new dadhood. 'Believe me when I say to you, I hope the Russians love their children too.' Nothing wrong with the sentiment, but no one ever danced to it at their wedding.

But I guess Sting wrote that because his son was precious to him. And I can relate to that now, just as I now understand why parents think their kids are unique and wonderful geniuses. It's simple: for the first six weeks or so, a baby is effectively little more than a screaming pet rock. It can't even hold its own head up, so any expectation you had regarding your child's abilities is instantly reset to zero. You get so accustomed to it doing nothing but yelling and defecating, the moment it does anything new – smiling or batting vaguely at an object – it's a miracle, like a chair has learned to tap-dance.

How clever, you think, forgetting that 'batting vaguely at an object' is hardly worth mentioning on a CV. All your baby has actually done – in geek terms – is receive the latest OS update, which fixes a few bugs (it goes cross-eyed less often), clears up some performance issues (it feeds more efficiently), and enables new features (object-batting now included).

Of course, everyone on the planet gets the same OS updates, at regular intervals, for their entire lives. Before long, he'll get the crawling update. The talking update. The walking update. And so on.

Personally, I downloaded all of those years ago. I'm way ahead of the little idiot. Way ahead. I've already got the hair-greying update, and am hoping to collect the complete set of related physical 'improvements', such as weaker eyesight and sagging flesh. Eventually, in a glorious climax, I guess I'll install and run the 'afterlife' routine, encountering the inevitable fatal system error halfway through.

Unless by then they've ironed out that final, unfortunate, inescapable glitch.

* Not that you'd know I'd grown my hair a bit from my obnoxious byline photo, which dates from 2006 and is a constant source of shame.

Moving on from Ms. Pac-Man
18/6/2012

In the early eighties, the arcade game *Pac-Man* was twice as popular as oxygen. People couldn't get enough of the haunted yellow disc with the runaway pill addiction and soon clamoured for a sequel. Namco, the Japanese creator, was working on a followup called *Super Pac-Man*, but this was taking too long for US distributor Midway's liking. So it bought an unofficial modification of the original game, changed the graphics a bit and released it as *Ms. Pac-Man*: possibly the first female lead character in a video game.

I say 'possibly' because no one knows what gender the shooty-bang thing you controlled in *Space Invaders* was because it didn't have stubble or knockers to define itself by. But then nor did Ms Pac-Man, whose name was confusing: at the time the prefix 'Ms' was a clear nod to feminist independence, whereas the surname

'Pac-Man' – not 'Pac-Woman' – screamed of subjugation to the patriarchy.

This intense paradox often caused gender studies students who encountered the *Ms. Pac-Man* cabinet to suffer such cognitive dissonance they fell to the ground, fitting and flapping like panicking fish. Arcade owners had to shove sticks with rags tied round them into their mouths to stop them chewing their own tongues off and distracting people from their game of *Q-Bert*.

'*Pac-Man* was the first commercial video game to involve large numbers of women as players – it expanded our customer base and made *Pac-Man* a hit,' claimed a Midway spokesman at the time. 'Now we're producing this new game *Ms. Pac-Man* as our way of thanking all those lady arcaders who have played and enjoyed *Pac-Man*.'

Thanks, men! But was the game itself a compliment? Pac-Man himself had no visible gender-specific features, presumably because his penis and testicles had been chafed away by years of sliding around on the floor of the maze – which explains why he was constantly necking painkillers. Yet Ms. Pac-Man had to wear lipstick, a beauty mark, and a great big girly bow on her head. Despite being a limbless yellow disc, we were expected to find her 'sexy'. Some men will screw anything.

As well as being superior to the original game, this 'female-friendly' incarnation actually had a story. Between levels, a series of simple animations turned *Ms Pac-Man* into a rom-com. In 'Act 1', her and Pac-Man meet. In 'Act 2', they take turns chasing each other. Finally, in 'Act 3', a stork flies across the screen and drops a baby Pac-Person in front of them. You can find this patronising or charming or both, but the startling thing is this: thirty years on, the depiction of Ms. Pac-Man in those basic cut scenes is actually more progressive than the depiction of the vast majority of female game characters today.

Last month the creators of the game *Hitman* drew widespread criticism for a grisly promotional trailer that showed the main (male) character slaughtering a group of S&M killer nuns. Since this was merely the logical conclusion of a deeply boring trend for rubberised female assassins that's been going on since the 1990s, some gamers were surprised by the outcry, and became indignant and defensive, as though someone had just walked in and caught them masturbating to the same goat porn they'd been innocently enjoying for decades, and judging them and making them feel bad.

When they're not seven-feet-tall high-heeled dominatrix killers, women in games tend to be saucy background-dressing or yelping damsels in distress. A rare exception is Lara Croft, the female star of *Tomb Raider*, who – in Pac-Man terms – is Ms. Indiana Jones.

But whoops. Last week the forthcoming big-budget *Tomb Raider* reboot made headlines after its executive producer apparently told the gaming site Kotaku that players would feel an urge to 'protect' Lara after she faces a series of ghastly trials including an encounter in which she kills a would-be rapist. The subsequent outcry necessitated a speedy clarification from the developers about precisely what kind of game they're making.

The irony about the *Tomb Raider* fiasco is that when you actually look at what's been revealed of the new game thus far, the creators' intention is clearly to transform Lara Croft from a heavily armed big-titted wank-fantasy into a grittier and more plausible heroine. It's an 'origin' story in which an inexperienced 21-year-old Lara crashlands on a remote island and has to fight the elements as well as the baddies in order to survive. Whether it's essentially *I Spit on Your Grave* in pixels remains to be seen, but the 'new' Lara looks less stereotypical than 99 per cent of female game characters.

But then, some people cling to those stereotypes as if their goolies depend on it. Last week, a female culture critic trying to raise funds on the Kickstarter website for a series of short films exploring the stereotypical treatment of women in games was subjected to a bewildering level of harassment from a peculiarly angry slice of the gaming community. As well as trying to have her Kickstarter account frozen or banned, they subjected her to a barrage of abuse that must have felt like running face-first into a muckspreader.

'Fucking hypocrite slut,' quipped one gallant observer. 'I hope you get cancer,' chortled another. To be fair, it's probably not the notion that games misrepresent the sexes that enrages them. They probably shout this sort of abuse at anything female.

I say 'shout'. I mean 'type'. And not in person. Whenever there's an actual woman in the room, they stare intensely at their shoes, internally composing their next devastating online riposte to uppity vaginakind. 'WHY MUST THEY TORMENT AND BEWITCH ME SO?', they think, in tearstained capitals.

Just as rubberised assassins represent a tiny proportion of women, these idiotic pebbledicks represent a tiny proportion of men. The trouble for the games industry is that on some level it believes it has to pander to these monumental bellwastes. It doesn't, and it'll only gain widespread acceptance when it learns to ignore them. In thirty years, it's scarcely improved on *Ms. Pac-Man*. Time to push forward.

The noblest people in Britain
2/7/2012

A curious sensation swept over me the other day when I was idly flipping through TV channels and found myself accidentally striding brain-first into an episode of MTV's *Geordie Shore*. If you've never heard of it, it's a 'structured reality' programme in which a gaggle of unbelievable idiots are stuck in a fancy house and intermittently hosed down with alcohol.

I use the term 'unbelievable idiots' for good reason. I don't believe they exist. For one thing, their level of idiocy is hard to accept on a human level. There's a reason the show isn't called

Cleverclogs Corner. You'd have more chance of decent conversation if you sewed a larynx into a lamb shank and asked if it'd seen any good films lately. They communicate using facial expressions and farts, with the occasional howl of rage thrown in for good measure. Even when attempting to mate.

I say 'attempting to mate'. I mean 'thumping away at each other's goolies like a builder grimly trying to knock a hole in a wall before lunch'. Since *Geordie Shore* is broadcast on television, where graphic footage of penetrative sex is only permitted in an educational context (or when Ofcom isn't looking), the camera stands back a bit for these interludes. There are a lot of shuddering duvets: sex is depicted beneath-the-covers, in a locked-off wide shot, night-vision style, just like a wildlife programme about rutting bison, but less romantic.

But let's not judge them by the content of their character. Let's judge them by the colour of their skin, which is terracotta. Mostly. Apart from the pale ones.

The way they look is the second unbelievable thing about them. Not all of them; most of them are sort of normal. But one or two of the men look ... well they don't look real, put it that way. They've got sculpted physiques, sculpted hairdos, sculpted eyebrows, and as far as I can tell, no skin pores. They're like characters from the Japanese fighting game *Tekken* – which, if you're not familiar with it, is not noted for a documentary-style slavish adherence to realism.

The most unsettling of the Geordies is a man called James, who looks precisely like a terrifying vinyl sex-doll version of Ricky Gervais. Or possibly a CGI Manga impersonation of a young Ed Balls. I've been to Newcastle. There's no way James is from Newcastle. He's from space. Deep space. My guess would be he's actually some form of sentient synthetic meat that crudely disguises itself as other life forms, but only to an accuracy of about 23 per cent. He's awesomely creepy to behold. Seriously, if James popped up on the comms screen of the USS *Enterprise*,

Captain Kirk would shit his own guts out. And that's the sort of behaviour that can undermine a leader's authority.

As I watched, I suddenly realized that this reality contestant 'look' – the strangely meticulous hair, the overdone tan, the teeth, the eyebrows – this is what we'll be laughing at in thirty years' time. Just as people still insist on finding seventies sideburns or eighties 'big hair' hilarious, so the fancy-dress partygoers of the future will be staggering drunkenly down the high street looking like a cross between Peter Andre and a sexually ambiguous robot.

Ah, you say, but we already laugh at that look now. And you're right, we do. But try telling that to your offspring, thirty years from now. They'll assume it was all taken sincerely at the time, like those seventies sideburns were.

What's more, they'll think *everyone* looked like that. There won't be any photos or videos around to prove otherwise. Ah, you say a second time, but we film and photograph every waking moment of our lives! And once more, you're on to something. But nothing we film and shoot now will be compatible with whatever holographic hand widgets we'll be using in the future. And the quality will seem appalling. Think of the first phone you ever got with a built-in camera. Still got all those pictures, have you?

Of course not: the quality is appalling. Some of those pixels are the size of your fist. And, besides, you lost them years ago. That phone's probably in a drawer somewhere, surrounded by defunct chargers and a hole punch you used a grand total of once.

What I'm saying is the inmates of *Geordie Shore*, *The Only Way is Essex* and *Made in Chelsea* represent our generation's 'time capsule' for the future. That's how the people of 2042 will think we look, spoke and behaved.

Which is a shame because they're not supposed to be representative. They're supposed to be different from 'normal people'. They're walking caricatured receptacles for spite. Their job is to make absolutely everyone who tunes in hate them. Instantly hate them. Hate them so much they can't take their eyes off them.

Those plucked eyebrows make it 5 per cent faster to form a grudge, which makes James something of a genius. Turns out you *can* polish a turd.

People no longer simply aspire to be famous. They aspire to be hated. 'Authorised media hate figure' is now a valid career. Which brings me to the curious sensation I mentioned at the start. I realised that maybe we need these people. Maybe we're all so angry and disappointed and bewildered, we need a free bunch of people to look down on and despise: they're a handy vessel. This is a noble public duty they're carrying out. They're our stress balls. Our punchbags. Our ballbags.

Face facts: if it wasn't for the cast of *Geordie Shore* and countless others like them, you'd be killing your neighbours with your bare hands.

Acknowledgements

Not that you care, dear reader, but thanks are due to the following human beings:

For the words in this book: Tim Lusher and Malik Meer at the *Guardian*, Jo Unwin at Conville and Walsh, and Julian Loose at Faber and Faber.

For co-writing my *10 O'Clock Live/2011 Wipe* pieces: Ben Caudell, Alan Connor, Shaun Pye, Jason Hazeley and Joel Morris.

For sorting out all manner of bibble: Annabel Jones at Zeppotron.

For putting up with me *the whole bloody time*: my wife, Konnie.

Index

explain their hatred of Norway,
270–1

Nail, Jenny, 72
Naked, 130
The Naked Office, 130
Nando's, 172, 174
Nature, 192
'Naughty' or 'Nice' list, 62–3
Nautilus, 288–90
Nazis, flippantly compared to popular
high street retail chain, 48;
apparent alliance with Smurfs, 134;
fought by old man in misguided
AV campaign advert, 246; used by
cape-wearing chin-stroking aliens
to put Captain James T. Kirk on
the defensive, 289
Nectar points, 278
Need for Speed, 298
Nesbitt, Shames, 50, 222–3
Nescafé, 291
Nevermind (Nirvana), 219
New Year's resolutions, 326–9
New York. *See* Ground Zero
mosque
New York Times, 338
News International, 10
News of the World, 11, 93, 241, 269;
makes its excuses and leaves,
264–6
Newsnight, 19, 213
newspapers, 108–9; as mindwarping
shitsheets, 122; tabloid, 92, 241–
3. *See also individual titles*
Newswipe, 261, 284
NHS reform bill, 350–1
Nicholson, Shakatak, 206
Nicola T, 67
Nilsen, Denise, 63
Nintendo DSi, 74
Nolans, The, 62
Non-existent feral cats, etc, 347

Nookie Bear, 137
Norris, Shucks, 314
North Korea, 139, 197
Norway, bad news from, 270–3
nose, slicing off in act of deliberate
face-spiting, 191
the 'Noughties', 23
nuclear war, 132, 259; unprovoked
nuclear attack on Berwick-on-
Tweed, 190–1
numbers chosen at random, 56, 87–
9, 161, 167, 210, 220-5, 317
Nuts magazine, 339

OAPs, 29
Obama, Bollock, 169
Obama, Miguel, 329
Ofcom, 10, 33, 207, 257, 381
The Office, 181
Oklahoma bombing (1995), 271, 272
Oliver, Jumpy, 51, 221–4
Olympic Games, London 2012, 188,
362–5
The Omen, 10
The One Show, 334
Only Fools and Horses, 67
The Only Way is Essex, 321, 382;
Royal Wedding Special, 247
Oral-B Olympic electric toothbrush,
363, 364
O'Reilly, Bell, 11
Osborne, George ('[Prince]
Gideon'), 28, 30, 134, 185, 186,
261, 263, 273–4, 365, 366
Over the Rainbow, 119
Ovett, Siff, 363
OXO TV ad campaign, 60

Pac-Man, 377, 378
Paddington Bear, 331
Paddington Beer, *see* Paddington
Bear, you were nearly right the
first time